Crime

An Analytical Appraisal

Crime
an analytical appraisal

Manuel López-Rey

PRAEGER PUBLISHERS
NEW YORK · WASHINGTON

BOOKS THAT MATTER

Published in the United States of America in 1970
by Praeger Publishers, Inc.
111 *Fourth Avenue, New York, N.Y.* 10003

© 1970 *in London, England, by Manuel López-Rey*

Library of Congress Catalog Card Number: 73–130457

Printed in Great Britain.

To Grace

Contents

Biographical note

Manuel López-Rey, LL.D. University of Madrid, post-graduate studies in criminology and related fields in Germany, Austria and France. Formerly County Judge, Professor of Criminal Law, Universities of Madrid, La Laguna and Salamanca, Member of the Commission for Codification and Director-General of Prisons in Spain. From 1946 to the end of 1965 with the United Nations, first as Chief of the Research and Treaties Section of the Narcotics Division and from 1952 as Chief of the Section of Social Defence; later as Senior Adviser on Social Defence in the Middle East. Professor López-Rey has represented the Secretary-General on several occasions at Congresses and regional meetings devoted to social defence and was instrumental in the organization of the United Nations Institute for Asia and the Far East for the Prevention of Crime and the Treatment of Offenders. As visiting Professor he has lectured in many parts of the world, and in the last thirty eight years he has become acquainted with the penal institutions of well over sixty countries. He has published several books and more than a hundred papers on penal and criminological matters. At present he is Director of the Criminological Research at the Social Science Research Center of the University of Puerto Rico and Visiting Fellow at the Institute of Criminology, Cambridge, England.

Introduction

Reality and appearance. Things do not pass for what they are but for what they seem. Few look within, and many are satisfied with appearances . . .
Gracian, *The Oracle*, 1647 (Translation by L. B. Walton)

What crime has lost in originality it has gained in extent and gravity. This is sometimes denied by those more interested in praising the *status quo* than in the objective appraisal of reality. Without seeking dramatic effects the fact is that in spite of scientific and material progress, or what is regarded as such, crime is an intractable problem in most of the developed countries and eventually it will be the same in others, developed or not. There are three reasons for this: crime has become a socio-political problem, criminology is to a great extent the result of professional aggrandizement, and the system of criminal justice is unable to cope with crime or criminals.

Crime will, in all probability, become more socio-political in character in the near future owing to the increase in number of dissatisfied youth and minority groups, and of corruption, so frequently linked to political patterns of every sort; the increasing number of crimes committed under cover of official position through political ideologies or as a sequel to revolutionary action and the expanding gap between the privileged and the under-privileged in developed as well as in developing countries. This means that what is usually called conventional crime, still the main subject of contemporary criminology, is only a relatively small part of the whole.

Criminology has not yet become a scientific and applied branch of knowledge. While its contribution cannot be denied in some respects, one may ask if humanitarian reasons have not sometimes been a more important factor than criminological theories in criminal policy progress. Criminology still persists in styling itself a natural or naturalistic science by borrowing more and more concepts, methods and techniques from natural sciences. This ignores the fact that natural science is unable to provide the socio-political approach at present required by the extent of crime. One may go further and say that naturalistic explanations of crime are philosophically an absurdity and have led to the present criminological impasse. I am fully aware that many professionals will smile at my bringing in philosophy, but the truth is that philosophy, particularly phenomenology, must constitute the substratum of any study of socio-political phenomena, of which crime is nowadays one of the most significant. Although experience and research are needed to gain knowledge of these phenomena they must be accompanied by logic, rigorous philosophical appraisal and political ideals, the latter not to be understood as those of a particular party or faction. With the exception of mathematics every science possesses its own philosophical and political problems which must be linked to the general ones. It is to be regretted that as a rule sociologists, psychologists and criminologists have ignored those affecting their respective disciplines. Empirical knowledge and judgment, so much praised nowadays, are less scientific than is generally supposed. What is mostly left in the criminological field is an impressive array of techniques and instruments aiming at an illusory measurement of crime, at the justification of a particular theory or sub-theory or at the expansion of often repetitive research programmes.

Criminologists have frequently overlooked the fact that the explanation of conventional crime, even if successful, would never be valid for the whole of crime, the greater portion of which is conveniently ignored not only by most of them but also by the vast majority of governments and agencies as well as political parties and politicians in developed and developing countries.

In fact crime has always been a socio-political problem but from the beginning criminology has confined itself to the narrow path of conventional crime, mostly in accordance with an individualistic conception, putting aside the fact that like love, hate, greed, power and dissatisfaction, with which it is closely involved, crime cannot be explained by a theory or an ensemble of theories which at best are no more than empirical abstractions of a part of reality. Actually, like love and hate, crime is inherent in the human condition and to reduce it to a theoretical expression or to a system of weights and scales in order to give the impression of more accurate measurement is as illusory as reducing love and hate to capsulized theories or numerical expressions.

One of the main tasks of criminology is to determine within reasonable limits the 'amount' of crime that a given society can stand without being seriously disturbed. The task is not easy; it would probably cost less than is now spent on criminological research, and control and criminal justice, both very different from what they are at present, will be the most important aspects. The increase and effectiveness of control will no doubt raise a series of questions particularly concerning the protection of human rights, individually or collectively. Both aspects have been overlooked in contemporary scientific and technological progress. As for criminal justice, its inability to cope with crime as a socio-political problem is obvious. The situation cannot be remedied by increasing the number of judges, courts, institutions and services or by reshuffling according to managerial criteria the existing organization of the 'administration of justice'. What is needed is a radical transformation so that criminal justice can accomplish the socio-political function demanded by the socio-political transformation of our time and the foreseeable future. This also raises the question of the validity of the aims at present assigned to criminal law such as defence, deterrence, protection and rehabilitation, all of which reflect a world which is receding. The same applies to the slogan 'law and order' which means little more than stronger enforcement and greater repression for the benefit of obsolete socio-political structures or 'establishments' whether capitalist or socialist.

In sum, of the three main subjects involved, crime, theories and criminal justice, only the first two are examined here, leaving the consideration of the last for the near future. Accordingly the book tries to restate the problem of crime in a different light and open the way for a different criminology, or a new and better criminal policy and justice more in accordance with the present and future evolution of mankind. Our penal needs differ considerably from those of the recent past in developed as well as developing countries and it is abundantly clear that neither contemporary criminology nor criminal policy can reasonably satisfy them.

In Chapter 1 the data concerning the socio-political character of crime and the frequent injustice of the 'administration of justice system' they reflect, are submitted and analysed. A comparison of the data with contemporary criminological research shows how peripheral the latter is in many respects, and that unless a serious effort is made governments will be unable to improve the situation as long as their political and economic policies relegate criminal justice to a secondary position. Mass production and consumption, expanding but always piecemeal welfare policies, economic penetration, spectacular scientific undertakings mostly for national prestige and the pursuance of political dogmatism as well as cultural and political nationalism in developed and developing countries will prevent the necessary reforms. Chapter 2 examines the theories of crime as a social problem which up to now has been the traditional approach even when psychology, psychiatry and psychoanalysis have tried to play a predominant role. In Chapter 3 the no less traditional and artificial distinction between crime and juvenile delinquency is considered. The reasoning, whether sentimental or scientific, that they are two separate phenomena, is now socio-politically untenable.

In Chapter 4 the expansion and distribution of crime as a sequel of material living conditions and population growth, the two main unsolved problems of our time are considered. Their impact on crime shows how closely related criminal policy is to general socio-economic policy, which does not mean that criminal policy should be regarded as an appendix to national or international socio-economic policies. At the end some final considerations are submitted.

Besides the acknowledgments in the text, I wish to thank all my friends, colleagues and the agencies, too numerous to be cited, who helped me in collecting data. I also wish to express my indebtedness to the United Nations, which for almost twenty years gave me the opportunity to study *in vivo* many aspects of the human problem of crime which cannot be learned from books or ascertained by sophisticated criminological research. Above all, my thanks go to my wife for her invaluable assistance in the long preparation of this book.

1 The extent of crime

Crime is increasing in developed as well as in developing countries. This increase is sometimes denied in the developing countries, partly because criminal statistics and other sources of information are lacking or inaccurate, partly because poor or primitive conditions or serious political unrest make crime less significant, and partly owing to political propaganda. Occasionally we are told that improvement in material living conditions will take care, not only of the increase, but of crime itself. Unfortunately, in practice, the improvement is often seriously handicapped by the pursuance of political policies which absorb most of the existing financial resources. As for the theory that crime may be reduced or even eradicated by the improvement of material conditions, experience shows that although this improvement may reduce some forms of crime, it creates others, sometimes more serious than those that previously existed. This does not mean that the improvement should be blamed, but simply that far more reforms than simply better living conditions are required before crime is reduced to what may be regarded as reasonable proportions.

In the developed countries, statistics as well as other information exist, but they are not always as complete and reliable as they should be. Generally, the increase and the seriousness of crime are admitted, although here and there attempts are made to minimize both by semi-scientific but comforting explanations. Sometimes the increase cannot be established because of the difficulty in determining the number of cases not brought to court or not prosecuted. As regards juvenile delinquency, a practice which seems to be gaining ground in some countries is that of considering as cases of civil law real cases of juvenile delinquency—a device which allows their exclusion from juvenile delinquency statistics.

The distinction between developed and developing countries,

although somewhat equivocal, is essential in criminal policy matters. It is equivocal because countries are always developing, even if slowly or in a haphazard way. It is acceptable if by 'developing' we understand a condition of retarded or insufficient development in certain respects. The term 'developing' is a terminological victory in the international arena for the less developed countries which resented being called 'under-developed'. Their feelings on the matter were stated quite clearly at the Second United Nations Congress in 1960 when the subject *Prevention of Types of Criminality resulting from Social Changes and Accompanying Economic Development in Less Developed Countries* was discussed. Shortly afterwards, following further complaints, the United Nations dropped the terms 'less-developed' and 'under-developed'.

The distinction is important because, owing to their characteristics and resources and the fact that crime differs from country to country, criminal policies cannot be the same for developed and developing countries or, for that matter, for all countries of the same group. It is illusory to maintain that the lack of development is confined to the economic field. The widespread belief among leaders, representatives, government officials and even professionals in developing countries is that as soon as their countries catch up in this field with developed countries, they will automatically reach the coveted category of developed. Certainly the developed countries will not be so obliging as to stop their development and wait until their levels are reached by the developing countries. Needless to say, in some ways the gap, especially in the economic field, may be considerably reduced or even disappear, but in some ways the constant process of development may even increase the gap between the developed and developing countries. In one way or another, the distinction between developed and developing countries is here to stay. This does not mean that the countries in each category will always be the same, but that victory in the battle of development is always difficult, whatever the efforts made or the bilateral or international aid received.

As far as crime is concerned, developed countries are far more vulnerable than developing countries. One of the reasons is that the greater the development, the greater are the individual and collective expectations and consequently the frustration, conflict and social protest. Some developed countries, such as the United States, have been unable to cope with crime as a social problem.

Since in one way or another all countries are developing, the question arises—and the answer is one of the main purposes of this book—of how criminal policy should be planned as part of public policy and what elements are to be considered in the planning. Admittedly, there are many difficulties in planning, and many difficult and opposing forces, but any planning is far better than no planning at all. With the aid of planning the problem of crime can be more easily handled. Nowadays it would be inexcusable not to plan for criminal policy matters, up to now almost exclusively dealt with empirically. What has to be remembered is that in planning the greatest priority belongs to the protection of human rights.

The point of departure of any criminal policy is to ascertain as nearly as possible what is the extent of crime. Fundamental to this is to know as exactly as possible what crime is, a knowledge that only criminal law is able to provide and without which no criminal justice would ever be possible. It may be argued that criminal justice can be dispensed with and replaced by something more in accordance with scientific knowledge. Putting aside the question of what should be understood by 'scientific', the fact is that although scientific findings can assist in reaching criminal justice, they cannot replace it. It has been suggested—a sociologically destructive suggestion—that the concept of criminal responsibility should be abandoned. I say 'destructive', first, because nowadays no society can reasonably function without justice, even if its meaning changes as a result of progress; second, because justice is an essential human need deeply felt by everyone, including offenders. As such, this need is inherent in the human spirit and cannot be put aside for scientific theories. In fact, quite a number of criminal offences reflect a quest for justice which, although erroneously pursued, cannot be ignored. It is equally true that offenders are primarily interested in getting justice and secondarily in being rehabilitated. The preference given to rehabilitation to the detriment of justice helps to explain the failure of contemporary criminology and penology. Third, because if the concept of justice is considered unnecessary, it will in all probability be replaced by social defence, protection or security, scientific treatment or something similar, all of which, although admissible as components of justice, are subordinate to it; and finally, because if the concept of responsibility is put aside in criminal matters, logically the same should be done in other fields such as parental care, administrative functions, payment of debts and compliance with obligations of any sort.

The theory that the legal definition of crime is conventional and its boundaries cannot be recognized by science makes little sense. To begin with, all definitions, including those having a fundamental character, are conventional, but conventional does not mean artificial, arbitrary or lacking a sound scientific basis. No less conventional than the definition of crime as a legal concept are in natural science the concepts of cause, causation, causality, result, law and species, to mention only a few. The same happens with personality, character, structure, system, type, model, etc., used sometimes too ambitiously in sociology, psychology, and psychiatry. The fact that the meaning of all these and similar terms is not uniform everywhere and to everyone, and that here and there their validity is denied, in no way reduces their importance as basic and indispensable conventional terms, without which it would be practically impossible nowadays to describe individual and collective life as well as socio-economic development and scientific and technological progress. Occasionally one of these fundamental concepts is replaced by a new one or emerges under a different label, but these and other changes only serve to confirm the necessity of fundamental conventional concepts. More specifically, as a non-causal but essentially attitudinal concept, crime is indispensable to society. Its main function is to express an extreme form of social reproach *vis-à-vis* certain extreme forms of behaviour. As such, whatever have been its modal variations, is has shown greater conventional stability than many other scientific concepts.

Social life requires fundamental definitions in many fields in order to make progress. Certainly their number should not be unnecessarily multiplied, but neither should it be reduced. It is possible that the term 'crime' may eventually be replaced by some other term—but the fundamental meaning will remain the same. Whatever name is used, a definition has to be given to ensure certainty and guarantees for the individual. An attempt has already been made by those using the terms 'deviation', 'deviant behaviour', 'antisocial conduct', etc., to designate in a generic term not only what at present is regarded as crime but also what is quite erroneously called social pathology. The most significant contributions to this naturalistic way of thinking are confusion, scientific wandering, social injustice and frequent infringement of human rights.

The mistake often made by those criticizing the conventional character of the definition of crime is to identify it as a fundamental socio-juridical concept with the numerous legal definitions given by criminal law. As the expression of an extremely severe social reproach, the concept of crime has changed less than is thought. As in the past, although with different contents in some respects, it is reduced to a few social commandments, the main beneficiaries of which are the individual, the family and society and the fundamental forms of their respective organization. Like sin and virtue, crime offers very little room for anything new. What may be new are the historical forms or modalities that the commission of crime adopts. These modalities are often given preferential treatment by criminal law through a series of definitions, the social value of which is doubtful in a number of cases. Among them is homicide: as a single, basic socio-juridical concept the definition of homicide should suffice to embrace all possible forms of killing. Instead, the criminal codes maintain a series of substantive legal entities such as murder, manslaughter in various degrees, reckless killing, involuntary homicide, homicide by negligent use of vehicle or weapon, homicide by an intoxicated user of firearms, homicide resulting from negligent control of vicious animals, etc. *Mutatis mutandis,* the same applies to the numerous cases of bodily injury, abortion, sexual offences, etc. Obviously these and many other historical modalities defined by criminal law are conventional and certainly not fundamental. It is hoped that many of them will eventually be dispensed with, but it would be erroneous to identify them with the basic sociojuridical concept of crime.

As a concept to maintain distinction between two main categories of offenders—juveniles and adults—'delinquency' is at least as equivocal as the term 'developing'. In most European and Latin American countries and in quite a few African countries, 'delinquent' applies to any person who has committed a criminal offence, and *délinquance* and *delincuencia* refer to crime or criminality. In English-speaking countries and their imitators, delinquency embraces not only crime in the strict sense but also any form of misdeed committed by a minor. The humanitarian and paternalistic reasons for the use of the term are praiseworthy, but it is obvious that the present extent and gravity of the problem of juvenile delinquency demands a different approach.

The matter was discussed at the 1955 and 1960 United Nations Congresses, where pleas were made for the definition of 'delinquency' and even of the more vague concept of 'pre-delinquency' so ably used to build up prediction techniques and tables. After detailed discussion, the 1960 Congress recommended 'that the scope of the problem of delinquency should not be inflated' and that 'the meaning of the term delinquency should be restricted as far as possible to violations of criminal law and that even for protection, specific offences which would penalize small irregularities or maladjusted behaviour of minors, but for which adults would not be prosecuted, should not be created'.[1] Unfortunately, for reasons which will be discussed in Chapter 3, many countries still maintain, and in quite a number of cases are entangled by, the present incongruous concept of delinquency as the counterpart of crime. In this book, unless otherwise indicated, the term 'delinquency' means the offences committed by juveniles for which an adult would be prosecuted.

Although the legal definition of crime is the only possible point of departure to determine the extent of crime, it should be kept in mind that as a fact crime may remain undetected or unknown, detected or known but unreported, or detected or known and reported. Each is related to the others but independent, inasmuch as it is determined by a series of factors which although sometimes identical, act in a different way; each raises its own problems and has to be studied by different approaches and techniques. The numerical extent of undetected crime may be guessed through sometimes elaborate methods, but not accurately determined. Whether it is greater than the other two kinds of crime put together is a matter for conjecture. Probably it is greater than either of them taken separately. Detected but unreported crime is crime found out by or known to the police, any other official, agency or individual, or brought up by criminological or other research. Due to many factors, its extent fluctuates considerably and cannot be definitely established. Detected and reported crime is not only known but also in one way or another acted upon by the police and certain public officials and agencies. With exceptions, sometimes important, it becomes the content of different types of criminal statistics.

These three aspects constitute the whole extent of crime, which is fluctuating enough owing to the number of variables involved. Even if all these could be determined and the approximate ratio between the three different kinds of crime established, it would be illusory to identify the total obtained with crime as a social problem. Certainly the fact of knowing the total numerical amount of crime would be of considerable help in tackling the problem it constitutes, but in dealing with social problems it should be kept in mind that the numerical expression is not the same thing as the social magnitude of the problem itself. The remark is made because, as a sequel of the growing transplantation into criminology of mathematical methods, there is a tendency to consider that the mathematical presentation of the crime problem is of decisive importance in dealing with it. There is no doubt that every effort should be made to ascertain as nearly as possible the numerical extent of a social problem, but there is no doubt either, that in view of the number and changeable character of the variables involved, no exact numerical presentation of a social problem is possible. Even if it were obtainable, its value would be transitory. Consequently, since other non-numerical and no less important elements should be considered, criminal policies should not, within reasonable limits, be restricted because an accurate account of the totality of crime is lacking.

Another question is whether the numerical extent of crime as one of the aspects of crime as a social problem should preferably refer to offences or offenders or both. Contrary to the criminological slogan that the offender and not the offence is what counts, as a social problem the numerical determination of crime is more relevant than that of the offenders. In order to avoid misunderstanding, it should be added that this preference for the numerical expression of crime as a series of acts does not mean that the corresponding figures about offenders should be neglected but on the contrary pursued as far as possible for comparison and policy reasons, nor does it mean that the treatment that offenders deserve should not be improved as much as possible.

Can the three categories of crime above be reduced to two—viz. known and unknown crime, reported and unreported, or detected and undetected crime? The temptation to reduce them is attractive, but like many other temptations it should be resisted, because no dichotomy is clear enough to convey the different kinds of knowledge about the factual existence of crime. Admittedly the three categories suggested are not sufficiently exhaustive or clear cut, but certainly this division is preferable. The two-term classification of reported or recorded and unreported or unrecorded crime is a deceptive oversimplification, inasmuch as it often requires involved and not always satisfactory explanations of what unreported or unrecorded is. In her excellent essay 'Recorded and Unrecorded Criminality in Finland' (1966), Professor Inkeri Anttila, after referring to the different meanings of 'unrecorded criminality' and giving some examples of definitions, fails to provide a clear concept of it and thus inevitably recorded criminality is equally confusing.[2] The impression obtained from these and other passages of her paper is that 'recorded' and 'registered' are used as interchangeable terms. Actually they are different, since according to general usage registered means a particular formal way of recording. In any case, the concept of 'unrecorded criminality' as equivalent to what 'nowadays usually refers to police statistics' is controversial, even if quotation marks are used to designate unrecorded crime. Apparently what is meant is that registered or recorded crime is that judicially adjudged as such. Here again, the erroneous identification already mentioned between crime and the legal status of the criminal appears. It should be noted that in an equally excellent essay, Christie, Andenaes and Skirbekk use the term 'officially registered criminals' to refer to those declared guilty by court or equivalent procedure.

The key to this entangled terminology lies in the still confused meaning of the expression 'dark number' and the meaning that the terms 'recorded' and 'unrecorded' should have for research purposes. Recorded crime should be understood as that for which written evidence is made by the public official or agency in pursuance of their duties, even if informally made and kept. Quite often in minor cases the police put down the particulars of juvenile offenders and the offence committed and take the offender to his parents for closer parental attention or supervision, without further action. In the case of a second offence the juvenile is brought before the court, but the particulars previously taken by the police are not produced. In France this practice is becoming more and more frequent, with results which I am told are satisfactory. For research purposes this type of recording should not be excluded. The same applies to similar practices with respect to adult offenders. The practice of destroying criminal records or invalidating them and making them inaccessible because legally they are non-existent, should be discontinued in the interests of research. This does not preclude the records being used for rehabilitation purposes. Putting aside the importance that any previous criminal record has for subsequent treatment, research into the extent of crime, of which recidivism is an important aspect, will be seriously handicapped as long as individual records are destroyed or cannot be examined because legally they do not exist. The difficulties of keeping criminal records for years are considerably reduced if, after a reasonable period of time, they are replaced by microfilm.

Indeed, research into the extent of crime is still influenced by the dark number theory which, as befits its name, was always somewhat obscure. N. Oba, its main pioneer, grouped together under this heading unknown crime, the undetected offender and the offenders who, although detected, were declared free because of lack of evidence or for any other reason evaded penal sanction.[3] An analysis of the categories involved and of the interpretation given to them mostly from a police point of view—*kriminal polizeiliche Praxis* or *kriminalpolizeiliches Interesse*—shows that the expression 'dark number' with such a mixed conceptual span is apt to be confusing. This is why Sauer rejected the term and used *Latente Kriminalität* which is, if anything, more confusing, while others interpreted the term *Dunkelziffer* in different ways.[4]

Whatever its shortcomings, the classification here suggested serves the purposes of research more accurately and systematically than any other.

1 Unknown criminal offences

In principle any criminal offence may remain unknown. The fact that some of them, such as treason, espionage, conspiracy against the State, murder and a few others, are more easily detected, does not necessarily mean that their respective unknown amount is small. The most frequent unknown offences belong to the large and heterogeneous group of crimes against property. Prominent among them are theft, embezzlement and vandalism. Lower in the scale but also widespread are larceny and burglary. Although apparently less significant, the following may also be mentioned: offences against justice, perjury, bribery, corruption, extortion, forgery, frauds, counterfeiting, smuggling, tax evasion, receiving stolen property, illicit traffic in persons and exploitation of the prostitution of others, illicit production of and traffic in narcotic drugs, bodily injury, sexual offences, insults and affronts, abortion, gambling, adultery and many others. I say apparently, because although criminological research on the matter provides little data, other sources of information lead to the conclusion that in many if not all cases the number of offences committed which remain unknown is very high. Such is the case with regard to fraud, smuggling, extortion, tax evasion, narcotic drug offences, violation of human rights, insults and affronts, sexual offences including rape, bodily injury (of which the injury of 'battered' children is one of the most pathetic forms), abortion and adultery. The latter still has in quite a number of countries the ambivalent character of being a criminal offence—if prosecuted by the offended party— and grounds for divorce. In some countries this dual character allows a series of abuses. One of them is that of 'criminal exposure' if divorce by mutual consent is not agreed upon.

The amount of unknown crime is considerably increased by two facts seldom considered in contemporary criminological research: one, the multiplicity of criminal offences created by special laws outside the criminal codes, and two, the bringing into the area of criminal responsibility of more and more cases of criminal negligence. The number of special criminal laws creating criminal offences, not only misdemeanours, whether in normal circumstances or emergency, is increasing, and these laws embrace every possible field. Political, military, economic, scientific and technological reasons are often used to justify the creation of these offences, the labels of which vary within a limited range of originality. The most favoured are crimes against the security or protection of the State; secrets and anti-subversive acts—equally practised but with different aims by democratic, socialist, dictatorial or semidictatorial regimes—espionage law, anti-economic activities, etc. As a rule the greater the number of offences created, the fewer the guarantees granted to the accused. To this 'security-minded' criminal legislation should be added the criminal offences—as a type apart from administrative offences—created by non-criminal laws dealing with health and food requirements, nationalization, financial, economic and currency matters, transport and communication, speculation, etc., which often carry long terms of imprisonment or heavy fines. The extent of unknown crime is widened by

9

considering as a criminal offence the attempt or conspiracy to commit many of the offences above enumerated.

The expanding concept of State security, technological progress, scientific and industrial research, greater mechanization, huge construction or building undertakings, large scale chemical, pharmaceutical and food production, the growing role of the State or government as employer, partner or contracting party, etc., have all increased the number of cases of crime committed by gross or medium negligence and hence the corresponding extent of unknown crime. Undoubtedly this increasing number of cases of criminal responsibility is often justified and shows how difficult it is to admit that the concept of criminal responsibility should be dispensed with altogether. Actually, putting aside the misuse of criminal law for political purposes, this expansion of criminal responsibility tries to satisfy one of the most significant penal needs of contemporary, and in all probability future, society.

Can the extent of unknown crime be numerically established? Many attempts have been made and prominent among them is Dr Wehner's monograph on *Die Latenz der Straffaten* (1957) in the Federal Republic of Germany with special reference to 1956. Wehner submits a series of tables which includes the number of cases of a particular group of offences reported to the police as well as the number of unknown cases of the group. The latter may move between two limits corresponding to a proportional minimum and maximum respectively. Thus with respect to murder, which includes manslaughter as well as infanticide, the number of cases reported to the police is 1,029 while the minimum of unknown cases is 3,087 or three times as high, and the maximum is 6,174 or six times as high. Consequently the minimum of actual murders committed is 4,116, the maximum 7,203, and a medium figure would be 5,659. For abortion the numbers are 5,400, minimum a hundred times as high or 540,000, and the maximum five hundred times as high or 2,700,000. Therefore the actual number is not the statistical 5,400 but a minimum of 545,400 and a medium figure of 1,625,400. In table XI Wehner summarizes the previous ten tables and shows that to the total of 1,630,675 criminal offences of the 1956 police statistics correspond as a minimum of unknown offences 3,602,398 and as a maximum 10,748,737, therefore the total minimum offences actually committed is 5,233,073, and the medium figure is 8,806,241. His conclusion is that the total amount of unknown criminal offences, including the unreported, varies between a minimum of twice and a maximum of four-and-a-half times the number shown in the criminal statistics.

What is the value of Wehner's proportional minimum and maximum limits of unknown or undetected or, as he calls it, latent crime?

Both limits are the result of painstaking research, the main elements of which are figures on individual as well as general recidivism, case studies, incidence of crime reported to and cleared by the police, findings brought up by other authors and carefully analysed police experience. Of all the sources, the data concerning recidivism, either from individual records, admission by the offender or police knowledge are the most significant and the safest. A series of complicated operations is required in order to collate and compute data and I am not sure whether Wehner was able to carry this out. This explains why it is not always clear how he reaches the limits minimum and maximum of *Latente Kriminalität,* and one sometimes gets the impression of a reasonably well-founded guess. Can this guess be regarded as sufficiently well founded to enable us to go ahead in the formulation and implementation of criminal policies and programmes? The answer is not easy. Certainly better collating and computing will provide more accurate figures, and this should be done if only to check the figures already produced; other sources should be used for comparison and thoroughly studied as Wehner did. In any case, Wehner's contribution has not as yet been matched by any other research projects in the field of unknown crime—despite the huge cost of some of these projects.

While Wehner's remarkable piece of criminological research was intended mainly for the benefit of the police service, Hans von Hentig's book *Die Unbekannte Straftat* (1964) constitutes a detailed and vivid explanation of why some criminal offences never reach the columns of criminal statistics.

Following a traditional German method, Hentig explores the rich field of individual cases in a way that differs from methods practised elsewhere. In some countries, for example the United States, the individual case approach is being abandoned in favour of a more expensive and certainly less satisfactory system, that of the victim research approach. Hentig again shows that the thorough study of individual cases—a concept similar to but not identical to that of criminal careers—with the study of other sources, pays good dividends. As an introduction to any type of research in unknown crime, Hentig's book contains useful remarks on the obstacles raised by criminal law and the reality of life which prevent a better knowledge of the extent of crime. Equally useful are his considerations on the problems created by the suspension or abandonment of criminal prosecution, the statutes of limitations, the continuous character of some criminal offences, mental illness, escapes and death. His remarks about the problems created by protection of the different kinds of social forces or interests are valuable for a better understanding of some factors determining the extent of unknown crime. An interesting section is devoted to *Von Souvenirs*

11

und Kavaliersdelikten which were not scarce in the past and are far more numerous today. By *Kavaliersdelikten* the author refers to the stealing of tankards and beer mugs in beer halls and similar places in Germany, especially in Bavaria. The question raised here is whether these—the souvenir offences and the like—should actually be regarded as criminal offences or be reduced to some lower legal category. By being regarded (like shop pilfering) as real criminal offences, the extent of known and unknown crime as well as the corresponding offenders is unnecessarily increased. From an objective as well as a subjective point of view—social damage or anti-sociality—in my opinion they should be taken out of the penal code. The question, however, is how to do it so that all the main interests involved are satisfactorily protected. It should be noted that Hentig refers frequently to case histories and criminal statistical data, including the judicial, which in some respects are as important as police data, and also that in a number of cases the examples are taken from the United States.

In the last ten years the Scandinavian countries have undertaken a series of remarkable studies, some of them as part of a broad project co-ordinated by the Scandinavian Research Council for Criminology, on the extent of unknown crime. The studies concerning Norway and Finland have received enough publicity to justify their brief analysis.

The Norwegian report by Christie, Andenaes and Skirbekk is based on data gathered through a questionnaire distributed in 1961[5] to about 3,800 youngsters in three selected areas, taking advantage of the fact that they had been gathered for pre-military classification. Neither through the selection of persons nor of offences was any attempt made to present a representative sample of Norwegian criminality. The purpose was merely to acquire some knowledge of the still-obscure problem of unknown crime. The Finnish study, also part of the above-mentioned broad project, is similar in content, methods (including the questionnaire which, nevertheless, has its own characteristics) and purpose to that of Norway. The number of youngsters participating was a little over 3,000. As studies of self-reported crime, the findings rely heavily on the willingness, honesty and ability of the participants to answer the questions put to them.

Although, as the authors frankly admit, the reliability of the questionnaire method may be contested, their findings are of considerable interest, not only because they coincide with others made elsewhere, but also because they bring to light facts which deserve careful consideration before they are regarded as evidence of anything. Thus, when examining the general trend of unknown crime, the Norwegian authors say that it is 'in good accordance with data from crime statistics and other official sources'. One may ask if this condition of 'good' is not partly due to the better quality of Scandinavian statistics. On the other hand, the conclusion points to a parallelism which, with some fluctuations, frequently appears when the territory of unknown crime is explored. My own experience is that even in developing countries with a reasonably good statistical system the parallelism, although less marked, also exists. The only note of caution is that it should not be interpreted in absolute terms as embracing all offences, and that in certain instances it works in a different way. Take, for instance, among others, the case of abortion, the statistical figures of which are always far below those revealed by inquiries in the field of unknown crime. Apparently in this and similar cases, the parallelism has been broken inasmuch as the statistical data do not adequately reflect the extent of the offence. Actually, there is a kind of parallelism here with respect to certain offences, for the smaller the statistical figure the greater is the undetected amount. This is also the case with offences committed by professionals and public officials of many sorts and to a great extent with the so-called white collar crime. Both reports conclude that, contrary to what criminal statistics show, there are no clear differences in the trends and even rates of offences among social classes. More specifically, Jaakkola says that

> contrary to what the information provided by the crime
> statistics gives reason to expect, there are no clear
> systematic differences in the actual crime rates of the different
> social classes [and] members of the higher social classes and
> the better educated run a smaller risk of having to answer
> for their crimes. The social control of deviant behaviour
> thus shows a status-selective bias.

Similar assertions have already been made in the United States.

To begin with, the classification of social classes is, at present, deceptive, particularly as far as young people are concerned. One may ask if the traditional method of grouping social classes by referring to the father's profession or occupation corresponds to the independence and role of young people in the contemporary society of developed countries; and secondly the samples are too small and too subject to a series of variables to allow generalizations, especially when these are as sweeping as in the Finnish report. It might be said that by showing more lower than middle and upper class criminality, criminal statistics reflect the fact that the extent of the former is far greater than that of the other two. The same would happen if the numerical extent of the classes were reversed. Consequently, the so-called bias would be almost exclusively a question of numerical probability. Certainly bias in different forms and degrees, as a rule more apparent in developing countries, has to be considered, but it would be an oversimplification to regard the prevailing lower class content of criminal statistics as the sequel of biased attitudes or practices of the 'social control of deviant behaviour', or the more educated as more intelligent and skilful than the less educated. By showing more lower than upper and middle class criminality, the statistics accurately reflect the inter-mingled effect of a series of factors, not only socio-economic, which are at work in any particular society and in crime as a social problem. The modalities of a number of offences, although common to different social groups, may differ considerably among them. In this respect it should be kept in mind that the lists of offences of the two projects, although dissimilar in some respects since they had to be adapted to Norwegian and Finnish characteristics respectively, give the impression of a stereotyped image of the crime which may be committed by youngsters in rural and urban areas. The participants had no choice and except for some scattered references to vandalism which were brushed aside, answered accordingly. This explains why, on the whole, the criminality confessed is of a rather mild character and why, in spite of the vast extent of crime uncovered, the Finnish report confidently says there is no reason to panic. Obviously the youngsters had committed more serious offences than those confessed. By their choice of offences the authors narrowed not only the field of the enquiry but also auto-matically the validity of their conclusions.

While I support the statement in the Finnish report that studies of undetected crime show the necessity for a re-appraisal of criminal policies and programmes, it must be said that this requires more solid foundations than those provided by contemporary crimino-logical research into this aspect of crime. Concerning the bias, the Norwegian report concludes:

> if the existence of a bias in favour of the well-educated
> offenders is established, it is not thereby obvious that this
> has to be counteracted with *more* official contacts and
> registrations for the upper half of the population. It can
> equally well be argued that there should be somewhat *fewer*
> official contacts and more informal ones for the *lower half,*
> if equality in this matter is seen as a goal.

This tilting of the scales will not affect the question involved, which is not one of contacts or even of equality. The core of the problem is the socio-economic structure of society and it is thought by the police that medium and upper class families may deal better with juveniles than lower class families.

In the United States, research into the extent of unknown crime has received far more attention than elsewhere. Whether or not this has paid the dividends expected is a matter of conjecture. According to the approach followed, the studies may be roughly divided into three groups. The first, with variations, may be called the self-reporting system, in which the questionnaire and personal interview are the main methods used; in the second, which may be tentatively called the documentary system, somewhat methodologically heterogeneous, records, statistics, decisions, etc. are primarily used to gather information; and finally, there is the victim reporting system, in which persons are approached in different ways, frequently through interviews, and asked to provide information about unreported offences of which they or their households have been victims. Needless to say, there is always some overlapping among the three groups.

Among the first group are the Cambridge-Somerville, the Porterfield and Wallerstein-Wyle studies. The first (1936–45), although not especially aimed at the investigation of unknown delinquency, showed that there was a considerable amount among juvenile offenders. More significant, since it concerned crime and delinquency and men and women, was the Porterfield study published in 1946. The offences admitted were in many cases of a serious character, including one of murder and another of negligent homicide for which no charges were ever made. The discrepancy between detected and undetected sexual offences was extremely high, but here again it should be noted that the greatest proportion corresponded to extramarital intercourse followed by a far smaller number of cases of indecent exposure and by attempted rape in pre-college days. The study also showed that the number of undetected offences was greater among what are considered medium and upper social classes and that most of these undetected offenders, even if repeaters when they were young, were leading decent and respected lives as adults. The Wallerstein-Wyle study, 1947, used a questionnaire listing 49 offences, excluding murder, which was answered by 1,020 men and 678 women. Ninety-one per cent of the persons admitted having committed one or more offences excluding juvenile delinquencies. Men had an average of 18 and women an average of 11 adult offences. Larceny had been committed by 89 and 83 per cent of men and women; indecency by 77 and 74; assault by 49 and 5, and falsification and fraud 46 and 34 respectively. Although for several reasons the findings were not considered reliable in all respects, the inescapable conclusion was that the extent of unknown crime was far greater than expected. Although not quite corresponding to this group, the Kinsey reports on male and female sexual behaviour in 1948 and 1953 respectively, show that as far as sexual offences are concerned their concealed number is probably one of the highest in the huge area of unknown crime.

Particularly prominent in the second group is Sutherland's *White Collar Crime* (1949). Since then, the problem has received greater attention not only in the United States but also in Canada and the United Kingdom. The fact that the criminal character of many forms of white collar crime and even the whole concept have been criticized and denied does not affect the fact that the amount of undetected crime committed by persons of a certain social status taking advantage of these conditions and of their profession or occupation is not only widespread but in all probability rapidly increasing. This is a sequel of growing corporationism, penetration of foreign markets, industrial and technological espionage, monopolies, competition, etc., all main characteristics of well-developed or affluent societies. Criminologically, the term 'white collar crime' is unjustified. Sutherland never regarded it as definitive but coined it for purposes of convenience. Paradoxically some of the criminologists who regard legal definitions as conventional enlarge the already conventional meaning of white collar crime by including in it para-white collar crime.

The accusation that in this area criminal statistics are particularly biased is unfounded, as they reflect more than the realm of crime the realm of criminal law and criminal justice, i.e. the way in which the law is formulated and justice administered. To return to Sutherland, one of the most prominent American criminologists, it suffices to reproduce here what he said in 1940 in his first study on white collar crime: 'The crimes of the two classes differ in incidentals rather than essentials. They differ principally in the implementation of the criminal laws which apply to them.' The conclusion is clear: it is not the criminal statistics but the implementation of criminal law which reflects all too well the privileges of certain social classes. In short, criminal statistics reflect what the machinery of criminal justice—criminal law, police, courts, prisons and other agencies—provide.

Within the third group, the Washington, Boston, Chicago and University of Michigan surveys are significant inasmuch as their findings have been used by the President's Commission report, *The Challenge of Crime in a Free Society* (1967). Although for comparative purposes especially, other sources such as the *Uniform Crime Reports* and police precincts reports were used, the primary source of information of these surveys was obtained from answers given by people either as individual or as household informants. The general conclusion of the report is that the victim rates provided by the surveys show that the actual amount of crime in the United States is several times that reported by the Uniform Crime Reports.

More specifically, it is added that the amount of personal injury reported by the National Opinion Research Center of the University of Chicago, which surveyed 10,000 households, is almost twice that of the Uniform Crime Reports and the amount of property crime more than twice as much as that given by the latter for individuals. Rape was more than three and a half times that reported, burglaries three times, aggravated assaults and larcenies of $50 and over more than double, and robbery fifty per cent higher than the reported rate. It is significant that the amount of vehicle theft was lower than the reported figures—significant because it shows the importance that the car plays in a society like American society in which the tempo of life is so rapid.

Although the above-mentioned victimization rates give a glimpse of the extent of unknown crime as compared with reported crime, they are smaller than expected and very probably reflect only a part of undetected crime. As Biderman in an excellent study says: 'there are many indications that the survey interviews failed to measure exhaustively the victimization experienced by the citizens'.[6] The President's Commission report seems to be aware of this but devotes barely two pages to the crucial problem of unknown crime in the study of crime as a challenge in a free society. Although New York City is not typical, according to The Correctional Association of New York in its 1966 annual report, it is estimated that only one out of every ten cases of rape is reported to the police. Since approximately 1,500 rapes are known to the latter every year, this means that about 15,000 are actually committed. In 1966 the Annual Report of the Police Department of the City of New York listed 1,462. Because of its obvious bearing on the amount of unknown crime, it should be added that since approximately one out of 50 rapes result in pregnancy approximately 300 women conceive each year by being raped, a fact which, like that of incest with pregnancy, has a significant impact on the extent of undetected abortion. In my opinion, adultery, incest and rape constitute a trilogy which greatly increases the number of unknown abortions. According to The Correctional Association the ratio between known and unknown abortion is one to a hundred. This is also the minimum ratio—the maximum being one to five hundred— put forward by Wehner with respect to the Federal Republic of Germany in 1956. That for rape was between one to five and one to ten of the reported police figure.

The low ratios established by the surveys used by the President's Commission are mostly due to the disadvantages inherent in the victim approach at present favoured in the United States, as pointed out by Biderman, Reiss Jr. and others. Among other shortcomings, those arising from memorizing or recalling, what is inaccurately called time-telescoping and the varied impact of the different offences are usually mentioned.

The greatest shortcoming is the use of the victim as a reliable point of departure for research. Of the five basic subject matters of criminological research—crime, offender, victim, criminal justice system and society—the victim is the least 'reliable' and thus offers the least firm ground for research and measurement. This is because first, there are a number of criminal offences without a specific victim and many others in which offender and victim are the same person. Although in both cases society or its fundamental values or interests may be regarded as 'victims' the interrogation of the persons concerned will yield limited results. The same applies when the victim is a corporation, agency or any other entity. The cases in which the roles of victim and offender are played by the same person are numerous: such cases occur where drug addiction, self-inflicted abortion, bodily injury, suicide, prostitution, etc., are regarded as criminal offences. In all these cases, reporting or admitting the offence is infrequent. Secondly, the interview method, although in many respects preferable to the questionnaire, to be really effective requires not only repeated interviews but needs also to be followed up by other methods. Unfortunately this makes the already costly interview system very expensive and time-consuming. Thirdly, because human recollection, subject to various factors, quite often leaves out many of the intermediate but important offences between the extremely serious crimes and the trivial infractions. Even if remembered, they are frequently distorted or misinterpreted. And fourthly, because the concept of victim or victimization, especially when referred to a household, is either too narrow or too broad to bring up accurate or complete findings in the study of unknown crime; too narrow if restricted to actual personal experience, and too broad and uncertain when the individual acts as a household informant. It should be added that frequently the victim does not know he is a victim. This happens when organized and other forms of crime affect persons who are nevertheless ignorant of it. The remedy of making a distinction between victim, victimization and harm will merely shift the ground without making it firmer for research purposes.

The self-reporting or confessing method using interviewing techniques in order to uncover unknown juvenile delinquency has been widely used in the United States with varied and contradictory results. Following already standard concepts and techniques, in 1960 in Flint, Michigan, Martin Gold, with the cooperation of the public school system conducted an enquiry among 522 boys and girls, white and non-white, between thirteen and sixteen years of age, whether or not they attended public or private schools or were drop-outs.[7] The results submitted were obtained from the validation of 125 cases.

Since comparative research and methodology are of importance not only for the sake of research and methodology but more significantly for criminal policy, and there is, unfortunately, a tendency among developing countries to imitate and transplant techniques and methods, it seems justified to compare the Flint project with the Norwegian and Finnish projects already examined.

There is a marked contrast between the list of offences selected for the Norwegian and Finnish projects and that selected for the Flint project. While in the latter threats with or without a weapon, assault requiring medical care and arson are included, the Norwegian and Finnish lists do not include these or other violent offences. Many of the questions refer to different forms of shop-lifting, illegally taking things or producing alcohol, aspects of drunkenness, several forms of theft and sexual relations with girls under 16 years of age. The most serious offences are described as destruction of signs, telephone booths, etc., breaking and entering and taking anything by force. All in all the questions and the answers reflect a preconceived type of juvenile delinquency rather at odds with the age of the draftees. In this respect the Norwegian report says: 'The problems in choosing illegal acts are also very much smaller in working with young people than with adults.' Criminal statistics in general and those of Scandinavia in particular show that really violent crimes are not nowadays the monopoly of adults and that breaking street lamps, smuggling alcohol or tobacco, taking things from restaurants or cafés, destroying mailboxes or parking meters and the like, although extremely regrettable, do not characterize juvenile delinquency. From a policy-making point of view, the uncovering of particular forms of delinquency of a rather mild character does not help much in the study of the extent of unknown crime. One wonders whether the character of the offences listed has not influenced the willingness of the participants to answer the questions, so much stressed by both reports. Since apparently the whole Scandinavian project will be operated on the same lines, one may ask if, in spite of the fact that its aims are limited, the results obtained will not be misinterpreted at least as indirect proof that after all Scandinavian juvenile delinquency is not particularly serious.

Curiously enough, the more promising list of the Flint project has not yielded the information expected about the character of the offences committed, and this because the project is so engrossed in the relationship between social class and delinquency that everything is subordinated to finding out whether or not this relationship can be established. Certainly the tables refer to the weights assigned to the different offences but since these are numerical and identical for very different offences, and no indication is given about the answers received or the equivalents of the indexes and percentages, the writer failed to discover what are the specific offences committed and their approximate ratios. This is a serious shortcoming, and although the list of offences shows actual criminal offences, in the validated case No. 115 given as an example, playing truant and lying about age to get into the cinema are regarded as delinquent acts subject to indexes and accounts. One may question the value of the tabulations and indexes and whether at the present historical juncture the incongruous concept of juvenile deliquency still prevailing in the United States offers the firm ground required for useful research. What is the validity of findings based on such a mixed and unrealistic meaning of delinquency? In this respect the Norwegian and by inference the Finnish report, deserves praise as it clearly says that: 'Norwegian law does not—happily enough for this type of research—operate with the vague concept of "juvenile delinquency" and we escape the tricky problem of whether or not our acts represent real law breaking.'

As for the relationship between social status and crime, like the two Scandinavian studies the Flint study bases the social status of the juvenile offenders on the father's occupation. This technique, widely accepted in the United States, is an over-simplification of what social status is, whether referring to minors or adults. Admittedly, the discrepancies are less when teenagers are the subject of the inquiry but more obvious when these are draftees, i.e. young people of about twenty years of age.

Contrary to the findings of similar projects, Gold concludes that social status 'is indeed inversely related to juvenile delinquency, that more lower status youngsters commit delinquent acts more frequently than do higher status youngsters'. Qualifying this general conclusion he adds that 'while official records are selective in a way which exaggerates the relative delinquency of lower status youngsters, they may nevertheless approximate real delinquent behaviour'; 'that the more delinquent boys are more likely to be caught by the police'; 'that the majority of even the most delinquent boys are unknown to the police and courts. This comes as no surprise to the police'; 'that the data reveal no reliable relationship between delinquency and social status among girls', and as a final remark it is said that 'Data presented here do not permit us to choose among the various theories of delinquency which are based on its relationship to social status'. This helps to correct the occasional stress given to the question of social status in the project. Gold's conclusion, if taken in conjunction with similar projects including those following similar techniques and reaching different findings, shows that the importance attached to the relationship between delinquency and crime and social status, although significant, is losing importance as one of the main aims of criminological research. One of the reasons for this is that the way of thinking and acting of young people, individually and collectively, is becoming more and more dissociated from parental or family social status; this applies in different degrees to developed as well as developing countries.

In the developing countries research into the extent of unknown crime is more difficult than in developed countries where trained staff and financial resources are usually available. Moreover the findings are often ill received because they go against governmental points of view or stress the inadequacy of existing legislation. With respect to the methods used, experience shows that sometimes less sophisticated methods also yield satisfactory results with far less expense involved; as for the reaction of governments, agencies, officials and some local professionals, this is something to be expected by any seasoned expert coming from outside. On the other hand, a number of governments and agencies react favourably to the findings submitted, although they act slowly, mostly for lack of financial resources. In this respect, my own experience in more than one developing country has been extremely encouraging. What often happens is that governments still rely excessively on the thesis that improvement of material conditions will considerably reduce, if not eradicate, crime and juvenile delinquency. Unfortunately this improvement, which finds official expression in planning programmes of many sorts, is too often subordinated to the pursuit of nationalistic aims, panism of various kinds, political infiltration or propaganda abroad and the continuity of personal regimes under various labels. The whole picture is too often marred by serious political unrest. All this means that research into crime and undetected crime is rarely undertaken, and when it is, it is frequently the sequel to biased politico-social policies or programmes.

Since criminal statistics are not always available, and even when they are, their importance may vary according to whether they are police, judicial or prison statistics, and since research personnel is scarce, the information must be sought from other statistics and sources such as reports, enquiries and data of many sorts, published and unpublished, or administrative files, sometimes carefully kept but unused. As an example of well-kept but unused criminal data I should mention my experience in the State of Minas Geraes, Brazil, where I went on a short United Nations mission to assist with prison reorganization for which some criminal statistical data were required. With the help of several public officials, I was able

21

to locate a well-organized 'depot' of criminal data which had been kept for years and built up without anyone being interested in using it, not even the two institutes and the official agency which were supposed to take care of criminological research and studies.

Questionnaires, personal interviews and other self-reporting techniques are difficult to carry out, especially for foreigners, even if they have a knowledge of the language. In most cases the majority of the population are not educationally equipped to answer questions even if approached by their own nationals. If the purpose of the inquiry is understood, quite often deeply ingrained individual as well as collective attitudes, unmistakable expressions of prevailing cultural patterns, prevent people from answering or discussing questions which, according to these patterns, affect their dignity and right to privacy. Although not uniformly widespread, these attitudes constitute a serious handicap to criminological research in the field of undetected crime.

Referring to my experience in a number of developing countries, a few examples will suffice to demonstrate that in these countries the problem of unknown crime is as important as anywhere. As part of my duties as United Nations Adviser to the Government of Turkey, which wisely regarded the question of criminal policy as part of the planned development of the country, I was requested to provide data about the extent of crime. The question of determining as nearly as possible the real extent of abortion was brought up in October 1964 at the *Ayle Nüfus Planlamasi Konferansi* (Family Planning Conference) sponsored by the Government. The assertion that abortion was practically non-existent in Turkey was supported by the fact that police and gendarmerie statistical data, the former covering urban and the second rural areas of the country, contained only scanty data about abortion. Judicial statistics showed that between 1935 and 1960 the annual average number of cases sentenced by the courts was fourteen. Even if the dark figure coefficient—more or less uniform in some developed countries—was applied for speculation purposes only, the extent of unknown abortion would have been ridiculously low. This is because dark figure coefficients require reasonably good police statistics which were lacking in Turkey, and the reverse parallelism previously mentioned concerning certain offences is applicable to abortion in Turkey as well as in other countries. The reverse parallelism does not apply to murder and grievous bodily injury the ratios of which, between statistical and dark figures, are similar everywhere. One of the points of departure was the severe provisions of the Turkish penal code which, although promulgated in 1926, is still virtually the translation of the Italian penal code of 1889, in turn a reproduction to a great extent of the Sardinian penal code of 1859. Another is the fact that in Turkey no less than 12,000 women died every year of illegal abortion, and that some of them had endured it three or four times. Fortunately, hospitals and many doctors kept some records about these cases. A third point was to establish as nearly as possible the ratio between births and abortions according to medical data, some existing records and police experience. After a series of attempts, comparison of data from quite a number of sources, consultations and rectifications, I submitted as a tentative minimum and maximum that between 150,000 and 300,000 criminal abortions took place in Turkey, a country in which anticonceptional practices of any sort were resisted by the male and also largely by the female population. The figure was accepted and was to some extent instrumental in the adoption of the Family Planning Law promulgated on 10 April 1965.

In spite of some Turkish studies on juvenile delinquency, the general belief, even at governmental level, was that the problem was relatively unimportant. In support of this the argument repeatedly put forward was the number of minors sentenced by the courts or sent to special sections of the prison or to reformatories; some of the latter, like the one in Ankara, are well run since the reorganization between 1963 and 1965. In fact in one of the many valuable studies published by the Institute of Criminology of the Faculty of Law of the University of Istanbul, the figures for juvenile offenders sentenced by the courts clearly show that the problem was quite serious. In order to determine as nearly as possible the number of unknown juvenile offenders, I undertook a survey according to which the dark figure was no less that 80,000. In 1964, when the survey was concluded, the number of juvenile offenders kept in the special sections of the prisons and reformatories was 1,320.

In Iran the survey I conducted in 1965 showed that, taking into consideration the large age span assigned to juvenile offenders—between 6 and 18 years of age according to the 1959 law—the total number was in all probability 170,000. The total number of minors convicted by the courts of very serious offences such as murder, bodily injury, rape and burglary was 276; they were kept in the special sections of the prisons of Teheran, Mashhad, Tabriz, Shiraz and other towns. Despite the warnings of Mr M. Madjlessi, formerly Minister of Justice, and the views unanimously expressed by the Advisory Council on Juvenile Delinquency, the low figure was used to maintain that the problem of juvenile delinquency in Iran was non-existent or of minor importance.

I have conducted surveys in other developing and semi-developed countries, not only on juvenile delinquency, and in all cases, to the surprise of many of the authorities concerned, the extent of unknown crime, although only tentatively estimated, was many times larger than recorded crime.

What are the reasons for unknown crime? In varying degrees

and forms they are often enumerated in essays, reports and books. The President's Commission report mentions the following reasons given by individuals: 'felt it was a private matter or did not want to harm the offender, police could not be effective or would not want to be bothered, did not want to take time, too confused or did not know what to report and fear of reprisal'. Professor N. Walker in his *Crime and Punishment in England* (1965), refers to ten different reasons which may be regarded as additions to the above list, some coinciding with these and others, such as failing to realize that an offence has been committed, that those involved were willing participants, or that the offence is known only to the offender but not reported by him.

Although correct, these and similar enumerations have a marked individual flavour in the sense that they give the impression that whether or not crime is reported depends on individual circumstances. This may be true inasmuch as the act of reporting is ultimately an individual act. On the other hand, in order to understand better the complicated internal mechanism of unknown crime as an important aspect of the socio-political problem of crime, and reduce it as much as possible, one should go further and try to examine what are the general factors which facilitate unknown crime. These are: too many police forces with ill-defined jurisdiction; poor police organization and equipment, partly due to the diversity of police forces and partly to lack of financial or other means; growing use of police forces for public order or security matters in riots, political gatherings and demonstrations, sit-ins, and public protection of prominent visitors in parades and on tours; collective attitudes among people in general and officials in particular *vis-à-vis* crime; widespread poor living conditions, discrimination, political persecution, acceptance of or indifference to violence, brutality, defiance and rebellion; a general feeling that authority or discipline are lacking; corruption; incongruity, inflation and abuse of criminal law; slow criminal procedure and obsolete methods of investigations; political unrest; economic crises and general materialistic, sceptical and 'don't care' attitudes as a result of new ideas or patterns of life. These factors, more than the individual attitudes enumerated, should be the subject matter of policy-making decisions. Developed and developing countries alike suffer from the handicap of these circumstances which are the result of clumsy or politically biased policies or inadequate programmes and affect the extent of known but unreported crime as well as the reliability of reported crime.

The whole picture of unknown crime is discouraging, and although it could be considerably reduced, present control machinery will never be able to do away with it.

In some developing countries, the effect of the circumstances outlined is powerful. In others, mostly African, superstition sometimes contributes to the increase of unknown crime when acts such as 'staring' are regarded as criminal offences. My inquiries in such countries as Bolivia, Peru, the United Arab Republic, Syria, Turkey, Pakistan and India showed that in all probability the high number of reported accidental deaths, particularly in rural areas of difficult access, hides a sizable number of murders. In 1963 in Turkey, 2,589 cases of accidental death were reported to the gendarmerie, who often arrive several days later; these were mostly in rural areas where there are few medical officers. Arrests were made in ten per cent of the cases, but after a time the accused were almost all released for lack of evidence. Judges and public prosecutors know that many murders are disguised as accidental death. In many developing countries the machinery of criminal justice as it exists in the capital, towns and important villages, is practically non-existent in the rural areas. Even in 1967 in three Asian countries it was admitted to me that nothing was known about the extent of crime in large areas of them; the same can be said of some African and Latin American countries. Put together these areas show an enormous amount of unknown crime and the reported crime is insignificant.

Another source of unknown homicide is the number of the unsuspected natural deaths which are actually of a criminal character. In his excellent study *The Detection of Secret Homicide* (1960) Dr J. D. J. Havard shows that the inflated publicity given to some murders and the way in which the bodies were disposed of overlooks the fact that these methods are seldom used by the resourceful criminal. After studying the coroner's system still functioning in England and other countries, Dr Havard suggests a series of improvements. In developed countries, particularly where transport, anonymity and indifference account for the increasing number of missing persons, this is a further source of unknown homicide. The fact that in cities like New York the vast majority of cases appear as cleared in police statistics does not exclude the possibility that homicide is behind the clearance.

What is the real extent of homicide, taking into account police reported figures? In England and Wales the number of homicides (including infanticide) was 325, 364 and 412 in 1965, 1966 and 1967 respectively; in Canada 220 in 1966, Australia 271 in 1965, the Federal Republic of Germany 534 and 599 in 1966 and 1967, in Sweden (including infanticide) 181 and 184 in 1966 and 1967, Turkey 2,223 in 1963, India 12,310 in 1965, Mexico 10,446 in 1957 and in the United States 10,920 in 1966. Colombia, France, Japan, Pakistan, the United Arab Republic and Yugoslavia report over a thousand homicides annually. If Wehner's *minimum* ratio on unknown murder 1 to 3 is applied to these figures the result may come as something of a shock, yet it is a reasonable hypothesis in spite of the variables involved. The fact is that the amount of unknown homicide is greater than the known. If this happens with homicide, which is the best reported offence, it is also true of any offence and known crime as a whole.

The boundaries between unknown and known but unreported crime fluctuate and sometimes clearly overlap. This explains why much of what has been said about unknown crime is applicable to known but unreported crime which nevertheless has its own characteristics and problems. Known but unreported crime may broadly be grouped as follows:

Crimes against the person. Many of these offences are of the bodily injury type as a result of physical ill-treatment, family quarrels and feuds, vendettas or organized crime activities. The cases of battered children in developed as well as developing countries are often known but seldom reported to the police. In 1965 in England the National Society for the Prevention of Cruelty to Children investigated 39,000 cases involving more than 100,000 children. Apparently just over half were cases of child neglect and about ten per cent were bodily injury due to physical ill-treatment. The term cruelty means physical assault as well as mental impairment. Battered children are also numerous in the United States, France, the Federal Republic of Germany, but far less frequent in the Scandinavian countries. The reporting is mostly done by medical doctors, social workers, juvenile courts and welfare associations either public or private. The number of cases eventually reported to the police is less than that known to the above persons and services and considerably less than the number of cases which, although known, never reach doctors, social workers and the like. In the developing countries the number of battered children is probably greater because of sheer parental ignorance or rough living or the rigid interpretation of the parental right of correction. According to accepted opinion it was the American Dr John Caffy who, after devoting considerable time to the problem, coined the term 'battered child syndrome' to denote the condition of children who suffered from several types of injuries, not always easily seen, and often accompanied by undesirable psychological states, because of physical ill-treatment.

Although family members and neighbours are fully aware of the existence of these children the rule of silence is frequently observed, and even if reported to the police evidence is hard to get either because the parents lie and no witnesses come forward or because for obvious reasons the child is unable or unwilling to testify. In sum, the number of cases of bodily and mental injury in battered children is anyone's guess. But this does not mean that it is insignificant. On the contrary, according to the social workers in certain affluent societies the number is increasing. One of the reasons given is that the ill-treatment of children is one of the most significant symptoms of the family breakdown. Since the latter is becoming more frequent the number of battered children is on the increase. The reasoning is not very convincing, first because the expression 'family breakdown' is so much abused by social workers and medico-psychological professionals and secondly because, especially in developing countries, the family is often tightly united, without any kind of breakdown, and nevertheless the number of cases of battered children is by no means small. Possibly better living conditions, parental education and more widespread social services will help to reduce the serious forms of this treatment which appear in most criminal codes as an offence.

The slowness and expense of judicial proceedings, the inability to get a loan or immediate cash in certain circumstances, widespread usury and expanding organized crime activities have evolved two systems for prompt payment when the debtor is unable to pay. In both, threats, personal harassment and extortion are applied. One of them goes further by inflicting bodily injury on recalcitrant debtors.

The first system is the procedure applied by registered private agencies which, in consideration of a sizable percentage, assure the prompt payment of a debt. Threats of physical violence, of the disclosure of the debt or other facts and occasionally beatings are used. This disreputable system is not new but it is expanding, especially in affluent and semi-affluent societies. The second is the 'loan-shark' system evolved and almost exclusively operated by organized crime. The procedure may not only be physically more brutal but the victim—sometimes chosen and subtly induced to receive the loan—is compelled to commit a series of offences as compensation for his inability to pay the outrageous rates of interest. The most frequent of these offences are the granting of a concession or contract; protection from or assistance against the police; the acquisition of goods in bad condition at normal or higher prices; passing merchandise illegally to others and giving information about the contents and itinerary of trucks or lorries to be hijacked.

In many cases, not only the offences resulting from these two systems, particularly the second, but also the offenders are known to the police and other officials, but the number of those reported is small. Hearings conducted in May 1968 before the American Senate at which victims and public officials as well as known 'sharks' were invited or summoned to appear—all of whom claimed the privilege of the Fifth Amendment—disclosed that the vast majority of usury practices, loan-sharks and the inherent threats, harassment, damages, beatings and even killings were known by many, but seldom reported. New York and other large cities are regarded as what is called 'fruitful ground for loan-sharking'. In Manhattan, little more than ten cases a year are brought to court because evidence cannot be secured. Testimony given by police and public prosecutors shows that victims would rather go to jail for contempt than risk getting beaten or having their businesses or homes set on fire or even being killed. The hearings also showed that even lawyers are sometimes victims of loan-sharks. The 1965 New York law making it an offence to lend money at more than 25 per cent annual interest has not apparently yielded the expected results. Whether the 1968 Illinois law reducing the interest to 20 per cent will be more fortunate is open to conjecture. Incidentally, this law has been regarded as the model on which a Federal law should be based.

According to the report on Organized Crime of the President's Commission, loan-sharking is the second largest source of revenue of organized crime. The initial capital comes from the profits of gambling, which is regarded as the most important activity of organized crime. No comprehensive study has yet been made of loan-sharking but it is known to be closely connected with gambling losses, narcotic addiction, betting, small businesses, public officials and occasionally prominent persons. The rates vary from one to 150 per cent a week, which by itself constitutes the crime of usury. The lender is more interested in perpetuating interest payments or getting some other sort of compensation than in collecting the original loan.

All criminal codes contain provisions against the corruption of minors whether as a sexual offence or as a crime against the family. A perusal of criminal statistics will show that the number of cases reported to the police is so small that the inverse relationship already examined with respect to abortion probably applies. Although obviously as a result of new individual and collective attitudes the 'corrupted' minor is less innocent than criminal law assumes, as long as it is not changed, their number, known but unreported either because the family or the victim prefer to hide the fact, will be considerable.

Although not always specifically mentioned, slavery, included in the offences against individual freedom or deprivation of fundamental rights or reducing a person to servitude, is, in the vast majority of countries, a criminal offence. The exceptions are Saudi Arabia and the Trucial States. The 1926 International Convention on Slavery defines it as 'the status or condition of a person over whom any or all the powers attaching to the right of ownership are exercised'. This broad definition coupled with that of the slave trade given by the same Convention and certain provisions of the 1956 United Nations Supplementary Convention means that other similar institutions and practices should be regarded as forms of slavery.

The United Nations *Report on Slavery* (1966) by Mohamed Awad shows that in spite of the shortcomings inherent in the questionnaire system, particularly when addressed to governments, slavery and the slave trade are still practised in certain Arab and African countries. All of them deny the data submitted against them at the meetings of the policy-making bodies of the United Nations. Apparently in 1963 the Government of Saudi Arabia paid compensation to liberate 1,682 slaves when it is known that there are a quarter of a million in the country, 60 per cent of them of foreign origin. The data presented by the Anti-Slavery Society were refuted by the representative of Saudi Arabia on the Economic and Social Council, but no other data were submitted by him in rebuttal. In spite of repeated denials at the international forum when the voting comes up, slavery and human trade is not yet a vestigial problem in some Arab and African countries, all of which subscribe to the United Nations Universal Declaration of Human Rights.

Similar to slavery, and still practised in Arab and African countries, is the placing of children by their parents or guardians with prosperous people in return for a small payment. The practice, generally regarded as a criminal offence in these countries, has also been recorded in certain Latin American countries with Indian populations. Possibly it was relatively widespread in the not too distant past but my experience is that it has now stopped. The same cannot be said with respect to some forced labour practices which, according to national law and international conventions, should have been abolished. The above-mentioned Report on Slavery contains the statement by the Anti-Slavery Society that in Brazil the Kayabi Indians were tattooed with a number to facilitate their identification and capture in case of escape from forced labour. The representative of Brazil stated that the Service for the Protection of Indians of his Government had investigated the case, and no evidence to substantiate it had been found. The same Protection Service was accused in 1968 of several acts of genocide against the Indians it was supposed to protect, and this was admitted by the Government.

Crimes against property. Fraud, embezzlement, theft and damages are in many cases known but not reported. The most tangible result of the growing number of these offences is the increase in insurance rates or the reluctance of companies to insure. This has been called the criminality of honest people. If this is so, the question arises of whether a new concept of honesty more in accordance with accepted practices should be taken into account by criminal law.

Embezzlement and stealing are often committed by trusted employees and workers with no criminal records, leading respectable if modest lives and participating actively in civic crusades of every kind, including those aiming at better control of crime. In some instances the culprit or his family manages to make up what has been taken, and a transfer instead of dismissal is the decision taken. In a well-summarized report entitled *Why Honest People Steal* (1947) the Chicago Crime Commission published the results of an inquiry to determine the main factors of this criminality. In decreasing order of importance they were: gambling, extravagant living standards, unusual family expenses, undesirable associations and inadequate income. These and other factors, such as drinking habits, whether jointly or separately, account for a considerable number of known but unreported offences. Norman Japan and Hillel Black in their book *The Thief in the White Collar* (1960) have very well described the insecure executive who, after having committed a series of embezzlements, is eventually brought to court while many others are simply demoted or dismissed in order to maintain the reputation of the company. They point out that the glorified executive is far outnumbered by the small executive who is always overworked and badly paid. This type may commit offences against property for other reasons than those enumerated above—among them, the effects of overwork and the injustices of a promotion system which, although based on what may be called managerial-scientific appraisal of success and failure, is in many cases unjust. This raises the more general question of the extent to which industrial methods of evaluating individual and managerial success, so widely used at present and supported by spurious or mercenary psychology, may be regarded as contributing elements to a number of crimes against property, public economy and even health. While the criminality of employees has received considerable attention from insurance and survey companies and, needless to say, from criminologists, that of the employers remains practically unexplored.

In his excellent study *Offenders as Employees* (1962) J. P. Martin examines the problem in England where apparently there is a widely accepted distinction between 'pilfering' and stealing, the former being regarded as 'legitimate'. Pilfering is the stealing of small quantities of things of little value, while stealing is the illegal taking of more valuable things or greater amounts of cash. The distinction is sometimes almost irrelevant, inasmuch as pilfering may be so continuous that in the long run the total value may be very great) Martin raises the question whether the existence of small 'perks' may not be seen as the worker's equivalent to the boss's expense acount. The equivalence is hard to justify; although admittedly expense accounts may be misused, they are administratively authorized and granted, two aspects lacking in pilfering. Technically, pilfering is a minor form of stealing. The fact that it is overlooked and accepted in many countries raises the problem of the extent of criminal law. Although, as Martin says, the figures are absurdly low, this should not be regarded as proof that the number of these offences and their economic importance are also insignificant. On the contrary, if account is taken of the reluctance to admit them and the data gathered by surveys conducted by insurance companies, department stores, etc., known but unreported pilfering, stealing, embezzlement and the like are far higher than the statistics show. Moreover, as Martin also says, the offence constituted by not reporting a known criminal offence is also repeatedly committed by employers and supervisors. In examining this, he raises a number of pertinent questions such as the possible effects of taking the law into one's own hands and of leniency, which cannot be examined here. Suffice it to say that in my opinion repeated pilfering and condoning are forms of recidivism that society can apparently stand without discomfort, providing both remain within 'reasonable' limits.

Shoplifting, pilfering, stealing, frauds and embezzlement, minor and major, are frequently committed and known but not reported by businesses, stores, industrial enterprises, factories, governmental agencies and private individuals. There is the classic case in the United States of a company which asked its workers to gather together in the open yard one evening before leaving for home. The idea was simply to take a group photograph as a memento but the workers did not know this and suddenly the ground was covered with tools and equipment which was part of their daily takings. Such expressions as 'I am entitled to it', 'They owe it to me' and the more cynical 'Everybody does it' are all too frequently offered as justification) Other forms of offences against property, well known but unreported, are misuse of the telephone, the taking of souvenirs from hotels, unfounded insurance claims, etc. As *Time* also reported in one of the many interesting essays it publishes, in 1966 the Claims Bureau of the American Insurance Association estimated that 75 per cent of all claims are dishonest in some respect and amount to an overpayment of more than $350 million a year.

As for intentionally caused material damage, the number of known but unrecorded cases is certainly far higher than that shown in police statistics. Vandalism in private property, underground and railroad transport and installations, telephone boxes, shops, etc., has become such a common feature of contemporary society, especially in developed countries, that even if the authors are known or easily identifiable only a small proportion of cases are reported. Recently, riots of many sorts, whether or not socially or politically justified, have been a sizeable source of material damage and looting, not always reported because, among other reasons, the owners may not be covered by insurance.

In his charge to the National Advisory Commission on Civil Disorders, 1967, President Johnson requested advice on the 'proper public role in helping cities repair the damage' suffered in recent disorders. Experience shows that damage sustained by public or official property, services and installations remains unreported to the police more frequently than individual property damage. In the writer's opinion, the situation is likely to remain unchanged even if the Federal Disaster Act enacted in 1950 is modified to assist the 'community in man-made disasters'. In this respect the report says: 'There is a serious lack of property insurance. . . . Now riots and the threat of riots are aggravating the problem to an intolerable degree.' Among the remedies suggested are 'to call upon the insurance industry to take the lead in establishing voluntary plans in all States to assure all property owners fair access to property insurance'; 'that the Federal Government enact legislation creating a National Insurance Development Corporation to assist the insurance industry and the States in achieving the important goal of providing adequate insurance for inner cities'; and 'that the Federal Government enact tax deferral measures to increase the capacity of the insurance industry to absorb the financial costs of the program'. Putting aside the obvious difficulties involved in carrying out this well-intentioned programme, the fact is that unless a radical change in American society takes place, a change that will take more than one generation, it is difficult to see how the huge amount of compensation involved in a repetition of riots and civil disorders could be absorbed.

Crimes against public relations, order or interest. This broad heading embraces a group of assorted offences against well-defined community interests. As Marshall B. Clinard demonstrated in his excellent study 'The Black Market', recently reproduced in *Criminal Behaviour Systems* (1967) edited by Clinard and Richard Quinney, the black market flourishes during wars and afterwards, but for political and financial reasons black market offences are today as frequent as in war or times of distress. In any case, they are among the most widely known and accepted offences but seldom reported in spite of the severe penalties they entail in some socialist countries. In the U.S.S.R., in accordance with article 88 of the criminal code of the R.S.F.S.F., black market currency operations may be punished by deprivation of freedom for from three to eight years with or without confiscation of the currency or additional exile for from two to five years; occasionally the death penalty has been applied. In spite of this severity, or perhaps because of it, and the publicity given to certain cases in which foreigners were involved, I am sure the Soviet authorities are fully aware that a substantial number of known cases are not reported. Closer scrutiny of some of the reasons for punishing black market operations and for committing them confirms Clinard's view that the economic factors 'have been emphasized far more than evidence warrants' but also, in my opinion, that they cannot be explained as an expression of sub-cultural patterns or in accordance with the theory of differential associations.

Riots of many kinds are known and suppressed as quickly and effectively as possible, but this does not mean that all rioters, even if identified, are reported. The number of active rioters who are known but unreported will probably increase as long as social injustice, poor living conditions, forcibly imposed political regimes or ideologies, the rejection of certain governmental policies, deep dissatisfaction with work and industrial organization, educational systems and discrimination practices are the factors of collective behaviour. Riots are becoming almost a regular feature of contemporary society. In various ways they all advocate and practise violence, revenge, destruction, race hate and overt subversion if not revolution. In a different way the same happens with the 'intellectual rioting' of Russian intelligentsia inasmuch as the existing penal provisions, namely article 70 of the criminal code and its more lengthy version, section 7 of the law on criminal responsibility for crimes against the state, are not always applied. Yet technically and according to the ideologically inspired Soviet criminal legislation, they are criminal offences.

Another source of known but unreported offences is the illegal possession of fire-arms, which in many countries is overlooked. The resistance to tightening up the regulations on the acquisition of fire-arms, particularly in Mexico and the United States, helps to explain not only the high incidence of murder in these countries but also to some extent the murder of Presidents and prominent leaders in the latter.[8]

The crimes committed by secret organizations for patriotic, political, racist or other motivations are often known but unreported, especially when their criminal activities receive governmental support or support from public opinion. Among others the case of the Ku-Klux-Klan in the Southern States of the United States is well known. Related but actually constituting another type of known but unreported crime, is the administration of biased criminal justice by courts, judges and other authorities for political, racial and other reasons. This kind of 'justice' differs from that resulting from the application of outright biased legislation in that it consists in the racially distorted use of current criminal law and of the administration of justice system, while the other is corrupt justice as a product of a corrupt legislation. Such is the case with the racist legislation of South Africa and of some American States declaring as criminal offences inter-racial marriages. The fact that this legislation has been legally adopted stresses the distinction between legality and justice.

As criminal offences, drug addiction, homosexuality and prostitution are important sources of known but unreported crime. Quite often they are overlooked even if overtly committed. The number of these offences which is known but unreported is difficult to estimate. Certainly it is very high in the areas of cities in which they are tolerated.

Surgical interventions are also a source of criminal offences known not only to the victim and his family but also to the surgeon and his assistants and a relatively large number of colleagues and other professionals. The transplantation of vital organs, particularly the heart, raises the question more acutely. Certainly recent cases in which the death of the donor was contested or not verified shows that, even if small in number, the importance of organ transplants as a possible source of known but unrecorded crime cannot be ignored. The fact that an organ transplant is carried out in the performance of a recognized and legitimate profession does not necessarily justify it. *Mutatis mutandis* the same applies to other professional people such as lawyers, architects, chemists, pharmacists and contractors. Incidentally their offences, although committed by white collar people, should not always be identified with the so-called white collar crime.

Nowadays the so-called liberal professions are becoming less liberal and more occupational in character and purpose. In my opinion the present dualism between profession and occupation will eventually be solved *bellis-nollis* as far as doctors and lawyers are concerned, not in favour of one or the other but of a third, that of social function.

Organized crime. Close scrutiny of organized crime reveals two main forms, one the American type which is dominated by Americans of Italian descent, and the other, far less systematically organized and powerful and for the time being independent of any particular ancestry. They may coexist in any country and to a great extent reflect not only political, social and economic structures but also individual as well as collective attitudes *vis-à-vis* the fundamental values of the society in which they operate. The most widespread and at the same time the more socially dangerous is the American type, the main characteristics of which are hierarchical and disciplined organization, ruthless punishment methods, sustained efforts to subvert governmental policies against it, widespread use of corruption, protection and infiltration, constant expansion of activities, internal power struggles within the organization, and huge benefits. The characteristics of the second type are mainly loose organization, quite often of an *ad hoc* nature with subsequent dispersal, little reliance on corruption, protection and infiltration, less frequent use of brutal methods of disposal, limited range of activities almost exclusively in the form of crime against property, more reduced benefits and greater risk of being caught. Experience shows that this type of crime may evolve into more sophisticated forms of organization approaching the American type when gaming and betting, even if legalized, are widespread enough to offer criminal business perspectives. The only possible way to avoid this is to legalize gaming or betting and have them directly organized and exploited by a governmental agency.

According to numerous reports and studies on organized crime in the United States and the *Report of the Permanent Subcommittee on Investigations on Organized Crime and Illicit Traffic in Narcotics* of the American Senate, No. 72, 1965, and the President's Commission Report on Organized Crime already mentioned, the main activities of the *Cosa Nostra* are gambling, illegal traffic in narcotics, loan-sharking, commercialized prostitution, labour and management racketeering and infiltration into legitimate business.[9] Of these, the most international in character is the illicit traffic in narcotics, inasmuch as it requires the use of other countries either as consumers or as producing, manufacturing and transit countries. Also internationally important is commercialized prostitution, which requires the use of other countries either as victims or consumers or both.[10]

Like many other reports those here considered show that the extent of known but unreported crime is considerable and that several hundreds of members of the *Cosa Nostra* are well known, not only to the police but to other governmental agencies. With respect to murder, which, according to the Senate Subcommittee, is probably the most important crime of all, while in the past violent methods were frequently used, nowadays the more subtle system of simple disappearance is gaining ground. If the disappearance is reported, which by no means always happens, the case is recorded among those of missing persons. Consequently the number of unsolved murders is in all probability high, although difficult to determine, either because these cases are unknown, known but unreported or listed as missing persons, or because, if investigated, no evidence is found. The Subcommittee report and many others contain enough data to support this conclusion.

I have analysed these and other reports and data and reached the tentative conclusion that, putting aside the co-operation obtained when necessary from non-organized crime, the total membership of the *Cosa Nostra* does not exceed 10,000, of which perhaps a third are inactive members. Yet this comparatively small number have been able to maintain and expand their criminal and highly remunerative activities both against the police and staff of many public agencies of the most important urban centres of the United States which, at a conservative estimate, is well over 100,000 public officials whose occupation is to combat crime. Why? Although not particularly original, the answer has to be found in the undue reverence for power, money and manipulated politics which characterize the dominant groups in American society. The unavoidable outcome of this is political protection, police corruption, widespread indifferent or apathetic attitudes *vis-à-vis* crime and barely disguised resistance to attempts at required legislation. Needless to say there are many exceptions. Among governmental agencies, the examples of the Federal Department of Justice and the Federal Bureau of Investigation deserve special mention. The key, however, lies in the reverence for power so assiduously—one is tempted to say religiously—practised by leading groups. These, far more than society at large, quite often unjustly put in the pillory, are the moulders of many of the prevailing patterns and attitudes of what is called the American way of life, of which organized crime is one of the most salient features.

More than anything else, the reverence for power, money and politics explains why report after report is well received but ignored or put aside by those who should do their best to remedy the situation either at the legislative or administrative and judicial levels. The pathetic destiny of the sensational Kefauver report is typical. Taken as a whole the recommendations of the President's Commission seem to miss the point; nevertheless if implemented they would yield remarkably good results. Experience shows that the *Cosa Nostra*—the largest organization of the criminal underworld, as J. Edgar Hoover called it when giving testimony at the

House of Representatives Appropriations Subcommittee in 1966—will continue as long as American society is moulded as it is. There are already signs that some groups of society—often accused of being sick—are moving towards badly needed changes. To be effective some of them have to be radical or, since the term may be misinterpreted, deep enough to change the present patterns of American life.

Is organized crime really a social problem? The question has been raised by Professors Cressey and Ruth from two different points of view. They deny the character of organized crime as a social problem or criticize the way in which it is usually presented.[11]

Cressey maintains that it will not be easy to establish organized crime as a social problem for the following reasons: first, 'the American confederation of criminals thrives because a large minority of citizens demand the illicit goods and services that it has for sale', i.e. 'organized crime cannot become a social problem until a much broader segment of society perceives that the cost of the services provided is too high'; secondly, '. . . because a large proportion of the persons demanding illicit goods and services believe that they are supplied by criminals who are unorganized and who, for that matter, are not very criminal'; and finally because '. . . "organized crime" is not against the law. . . . Except when conspiracy statutes are violated, it is not against the law for an individual or group of individuals rationally to plan, establish and develop a division of labor for the perpetration of crime, whether it be bookmaking or murder'. Although dialectically attractive, Cressey's view is sociologically untenable. To begin with, the number and beliefs of victims are important, the former more than the latter, but the existence of social problems requires far more than a numerical consideration of the persons involved who, incidentally, are not only the victims directly affected. Cressey's initial misunderstanding is to regard organized crime as different from crime in general, of which it is an important part. Therefore, if crime as such is a social problem, it is obvious that organized crime is also. The fact that for investigation and even policy-making purposes, aspects of the same problem may be taken separately does not mean that they are not all parts of the same social problem in the same way that organized corruption of minors is part of the larger problem of moral corruption as contemplated by criminal law, or organized embezzlement or theft by a group of employees is part of crimes against property. As for not being defined by law, putting aside the refreshing fact that for once the importance of criminal law as a point of departure is admitted, Cressey seems to overlook the fact that social problems exist even if the law in general or criminal law in particular ignores them. Without denying that in some cases agencies or commissions may create social problems in order to justify their existence, it is obvious that as a general rule the problems existed before the agencies or commissions which are supposed to deal with them. In fact history shows that organized crime has always existed. To cite one example, the Italian Renaissance is typical. If conspiracy is punished only in certain cases, it is because to punish mental processes or preparatory acts is against the principle *nullum crime sine previa lege* almost universally recognized as a fundamental guarantee of human rights. What Cressey raises is a question of *lege Ferenda*. Should the rational planning of crime as a business or occupational enterprise be regarded as a form of criminal conspiracy? Among other forms we have conspiracy against the State. If properly formulated there is no reason why organized crime should not be regarded as a form of criminal conspiracy against society.

By stressing the primary importance of investigating the organizational linkages, fluidity and stability of organized crime's interaction with the world of respectability, Professor Ruth not only reduces the overall impact of the problem but what is more seems to contradict himself when he attacks the fragmented presentation of organized crime. It is true that the fragmentation is relatively frequent especially by the Press, which is sometimes more interested in sensational descriptions than in presenting a complete picture of a social problem. Therefore, the fact that commercialized prostitution is not now as important as it was does not affect the prevailing conviction among public officials and agencies and many researchers that organized crime is one extremely important aspect of crime in general. In this respect it should be noted that although organized crime uses crime in general, the reverse seldom happens. Although without giving total autonomy to organized crime, this significant fact shows that in some respects organized crime deserves special attention both in sociology and policy-making. The fact that by this attention some activities are stressed more than others does not imply fragmentation. In connection with commercialized prostitution which is singled out by Professor Ruth, two further comments are called for. The first is that since, like crime, organized crime reflects social evolution, its activities also change and fluctuate accordingly and may even disappear. Such was the case with bootlegging. This does not mean that some of these activities may not be revived. The second is that as long as prostitution is regarded in the United States as a criminal offence— curiously enough seldom mentioned in spite of its frequency in police and judicial statistics—commercialized prostitution will be a profitable undertaking for organized crime. The facts already known about interaction, linkages, etc., of organized crime offer the writer enough basis to go ahead, without waiting for answers which at the best will be as vague as the grounds on which they are based. What is far more important and is incidentally mentioned by Ruth, is the frustrating character of the evidence of organized crime.

The impact on society of the non-American type of organized crime is smaller but still important enough to require immediate attention. One is tempted to say that the stages of organized crime are loose organization, more definite and diversified organization of groups under different bosses often engaged in internecine fights, and the replacement of individual bosses by a 'director' who conducts crime as a business undertaking. Even if one of them is 'the boss under the table' the collective spirit predominates. The last stage requires receptive individual and collective attitudes to corruption at high levels and resigned or indifferent attitudes *vis-à-vis* certain forms of crime. Gaming and betting, even if legalized, facilitate passing to the second stage. As an expert called to give opinions on gaming and betting problems in several countries, I have always advised that if the principle of their legalization is accepted, both should be operated directly by the State and not by concessionaires. There is evidence that organized crime on non-permanent bases is frequent and developed. McClintock and Gibson's study *Robbery in London* (1961) although not dealing particularly with gaming, contains sufficient data to conclude that there is a considerable amount of known but unreported organized crime against property in London; the term 'professional gang' is used.

Crimes committed under cover of official position. Probably the greatest number of known but unreported crimes are those committed by people who, either as paid or unwilling accomplices, are engaged or used on behalf of those having an official position. Most of the offences perpetrated are against the person such as beatings, torture, maiming, deprivation of freedom and other fundamental human rights, and killing. Another substantial number is constituted by criminal offences against property, either individual or public, espionage of many kinds, rebellion and riots and instigation to rebellion and riots, corruption of officials, sabotage, etc. The most significant positions involved are intelligence or espionage services, diplomacy, security police, general police services, occupation armies and various official missions. Actually no country can claim to be innocent: the only differences among them are of skill, lack of scruple and the extent of the activities of the services concerned. The most unrepentant are the special branches or services. As for discrimination practices and policies for political, racial, religious or other reasons, they are often brutally implemented by developed as well as developing countries. Like colour discrimination, white discrimination has already found victims in Arab and newly independent countries. Political discrimination has also led to crime by officials in countries with nationalist regimes, dictatorships and most if not all of those claiming a people's democracy. Contemporary riots are also a frequent source of this type of crime by police and military forces.

Crimes committed under cover of an official position can sometimes be regarded as a form of organized crime, the main organizers of which are services very little known except through references in 'literature' and the Press. There is no question that an organization exists. It is more difficult to say whether the commission of crime, although not for pecuniary purposes, is its primary purpose. Only certain types of crime are regarded as part and parcel of the set-up, such as espionage, sabotage, corruption of officials, destruction of things having specific or potential value, disclosure of vital secrets, treason, criminal disloyalty, etc. With them homicide, bodily and mental injury and violation of fundamental human rights are quite often intermingled. Their field of criminal activities seems to be larger than that of the traditional American type of organized crime. Another difference is that while organized crime makes money, crimes committed under cover of an official position cost money, sometimes enormous amounts of public money. Even if the countries are wretchedly poor and the vast majority of the population is starving, they always manage to maintain an intelligence service or security police in order to pursue political aims.

The second important question is whether the crimes committed under cover of an official position are justified either because the persons involved acted on behalf of national law or following legal orders or because of political necessity or expediency as part of the *raison d'État*.

It is possible that in some cases there may be justification, but neither the law nor the legal order can be justified beyond the limits established by the respect due to fundamental human rights. The fact that they are often violated does not affect the position. Only in exceptional cases may the law and the legal order justify what is currently regarded as a criminal offence. This was the decision at Nuremberg and has also been the position maintained by the courts of the Federal Republic of Germany in the numerous Nazi cases judged by them. For years the traditional foundations of these two forms of justification have been challenged, and it has been maintained that in order to protect the individual and society against arbitrary law or policies, even if legally promulgated, the exemptions provided by criminal law must be considerably reduced. Otherwise legalized brutality would be the rule. As for the act of State or *raison d'État*, which has a rather unsavoury past, apart from the erroneous identification often made in pseudo-democratic countries between State, regime and person, there is the crucial question of whether the interests of the State or political necessity justify the crimes committed. Unfortunately, in many countries some official positions have become so degraded that the commission of criminal offences is accepted without question. This is the case with diplomacy; it is true that it has always been concerned with watching and getting information, but it now seems that it is frequently used as a cover for espionage. The increasing infiltration into the province of diplomacy by intelligence activities does not justify it. The expanding of these activities is partly the result of the inflated importance given to security, secrecy and risk. Science and technology have contributed to this inflation, but political aims play the dominant role, especially in countries where the lack of scientific and technological power is replaced by pan-isms or anti-isms of every sort, claiming expanded intelligence and security services.

In sum, there is in every country, always was and probably always will be, an area of uncertain limits in which what is called political necessity is the *ratio essendi* of policies, programmes and decisions which often require the perpetration of criminal offences. Although, admittedly, in exceptional circumstances, necessity may justify certain acts and divest them of their criminal condition, when necessity and politics combine they inevitably multiply the number of exceptions, and these remain common crimes. The condition of being political, which until recently implied extenuating circumstances, cannot be applied to them, for the simple reason that while in the past political crimes were usually committed against political oppression or brutal regimes, most of those committed nowadays are aimed at maintaining them. These crimes are known but seldom reported to the authorities in charge of the control of crime and the administration of justice. One of the reasons is that most of the pseudo-democratic countries of our time have organized a system of criminal law of a purely administrative character which works completely apart from the current system of criminal justice which, needless to say, is also pliable enough to serve political purposes. The frequent cases of political rehabilitation of men executed or sent to prison for long periods of time is one of the many examples. The most frequent official reactions against these criminal offences when they are made public are disavowal, obstinate denial, accusations that the whole thing has been invented, the transfer of the persons implicated or, at the utmost, the application of disciplinary sanctions. Seldom are the real culprits brought before the courts. The cases of crimes committed under cover of, or related to an official position are too numerous to deal with here. The following examples will suffice. According to information published by the Press and made known by official communiqués in recent years a substantial number of Arab foreign service officers, most of them from the United Arab Republic, have been sent back to their countries after being accused of subversive activities. Even assuming that some of these expulsions were in retaliation for similar expulsions, the number is significant enough to conclude that the subversive activities existed. The expulsion of diplomats from the United States, the U.S.S.R. and other countries are too numerous to mention. Here again retaliation may play a definite role, but in many cases there is little doubt that criminal offences of various sorts covered by the generic mantle of subversion or espionage have been committed. The record of these and similar criminal activities is still held by the United Arab Republic with her trunk-diplomacy, discovered by pure chance in 1964 when two secretaries of the Egyptian Embassy in Rome were expelled for trying to send to Cairo as *valise diplomatique* a specially prepared trunk in which Mordecai Luk was found. The investigation showed that it was not the first time that the trunk had been used with the same kind of contents.

In 1960 at the trial for the assassination of the Prime Minister of Jordan, it was revealed that Egyptian diplomats and intelligence agents, some of them identified, were implicated; similarly at the trials for the attempted assassinations of President Bourguiba and King Idris of Libya. One may assume that the amalgamation of diplomacy and intelligence services is a source of known but seldom reported criminal offences.

Kidnapping engineered by joint diplomatic and intelligence services has also been carried out by other countries. Some of the abductions by the U.S.S.R. are very well-known. More recent and no less significant are those in 1967 by South Korean diplomats and agents of workers, professors, writers, artists and students living in European countries, particularly in the Federal Republic of Germany, who were brought before South Korean courts to be convicted as criminals for the simple reason that they were regarded as political 'enemies'. The complaints made by the German Government were of no avail. American intelligence, with or without the connivance of diplomatic or other missions, has an equally unsavoury record. In this respect the CIA's activities are numerous; its widespread infiltration and corruption may occasionally transform common criminals of other countries into patriotic servants of the United States. Neither the ambivalent character of espionage activities nor the interchange of spies invalidates the criminal character of the acts committed.

The past and the present offer numerous examples of known but unreported crime committed more or less openly by special security police forces. The case of German Nazism is sufficiently well known; its atrocious crimes included experiments committed for scientific purposes by doctors and other professionals on human beings. In sum, the extermination of Jews and other minorities will always remain as patent examples of brutal political criminality. This was done on internal administrative orders, some of them secret, which legally did not invalidate the provisions of the German penal code according to which killing, bodily injury, deprivation of human rights, etc. were defined as criminal offences. The most sophisticated answer that I received when questioning Nazi professionals was that *der totale Staat* as represented by national socialism was based only on *Volk und Rasse*.

By definition, all dictatorial or authoritarian regimes, even if labelled people's democracies, require strong and tentacular security police which inevitably commit crimes by torturing, beating, depriving people of their fundamental rights, keeping them in prison in inhuman conditions, sending them to camps and when required, liquidating them. Here I am referring not to periods of revolution in which criminal justice and justice in general is given a 'revolutionary conscience', but to definitely settled regimes. The European, African and Latin American dictatorships are too numerous to be worthy of specific mention. In all of them, outside *ad hoc* criminal legislation, there are police security forces with enough autonomy to act as they wish following the dictates of political necessity or expediency. Particularly significant were the atrocities, including kidnappings, committed by the security police of the Dominican Republic in the Trujillo era. No less significant is the present case of Haiti. My experience after so many years attending and organizing international congresses and conferences on crime prevention and treatment of offenders is that often the representatives of dictatorial countries are hypocritically the most eager supporters, if not the initiators, of proposals to improve the treatment of prisoners. According to the United Nations Standard Minimum Rules, treatment should be equally humane and impartial for all prisoners without discrimination on grounds of race, colour, sex, language, religion, *political or other opinion*, national or social origin, property, birth or other status.

Police brutality and corruption quite often amounting to criminal offences exist in different forms and degrees in all countries. In some developing countries widespread corruption, although it reflects the general impoverished condition of the country, usually concerns only minor matters. In developed countries, as befits their socio-economic structure, police corruption is more subtle and demanding, and in some of them, too widespread for comfort.

Politics and organized crime play a definite role often exposed in the United States by the Press and official inquiries. Cases of policemen committing burglaries and several forms of extortion are periodically reported there and, far less frequently, in the United Kingdom. An analysis of the cases leads to the conclusion that the number of those known but unreported exceeds those which are known and reported and submitted to disciplinary action and to the courts.

More common is police brutality. A study of this problem shows that a distinction should be made between rough and even brutal manners, sheer brutality in attacking and counter-attacking demonstrators and rioters, particularly by specially organized riot police forces as is the case in France, and brutal or 'third degree' methods used to secure evidence, particularly confessions, also shooting with scant justification offenders when they try to escape. In varying degrees all these forms reflect what may be called police mentality which, in my opinion, corresponds to the socio-economic factors and politico-cultural attitudes prevailing in the area concerned. In countries such as England, the image and function of the police responds to some general characteristics such as dislike of violence, restraint and patience, and a certain disregard for material comfort and amenities as status symbols. In countries such as the United States, police violence is more frequent because violence is a pattern of life, and restraint and patience do not accord with the rapid tempo of life. The importance attached to the possession of material things as symbols of social status should also be mentioned. In France the police are inclined to regard themselves as being apart, as living incarnations of law, order and above all, of a powerful administration, which is not always inclined to stand behind the responsibility incurred by its servants. Perhaps the way in which the terms 'bobby', 'cop' and 'flic' are used with their different intonations may convey better than anything the three images outlined.

The first form of violence is to be regretted, but by itself does not constitute an offence. The second is often regarded as a legitimate reaction against brutal attacks by demonstrators. This is possible but does not explain the cases in which the police, particularly the riot police, are the attackers and the rioters respond, or the ill-treatment inflicted on by-standers or people who have little to do with public disorder. Putting aside whether or not they were justified, recent public disorders and protests in many countries such as Spain, Italy, France, the Federal Republic of Germany, the United States, Yugoslavia and Japan have been the source of criminal offences against the person widely known but for obvious reasons seldom reported.

As a source of known but unreported crime especially against human rights, the brutal methods still used to get evidence are particularly important. The instances are more frequent in cases of felony when the suspected person is without influence or not prominent either in politics, professional standing or business. The most current practices are trial and error arrest, taking undue time for investigation, third degree methods and deprivation of counsel or medical assistance when they are needed. It need hardly be said that in every country criminal procedure and special rules prohibit these practices, often defined as criminal offences, and that not all police forces or all the members of a particular force engage in this form of criminality. It should be added that this is partly facilitated by complacent public prosecutors and judges. Moreover, when the offences are denounced the complaints are often dealt with by Police Boards or authorities, a practice that makes the police judge and party at the same time. Boards or Commissions constituted by civilians are resisted not only by the police but even by the public, as happened in New York in 1966 when this type of board was rejected by public referendum. Another contributing element is collective apathetic attitudes *vis-à-vis* illegal police practices. As for the members of the underworld who are also frequent victims of criminal offences in the form of physical ill-treatment or violation of human rights, they regard both as something inherent in their profession. Finally but far less common, the faking of evidence is also an offence which, although known and even occasionally reported, is seldom acted upon.

In the United States the devoted efforts of Vollmer, Wilson, MacCormick and many others have considerably reduced these practices in many states. By introducing better selection, training and remuneration, police mentality and practices have improved. Particularly decisive in this respect have been the last decisions of the United States Supreme Court dealing with or touching police practices and the obtaining of evidence. Yet important segments of public opinion openly maintain the necessity of preserving or reinforcing police prerogatives. Indirectly, this attitude gives support to the thesis of many policemen and lawyers that the rights of criminals are overprotected.

Another source of known but unreported criminal offences is the ill-treatment and deprivation of fundamental human rights of prisoners by guards, especially in large institutions. Less serious but also criminal in character are the numerous forms of extortion to which prisoners have to submit if they want to get privileges or even the simple application of prison regulations granting them certain benefits. In many prisons in developing as well as developed countries, strolling in corridors or yards, going out on errands, getting a particular assignment, receiving cards, dice, liquor and even women has to be paid for according to a well-established tariff. Sometimes these rackets are operated by prisoners with the connivance of the guards, sometimes by guards with the help of the prisoners. It took no fewer than three inquiries to eradicate the prison racket in 1955 in The Tombs of New York City which was operated by several guards, three of whom already had criminal records when they were appointed. An inquiry conducted in 1959–60 in the prisons of Florida elicited the fact that 'Prisoners were forced to sit on the floor, some on piles of salt with their legs protruding between the bars over the lower horizontal bar cuffed in that position while their hands were also drawn through the bars and handcuffed'.[12] The grisly record of the Arkansas prison system was publicly disclosed by the Press when a series of inmates' bodies were discovered buried in the grounds of the State Penitentiary in 1968. Official and Press inquiries were conducted; the police report was never made public, but according to the Press findings, killings, brutal felonies, ill-treatment, gross neglect and serious infringements of human rights had for many years been features of the prison system. In March 1968 the United States Supreme Court unanimously declared that Alabama's discrimination in the correctional system was unconstitutional. Alabama authorities had contended in 1966 before a Federal Court that discrimination was necessary to maintain order, and that inmates forfeited their rights when they were found guilty of crimes and they appealed against the decision. Curiously enough, this mediaeval point of view still finds supporters in the United States.

Overcrowding, poor professional training, poor selection and remuneration of guards pompously called 'correctional officers', obsession with security measures and the viciousness of some prisoners explain why many crimes remain unreported.

In 1966 prisoners of the Hamburg main prison were 'disciplined' by being kept naked and having streams of alternately freezing and hot water turned on them. Brutal physical punishment is used in many countries by prison guards, with or without the knowledge of supervisors or wardens. This is particularly the case with juvenile offenders.

Prisoners themselves commit many offences which are sometimes known and reported and punished, sometimes unreported or over-looked.

This is particularly the case with forced homosexual practices. Among many other examples the case of Villa Devoto, Argentina, where they were practised on almost every newcomer in the presence of all the members of the huge collective dormitories is significant, not of the lack of sexual satisfaction but of the brutality that often

46

permeates the atmosphere of the large prisons. This brutality by both prisoners and guards was at its height in 1962 when the prisoners' riot was followed by the massacre of some of them by the guards. Forced homosexual practices are common in all the prisons in the Middle East. As for extortion against fellow prisoners, this is practised on a major or minor scale in all institutions by prisoners holding such small official positions as trusties, clerks, assistants to doctors and other posts. One may argue that homosexuality is not an offence and that the extortions are often insignificant. This is possible, but in the vast majority of countries homosexuality is still regarded as an offence, particularly when committed by force and quite often by several persons on the same victim. As for being insignificant, anyone knowing prison life knows that what in many cases is insignificant for outsiders is very important for a prisoner.

Brutality frequently amounting to maiming, torturing, bodily and mental injury, ill-treatment, deprivation of fundamental human rights and occasionally murder, is committed against political prisoners by the military, special police forces or security services in charge of penal institutions, and on a minor scale by regular prison staff against common offenders, especially when, as happens in developing and even certain developed countries, that staff is made up of members of the police, gendarmerie or civilian employees with no qualifications whatsoever. The Press inquiries conducted by organizations or committees and other sources have fully revealed the existence of this type of known but unreported criminality, always denied but always present in the prisons of dictatorial regimes. Under Franco, the Spanish prisons offer numerous examples, and Portugal still offers them in spite of public protest. Examples are provided by Greece and Brasil.

In the socialist countries the cases are less well known, but it would be illusory to think that they do not exist. The report of the International Commission of Jurists *Justice Enslaved* (1955) provided ample evidence. Since then, in spite of some liberalization, the situation remains essentially the same. Continuous suppression or serious limitations on freedom of dissent, speech, thought and expression—proclaimed by the different socialist constitutions— even if carried on under cover of judicial trials against intellectuals, are a source of official criminal offences, not only against individuals but also against the due process of justice recognized by the constitutions, criminal codes and laws of these countries. The still recent trial of Bukovsky, denounced by Litvinov and others, is one of many examples. The fact that references to this and other cases were erased from the records of the Commission on Human Rights, March 1968, at the request of the Soviet Union with the support of other socialist or complacent countries does not mean that the criminality of the offences has also been erased. Recent disclosures in Czechoslovakia have demonstrated the frequency of these known but unreported offences. Those made by A. London in his book *L'Aveu*, 1970, show how widespread this kind of crime is.

The foregoing does not exhaust the number of cases either with respect to countries or to criminal offences committed under cover of an official position. Traffic of influence, corruption and venality, defined in most countries as crime under special laws, are becoming more frequent. In the developing countries, political instability and growing industrialization seem to contribute to their increase. The former implies insecurity and the tenure of a post (whether minor or not, but usually poorly remunerated) for a short period only; the latter means abundance of concessions, contracts, etc. in which large amounts of public funds are involved. As for other countries, corruption, kick-backs, graft, etc., although punished by criminal law, are frequent in the dealings of the public administration of big cities in such different types of countries as Argentina, Brazil, Italy, France and the United States. In the latter, the Marcus Reservoir scandal of New York City in December 1967 is one of the many examples. Economic crimes involving corruption, venality and traffic of influence are not infrequent in the Soviet Union, and this is in spite of the fact that capital punishment has been imposed in some cases.

Crimes against international law. These are crimes against international agreements such as those on genocide and the four Geneva conventions on prisoners of war, interned enemies, civilians living in occupied territory, etc. Even with respect to armed conflicts of a national character, the conventions specifically provide that persons not taking an active part in the hostilities, including members of armed forces who have laid down their arms and those placed *hors de combat*, shall in all circumstances be treated humanely without discrimination of any sort. Accordingly, violence to life and person, in particular murder of all kinds, mutilation, cruel treatment and torture, taking hostages, the passing of sentences and the carrying out of executions without previous judgment pronounced by a regularly constituted court according all the judicial guarantees which are recognized as indispensable by civilized people, are prohibited. Furthermore, the wounded and sick shall be collected and cared for.

Countries such as China, North Vietnam and North Korea maintain that since they are not parties to these and other international conventions, they are not bound to respect their provisions, which actually require only a minimum established and accepted by civilized people. If they choose to ignore these minimum requirements, only two conclusions are possible: either they are not civilized or, while they profess to maintain dignity and freedom, they violate both. The brain-washing of prisoners is one of the most obvious proofs of lack of civilization. Even if national criminal codes do not declare such acts crimes, *juris gentium* principles and practices are against them, but here again the question of being civilized seems to be decisive. It is worth noting that while in the *Quotations from Chairman Mao Tse-Tung* (Peking, 1966), frequent references are made to patriotism, frugality, courage and heroism, nothing particularly significant is said about justice and human dignity. Apparently, within the framework of 'democratic dictatorship' they are irrelevant. One may understand the brutalities of past centuries but be baffled and pained by those committed in our time, particularly when the culprits are countries which claim to have committed themselves to building up a better world. The theory that in order to achieve this, the death or liquidation of individuals is unimportant is not only unconvincing but in the long run fruitless. Whatever is done to man, the individual re-asserts himself and fights back. The present reaction against oppressive regimes in socialist countries confirms this. The tragedy is that in the meantime numerous crimes are committed, followed here and there by rehabilitation and release which, besides being proof of past crimes, is of no help to the dead, the maimed or the morally or psychologically ruined. The conclusion is twofold: first, that to greater political promises, even if accompanied by scientific and technological progress, corresponds greater political brutality against individuals, groups and countries; and second that, as the inevitable sequel, criminality will increase. What has been said does not mean that socialism, which has contributed in many respects to the improvement of human dignity, is to be blamed and banned, but that the way in which it is interpreted and imposed in certain countries increases crime.

With respect to genocide, the cases of the Armenians, Biafrans and Brazilian Indians are illustrative enough. The first were the victims of the deliberate policy of brutality of the Turkish Government for almost five years. One million Armenians were slaughtered without compunction or interference of any sort. Certainly, individual criminal responsibility for the crimes committed was never envisaged. The same happens in Nigeria against Biafrans and other countries where minorities are brutally persecuted or liquidated. The case of the Brazilian Indians has been going on for years on what may be called the genocide instalment plan. Only because the Brazilian Office for the Protection of Indians recently went too far and increased the wholesale liquidation of Indians, was public and then official opinion aroused and action taken. This does not necessarily mean that the culprits will be punished and all crimes investigated. Politically and economically, the Indians of Brazil, like all other Latin American countries, have always been regarded as expendable. It is interesting that the Spanish and Portuguese methods of exploitation look clumsy and almost benign when compared to the methods used by Latin American countries. Argentina, Peru, Ecuador, Colombia, Venezuela, Guatemala and Panama offer vivid examples.

Army occupation is a frequent source of known but unreported crime and criminal impunity. Here again, without going too far into the past, the examples are numerous. Japanese atrocities against civilians and prisoners during the last war are too well-known to warrant detailed inclusion. Differently motivated but still important because of the involvement of 'people's democracies', were the crimes committed against the Hungarian people during their legitimate uprising. Although couched in restrained terms the *United Nations Report of the Special Committee on the Problem of Hungary*, 1957, leaves little doubt about these crimes. In Algeria the Secret Army Organization and its supporters committed a series of atrocious crimes against the Algerian people, most of them known but unreported to police authorities. In 1961 the Bizerta (Tunisia) atrocities exposed by the report of the International Commission of Jurists confirmed much of what had been said about the crimes committed in 1958.

On a minor scale, but still serious enough to be taken into account as proof of the extent of known but unreported offences, are those committed by the occupation armies in Austria and France in the recent past. In Germany, far less important as far as extent is concerned, the protests made by local authorities moved American and British commanders to cancel all military passes in certain areas. Although traditionally army occupation implies unpunished criminality, it is still out of proportion in view of the 1949 Geneva Conventions. There is no doubt that the armies involved in the war in Vietnam have been sources of common crimes. Many of them will remain unknown, and others, although known, will remain unreported. A few, like the massacre of Pinkville, are eventually brought before a military court. The possibility of crimes committed by the Vietcong being brought before a court is, for the time being, remote.

Crimes committed as the sequel to patriotic, political or revolutionary action. Resistance organizations against enemy occupation, political organizations in favour of national independence and revolutionary movements have accomplished many good things, but these do not always justify the crimes committed on their behalf. It may be argued that to a great extent they were inevitable, but inevitability is not justification. In these and similar cases, what is euphemistically called 'political casualty' is actually a criminal offence and shows how crime is inherent not only in historical and political processes but in human nature as well. In sum, these crimes retain their condition whatever political purification is offered. The Spanish Civil War is one of the most typical cases of the failure to purify the crimes committed, even if religion is used to that effect by one of the sides.

Resistance organizations against the enemy fulfil a patriotic duty, but one cannot assign to patriotism a total purifying condition, since the occupying forces could claim it as their justification. Some of the actions of resistance fighters were motivated by other than patriotic reasons, and often others than enemies were victims of their activities.[13] *Mutatis mutandis* the same applies to movements in favour of independence against colonialism. The crimes of the Mau-Mau cannot be justified either politically or criminologically. Obviously, in fighting for independence a patriotic role is fulfilled but this does not mean that everything is permissible in the name of patriotism. Probably, to some revolutionary minds the question of justification is purely academic, but not to history and the individuals who suffer. This is because justice is the most powerful need of the individual and mankind in general. Not even the promise of a better world can justify crime or divest it of its condition. This is why the study of crime cannot be confined to that committed by what may be called the conventional criminal.

Revolutionary periods usually create their own legal systems. Technically what is done under them is legal, and it would be difficult to demonstrate the contrary. On the other hand, it is obvious that outside this legal system, and sometimes against what it proclaims, political and many other crimes are committed and tolerated. What is significant here is not that an ideologically inspired definition of crime exists, but that the revolutionaries quite often know that the facts do not conform to the legal description and yet use it to judge and condemn. Since by themselves political aims have not a justificative character, the use of legal machinery and justice to achieve these aims is a crime. Here again, the ugly juridical ghost of the rehabilitation of executed or imprisoned persons provides the evidence required to demonstrate the series of crimes committed by using the machinery for political purposes. Contrary to the 19th century's sentimental and ambivalent conception of political crime, owing to the distortion of the term democracy, the content of political crime has been so adulterated that it cannot be justified as it occasionally was in the past.

Finally, terrorism whatever its forms and purposes, has always been regarded as crime. An international convention against terrorism failed many years ago because no sufficiently clear-cut definition of the term was found. As an instrument of political ideology it has always been used against certain regimes or groups. As a source of crime against innocent people it is becoming more serious, inasmuch as it is regarded as a complement to guerrilla warfare, infiltration in neighbouring countries, etc. It may be practised by specially organized units or as individual acts. The Vietnam war offers examples on both sides of a variety of forms of which the most frequent victims are non-combatants. Although well-known, the criminal acts are so frequent that often they are not reported. A typical example of an individual act of terrorism was the public murder of a Vietcong prisoner by the chief of police of Saigon. Although obviously a common crime it was never reported as such. Whatever its patriotic motivation, Palestinian terrorism is as criminal as any other. The same applies to the cases of torture of Arab prisoners in Israel, the kidnapping and murdering of individuals for political reasons and the brutal beating, wounding and killing by police, national guards, etc. against rioters and protectors.

2 Reported crime

Reported crime is the information received or gathered about the commission of a criminal offence taken down by an authority for verification purposes. The definition implies a distinction between reported and statistically reported crime. The former means acquisition of a knowledge which at a certain stage has to be formalized according to existing regulations, the latter the systematic presentation of reported crime duly verified. In sum, while statistical crime is reported crime, not all reported crime is included in the statistics. Several reasons may account for the exclusion: one the triviality of the offence, another that, as previously stated, in France and other countries some juvenile offences, although taken down by the police, are not formalized but kept for future reference. Occasionally the same may happen with adult cases. Generally the expression 'reported crime' is identified with crime known to the police. This is only partly correct, inasmuch as apart from the fact that crime may be known first by another public authority and afterwards reported to the police, judicial and penitentiary data are also important aspects of reported crime. Verification of the information received or gathered does not mean that the offence has been solved in the sense that there is an accused person. It means that the offence has been established. It is here that although constantly related, fact and person, or better, crime and offender, often part company. Police statistics on cases refer to facts and are more reliable than police statistics on arrests, which refer first to accused or suspected persons and indirectly to facts or offences. The content of reported crime, particularly when statistically presented, may refer to offences and offenders and each of them may be classified in different ways.

As soon as a crime is reported, the long procedural itinerary as well as the thinning-out of the offenders involved begins. The procedural itinerary varies from country to country, although not essentially. Those interested in having a detailed view of the itinerary that the penal system imposes may study the well-presented schema of the *Task Force Report: Science and Technology* (1967) of the President's Commission report which, with some imagination, may be applied everywhere. Schematically the main stages of the itinerary are police action (verification, arrest, solved and unsolved cases); indictment or prosecution (accused persons whether or not awaiting trial or detained); trial (preliminary hearing, if any, probation or suspended sentence, charge dismissed, acquitted or sentenced); imprisonment (parole and release). With some modifications the schema applies to juvenile offenders. Every step taken means that the number of persons who will eventually reach the end, i.e. be sent to prison, is getting smaller. What is the proportion of those who reach this point as compared with the number of persons who initially appear as suspects or are arrested by the police? With respect to the United States, Max Hubner's paper 'Crime Does Pay' in *The Journal of Criminal Law and Criminology,* 1939, said that 'only 15 per cent of the perpetrators are ever brought to trial and that only 2 per cent are committed'. His conclusion regarding committed persons, reached with far fewer facilities for research than those available at present, has been confirmed by the data gathered by the President's Commission, according to which the 'funnelling effect from reported crimes through prison sentence' shows that 2,780,000 index crimes reported led to 727,000 arrests, these to 177,000 formal felonies complaints, these to 160,000 sentences of which only 63,000 or 2·27 per cent of the grand total were sent to prison. The percentage may appear too low to those asking for greater severity and punishment and very promising to those advocating the total suppression of prisons. The question, however, cannot be solved within such narrow emotional limits, but by examining whether or not at the present juncture the 'funnelling process' which, with some variations is working in the same way in the vast majority of countries, is the correct one. Pending discussion of the matter, it may be said here that this process, which is almost universal, is based on a criminal justice system the conception and functioning of which is virtually what it was two centuries ago. It should be added that, according to my own estimates, in some semi-developed and developing countries the percentage may reach as high as twenty, mostly owing to the great number of people sent to prison as short termers. In those with dictatorial regimes, whether or not they are labelled as democracies, the percentage is in all probability higher.

The procedural itinerary of crime explains the traditional classification of criminal statistics into police, judicial and prison statistics and their subsidiaries in arrests, probation, acquittal, parole, etc. Part of this growing statistical world are juvenile delinquency statistics, often less reliable than those for adults.

Geographically criminal statistics may be classified as national and international. The former are not always as satisfactory as they should be, and the latter have not as yet taken proper shape. The shortcomings of national criminal statistics are due to many factors, the most important of which is the lack of a central statistical office for their preparation. It is not true that criminal statistics require special preparation techniques. My experience is that countries with central statistical services usually publish good criminal statistics. This is so in Canada, Sweden, Spain, Italy and Japan, to cite only a few. Police statistics are not easy to obtain in France, but judicial and prison statistics are excellent. For reasons best known to themselves, in some countries, including Spain and Turkey, police statistics are outside the competence of the Central Bureau of Statistics. In federal countries, centralization is often resisted; here again the situation varies and for very different reasons. In the United States the reasons have been analysed by Sellin, Lejins, Beattie and many others. The necessity for uniform general statistics was forcibly put by Sellin in his excellent study 'Uniform Criminal Statistics Act' in *The Journal of Criminal Law and Criminology,* 1950. The *Uniform Crime Reports,* which are not based on a uniform criminal reporting Act, are issued regularly by the Federal Bureau of Investigation and are virtually national in character. Without them it would be difficult to imagine the study of crime in the United States. The recent analysis by Lejins, 'Uniform Crime Reports' in the *Michigan Law Review,* (1966) shows that the shortcomings are not in the *Reports* but in the unjustified demands made by many professionals who apparently have not as yet realized their purpose. This has been repeatedly explained by the *Reports* themselves, the last time in the Introduction to the 1966 issue. The reason for maintaining the current method of gathering data instead of the accommodating but frustrating sampling procedure requested by the critics is that, as Lejins pointed out, the *Reports* have by now achieved almost complete coverage. This is confirmed by the 1966 *Report*, which is based on 'crime reports received from law enforcement agencies representing 97 per cent of the total United States population living in standard metropolitan statistical areas, 88 per cent of the population in other cities and 75 per cent of the rural population. The combined coverage accounts for 92 per cent of the national population'. If this coverage is compared with that of the *Annual Bulletin for 1944*, the oldest in the writer's collection of *Uniform Crime Reports,* one can see the enormous progress achieved by the perseverance and ability of Hoover and his colleagues in trying to provide national police criminal statistics. According to my calculation on the available data in 1944 only 40 per cent of the population was covered.

In other federal countries, the quality and availability of criminal statistics vary greatly. In Mexico, criminal statistics of any sort either at state or national level are irregularly published and not very reliable. In Brazil, some national prison data may be found in the official Statistical Yearbooks. Judicial statistics in Yugoslavia are fairly good; the most serious shortcoming is that the equivalents of terms given either in English or French are not always clearly rendered. If all the circumstances are considered, the statistical data compiled in India deserves praise for the effort they represent. In Switzerland, the Federal Statistical Bureau (from 1946 to 1966 it was the Central Bureau of Police) has taken over the publication of criminal statistics which are actually judicial, inasmuch as they are based on the registration of sentences kept by the Central Bureau of Police. In the Federal Republic of Germany the *Bundeskriminalamt* (Federal Criminal Bureau) also ensures good national statistics of different kinds. Canada, with a Federal Bureau of Statistics which regularly issues police, judicial, juvenile delinquency, etc. statistics, deserves special mention. Judicial statistics are published late in many countries; this is so for example, in France, Spain, Italy and Turkey. The General Direction of Judicial Statistics of the Ministry of Justice of the United Arab Republic publishes good judicial statistics with excellent translations in French of the Arab text. National judicial data are hard to get in the United States; at the state level, the statistics published by the Bureau of Criminal Statistics of California deserve particular mention for their high quality. In the United Kingdom, the usefulness of existing criminal statistics whether on police, judicial or prison matters, for England, Wales, Scotland or Northern Ireland, would be greatly improved and allow more general comparisons and conclusions and better research if they were presented in a more uniform methodological and systematic way. In spite of the different jurisdictions and authorities involved, it would be possible to make some progress towards a system of national statistics, a matter already explored in 1966.[14]

As for international criminal statistics, the United Nations have not been very successful, in spite of the efforts of the Secretariat. The need for a system of international criminal statistics and the difficulties involved were brought up at the General Statistical Congress held in Brussels in 1853. Nowadays the need is more acute, among other reasons because of the growing interdependence and cooperation among countries, and as a ground for comparative criminological research. On the other hand, the pessimistic school of thought, reinforced by the opinion submitted by the Mixed Committee of the International Statistical Institute in 1937 to the International Penal and Penitentiary Commission that international criminal statistics constitute an impossible task was, in 1960, still strong enough inside and outside the Secretariat to prevent the completion of the project described below. The difficulties usually mentioned are national differences in the legal definition of criminal offences, police methods, criminal procedure, and lack of uniformity in compiling crime figures.

From the outset, the United Nations included in its programme of work on the prevention of crime and the treatment of offenders —administratively called social defence—the item of international criminal statistics. The matter was first discussed in 1950 by an international committee of experts which had at its disposal excellent working papers prepared by Messrs. Ancel, Beattie and Verkko. Verkko's paper may still be regarded in some respects as one of the most comprehensive studies on this matter. The item was discussed at successive meetings with the co-operation of other international experts, among them Professor Sellin, whose support was invaluable. Eventually the Secretariat was requested to prepare a study on the feasibility of a system of international criminal statistics. This was the report *Criminal Statistics, Standard Classification of Offences* (1959) in which the offences of criminal homicide, aggravated assault and robbery-burglary had been selected as basic offences for a tentative system of international criminal statistics. Previously the report had been submitted for comments to all United Nations correspondents in social defence matters and other experts. Part of their comments were incorporated in the final drafting of the report, which was a highly technical paper and represented the most exhaustive inquiry. It was submitted for consideration to the Social Commission, and that was the end of the matter. The project was never discussed but for obvious reasons put aside and never revived, in spite of the efforts of the Section of Social Defence.[15]

Although highly technical and requiring long and careful preparation, the organization of an international system of criminal statistics is not the impossible task the Mixed Committee thought in 1937. There are more complex matters than legal definitions, on which international statistics are produced with a reasonable degree of reliability—for example, those issued by the International Labour Organization and the World Health Organization. The main operations involved are the choice of a small group of countries with a reasonably good system of police statistics; the selection of only a few offences (those chosen by the United Nations are the best inasmuch as they are relatively easy to detect and are frequently reported); the 'compression' under the headings of these offences of the different modalities described by the corresponding criminal codes and the classifications used by the respective police statistics; and finally, the assignment to the United Nations, where there is a statistical office and a section of social defence, of the supervision and assistance required by national reporting operations and the preparation of the international criminal statistics. It would be for the Secretariat of the United Nations to decide when the policy statistics of a particular country could be used for international purposes.

Admittedly the outline does not convey the complexity of the operations involved, but certainly a system of international criminal statistics is feasible, provided that effective co-operation is established at the international level. The 'compression' of legal modalities of the same criminal offences under a single heading is already made in the preparation and presentation of police statistics, which frequently prefer broad meanings to the particularized classifications of criminal codes. As examples, the police statistics of Sweden, the Federal Republic of Germany, the United Kingdom, Canada and the *Uniform Crime Reports* of the United States may be cited. In the Swedish statistics a series of categories are quite often presented under a broad heading which gives a good idea of the contents of the particular chapter or section of the criminal code dealt with. In the German statistics, the categories used are broad enough but also close to the main headings of the criminal code. Partly owing to the lack of a criminal code and the chaotic condition of English criminal legislation, English criminal statistics occasionally use a broad classification of offences in six groups which, although in need of improvement, also shows the feasibility of the 'compression system' at the international level. The same may be said of the police classification in the Canadian *Crime Statistics* (1966) which, when they deal with Canada as a whole, use only twelve headings, while for the provinces there are twenty-two.

The *Uniform Crime Reports* have succeeded in setting up a 'compressed' classification of offences which deserves praise if it is remembered that there are fifty criminal jurisdictions involved. In this respect, it should be noted that the refusal of the Federal

Bureau of Investigation to accept state police statistics which do not comply with its standards has led to the success of these reports. There is no reason why the same policy cannot be applied at the international level.

Following a more simplified procedure and with a far more ambitious coverage of offences and countries, the International Criminal Police Organization—Interpol—publishes a series of International Crime Statistics; the last covers the years 1963–64.

Police statistics.[16] These constitute the largest although not always the most reliable presentation, especially in developing countries, of reported crime. Since they are the most widely used, the following remarks may help the reader to understand them better.

Although reflecting in a substantial number of offences the fluctuations of crime, police percentages, especially those concerning arrests, should not be interpreted as indicators of the general increase or decrease of crime. In most cases, what they represent are the variations of a police statistical world which is affected by many variables such as improvement of reporting, attitudes and activities, changes of legislation or police reorganization. The extent and fluctuations of abortion, adultery where it is an offence, frauds, embezzlement, minor thefts and even rape do not always reach the police. Yet in spite of these and other shortcomings, police statistics are the greatest source of knowledge about the extent of known crime.

On the other hand, either because of their triviality or for other reasons, not all offences brought to the attention of the police are included in their statistics. As previously stated, this happens with some minor offences committed by juveniles; in practice also with some committed by adults. To this should be added reporting errors and omissions. More significant is the practice of upgrading or downgrading offences as part of a deliberate policy. Upgrading is frequently used to justify demands for more staff or better equipment, or simply to boost police functions politically. Downgrading may also be politically motivated, but is more frequently done in order to dispense more easily with a series of offences such as burglaries and larcenies which are 'transformed' into minor larcenies. The same happens with a number of sexual offences, affronts, threats, etc. which, although included in the statistics, are disposed of with a warning.

One of the most debated questions is the value of crime indexes, to which some attach great importance while others deny their usefulness. To the writer, general crime indexes have relative significance only. To begin with, although large, the amount of crime known to the police is too small when compared with the whole extent of crime to be used as a reliable basis to set up a crime rate; secondly, when referring to the latter, quite often no qualifications are made with regard to type of population, which should be the other term of reference; and finally, very often the offences shown are too broadly expressed to have any significance other than for readers of the popular press. Such is the case with the categories of crimes against the person, sexual offences and offences against property. In sum, what is frequently offered is a numerical ratio which is unrealistic. More realistic but still subject to some reservations are the crime indexes with respect to a particular offence, the system used by the *Uniform Crime Reports,* which has been examined and reported on favourably by Professor Lejins in his study. In its 1966 report, the F.B.I. justifies the system as a count of victims and as an expression of the risk met by the population which, if account is taken of the previous indexes, is increasing every year. The offences selected are murder, rape, robbery, aggravated assault, larceny $50 and over and auto theft. Their respective ratios are calculated per 100,000 inhabitants. Although widely used, in my opinion the system is somewhat misleading and in certain cases presents an index of risk which lacks real foundation. Admittedly, the probabilities of risk can be computed independently or on the basis of experience. In the first case the 'law of large numbers' is used as an *a priori* method, the application of which is very limited in criminal statistics. These are mostly based on the repetition of a large number of experiences or cases of the same event. Accordingly, what may happen in the long run can be predicted in the form of a numerical ratio. On the other hand, as far as some crimes are concerned, the experience they imply differs considerably from that of others. This means that the probability of risk or of becoming a victim of a particular crime is not determined simply by the numerical consideration of the two variables involved, total amount of a particular offence and entire population of the country, but that before establishing the numerical rate, the character of the repeated experience has to be considered. Thus while in the case of murder, sex as an experience requirement plays a limited role, that of rape is quite different, inasmuch as the victims are always females. Even among females, as a rule, the extremely young and the extremely old should be excluded. Accordingly, it seems that the rate 12.9 per 100,000 inhabitants without further specification assigned to rape in 1966 by the *Uniform Crime Reports* cannot be presented in the same way as those corresponding to the other six groups of offences, and that the rate of risk of becoming a victim is not based on the repeated experience of cases. According to available data, the population of the United States is almost evenly divided between women and men, and the reference without specification to 100,000 does not make much sense, in spite of the fact that in subsequent pages some explanations about rape are given. More in accordance with the requirements of the system of specific categories of crime—although too broadly expressed— and the character of the repeated experience, the statistics for England and Wales make the necessary sex and age distinctions when dealing with the offences of violence against persons, sexual offences and receiving, frauds and false pretences, without trying to set up indiscriminately crime indexes with respect to the entire population. Needless to say, the study of repeated experience as far as specific crimes are concerned shows that elements other than sex have to be considered, but it would take too long to deal with them here.

The foregoing considerations also raise the question whether the assertion that 'the risk of becoming a victim of crime' used by the *Uniform Crime Reports* is not a misinterpretation of the term 'risk'. Suffice it to say here that the ratio of frequency of a particular event with respect to a group as a numerical whole is not the same thing as the risk of being the victim of this event with respect to the individuals constituting the group. In the case of rape, the ratios, although related, show clearly that they operate in a different way. In other words, frequency and risk should not be regarded as interchangeable terms.

In view of these remarks, one may ask why crime indexes are still so much in favour. The most important reason is that in a general way they may represent trends of a certain value for policy-making and research purposes. Another is that psychologically they may be regarded as valuable devices to impress the population and change its negative or indifferent attitudes *vis-à-vis* crime, and in this way get badly needed co-operation. A third reason is the growing tendency to numerical manipulation of data, and the belief that everything can be numerically ascertained. Certainly, crime indexes could be useful if their preparation were more refined and good criminal and non-criminal statistics were at hand. This is why the statement, 'A study to help devise methods and techniques for the establishment of crime indexes and the development of indicators to determine the extent and trend of crime without recourse to elaborate crime statistics', included in the report of the Secretariat of the United Nations, *International Action in the Field of Social Defence* (1966–70), 1966 is somewhat puzzling. In order to be useful, criminal statistics have to be elaborate in preparation and presentation, otherwise they are merely compilations of data which can hardly be used for devising crime indexes and indicators.

Another important question in policy matters is the rate of cases cleared up by the police. As a rule a case is considered cleared up when the offence and the offender have been ascertained and there is enough evidence to charge the latter, irrespective of whether or not he is taken into custody. In England, the concept includes the offences which the offender asks to have taken into consideration by the court when he has been found guilty of some crime. Although the police themselves have not cleared up the crime, the statistical usage is sound and it can be used, as it was in Germany, as one of the elements to be considered in the study of dark figures of crime. A more elaborate concept is used by Swedish police statistics which include the cases in which the public prosecutor decides to stop or forgo prosecution. Although there is not much harm in this wide interpretation of the term, it is obvious that these two instances are outside the range of police activities and reporting, and therefore they seem to belong to judicial and not police statistics.

For England and Wales, the *Report of Her Majesty's Chief Inspector of the Constabulary, 1967* gives as cleared up percentages, excluding the Metropolitan Police District, for the years 1967, 1966 and 1965, 46.25, 45.79 and 45.02. For the Metropolitan area the *Report of the Commissioner of Police for 1967* gives, for the same years, 24.3, 22.3 and 21.3 per cent. In Scotland, where the statistics make a clear distinction between crime and offence, the *Criminal Statistics, 1966,* give 36.9 (36.0 in 1965) for crimes and 94.7 (94.4 in 1965) for offences. The combined percentage was 72.8 in 1966 and 71.9 in 1965. In Canada, according to *Crime Statistics* for 1966, the percentage was 57.5; in Sweden, the *Kriminalstatistik 1967* gives 33.65; in the Federal Republic of Germany, the *Polizeiliche Kriminalstatistiks* for 1966 and 1967 give 53 and 52.2 respectively; in the United States, the *Uniform Crime Reports* for 1966 and 1967 show percentages of 23.3 and 22.4, and in Japan, the *Summary of the White Paper on Crime* published in 1966 and 1967 gives 66.7 and 66.1 for the years 1965 and 1966 respectively.

Like general national crime indexes, general cleared up percentages, although having a certain indicative value, are misleading, do not reflect the real state of affairs and often convey too gloomy a picture of the situation. Here again the percentages of certain categories of offences are far more reassuring than others. Thus with respect to homicide, which for comparative purposes excludes infanticide, the cleared up percentages for 1967 in England and Wales, the Federal Republic of Germany, and Sweden, were 93.3, 95.7 and 80.5 respectively. For Canada and Japan in 1966, the percentages were 83 and 96.6; and for the United States in 1966 and 1967, 89 and 88 respectively. Far less reassuring are the percentages for not very serious offences against property, minor sexual offences and other criminal infractions of relative gravity. Since these offences are increasing rapidly everywhere and in most cases

61

the police cannot cope with them, there is little doubt that the low percentages of those cleared up—sometimes below ten per cent—encourage this type of criminality. The question is, does this type of minor crime constitute a serious social problem? The answer is in the negative. The fact is that, to a certain extent, crime in general and more specifically minor crime has always been a normal feature of society. This does not mean that criminal law has not a deterrent effect but only that it has its own limitations, partly imposed by criminal law itself and partly by many other factors outside it. The question not as yet solved is what is the approximate amount of minor crime that a given society can stand without being seriously disturbed from a public safety and economic point of view. Many minor property offences are at present absorbed by insurance schemes, others are simply endured by the victim. In my opinion, minor sexual and other minor offences against the person could be financially compensated by State or other insurance schemes, making unnecessary in many cases criminal proceedings and the imposition of a penal sanction. The idea is to introduce within certain limits in the area of criminal justice the principle of criminal risk and due financial compensation in the case not only of minor offences against property but also against persons, and possibly in other minor cases which constitute a sizable part of current criminality. Tentatively, it may be said that although financial considerations are not paramount, the insurance scheme system against minor crime would be far less expensive than the increase of the police forces in order to raise the percentage of minor offences cleared up to a satisfactory 75 or 80. If achieved, these percentages would necessarily imply the expansion of the court machinery, with results which would probably have a no more practical and deterrent effect than that attained by an insurance scheme.

Judicial statistics. As a rule, judicial statistics are less exposed than police statistics to the influence of factors outside the field they cover, such as individual and collective attitudes about crime reporting. The main aspects they should cover are the number of cases filed before the courts with indication of the offence; dismissals and waivers; persons kept in prison awaiting trial; acquittals and convictions; types of sentences imposed; socio-economic, geographical and other data on convicted persons; probation, suspended sentence and fine cases; length of proceedings with indication of the time spent by detainees in prison; appeals submitted with mention of those confirming or reversing the sentence previously imposed, and extradition cases. Obviously other aspects required by national characteristics or systems of justice may be added; unfortunately, few judicial statistics cover those above mentioned. Judicial statistics take a long time to prepare and delays of three or more years are frequent. Nevertheless, as indicators of how criminal justice is administered and as a source of proposals for its improvement, they are important. The most significant questions they raise are inflation of the term criminal offence; justification of the excessive numerical difference between police arrests, judicial indictments or prosecutions, and convictions; wholesale or individual use of waivers and probation; use and abuse of detention awaiting trial; undue delay of judicial proceedings; disparity of judicial decisions; frequency of short-term imprisonment sentences; severity or laxity of sentences of imprisonment with respect to certain offences; correlation between police and judicial trends of crime, prevalence of demographic, social, economic and other characteristics among sentenced offenders and appraisal of the role played by the courts as an intermediate stage between the police and the prisons in the administration of criminal justice.

With respect to the inflation of the meaning of criminal offence, judicial statistics often present a mixture of serious criminal acts and small infractions of by-laws, regulations and ordinances. English criminal statistics are typical; in 1966 and 1967 for England and Wales the total number of persons found guilty of *offences of all kinds* was 1,445,948 and 1,579,653 respectively. Although the expression is equivocal in the sense that it may be interpreted as referring to criminal as well as to non-criminal offences, the fact is that all appear as forming part of the Criminal Statistics of England and Wales, and as such all are regarded as criminal in official documents, legislation, comparative studies, etc. and dealt with by police, magistrates and judges. The main classification between indictable and non-indictable offences may imply different kinds of proceedings, but the 'criminal' condition remains unaltered. The inflation of the term 'criminal' is obvious inasmuch as in round figures in 1966 and 1967, 84 and 85 per cent of all criminal offences were non-indictable offences which are extremely varied and run from adulteration of food, drugs, etc. and assault, including aggravated forms, to offences against Wireless Telegraphy Acts, unlawful meetings at Westminster, motoring offences—well over a million in 1967—juvenile smoking, playing games in the street, offences in relation to dogs, begging and sleeping out. The main indictable offences are violence against the person, breaking and entering, robbery, larceny—which accounts for more than half—frauds and false pretences, receiving, sexual offences, forgery, offences against the State and Public Order, perjury and libel. The inflation would not be avoided by regarding as criminal only the present indictable offences. There are two reasons for this: one is that a number of these offences require a specification which is not provided by law before being considered *prima facie* as real criminal offences, such is the case with cheating, theft, frauds, etc.; the other is that a substantial number of assaults, cruelty to children, adulteration of drugs, etc. at present regarded as non-indictable offences are, in certain cases, actual criminal offences. In all probability, only about 20 per cent of the million and a half persons found guilty in 1967 were truly criminal offenders. More technically, the Criminal Statistics for Scotland make a distinction between crimes and offences which only apparently reduces the inflation, inasmuch as both types of offences are eventually considered as criminal. A similar technique is used by Canadian criminal statistics, by making a distinction between criminal offence (indictable offence) or criminal act and offence or infraction. Hence the title *Statistics of criminal and other offences* given to what are actually judicial statistics. In 1965, 46,662 persons were charged for indictable offences or criminal acts and 3,991,657 for offences or infractions. It is important to note that out of this amount only a little more than 100,000 were offences described by the criminal code. All others were federal, provincial, municipal and parking offences. Curiously enough, drunkenness is punished by three different jurisdictions: the criminal code, federal and provincial. The inflation of criminal law is still more visible in France where, in 1965, well over seven million criminal complaints, denunciations and police proceedings were brought before the corresponding police and judicial authorities. Even if the increase of police cases is partly the result of recent reforms, the fact is that police and judicial criminal cases are steadily increasing in France. Although well over one million cases were dismissed, the remainder, totalling almost six million, were referred to judicial and police courts; the latter amounted to more than five million. In 1965, the *Cours d'Assises* sentenced 1,497 persons, the *Tribunaux Correctionnels* 256,701 and the *Tribunaux de Police* 1,599,999. In Italy in 1965, the number of cases brought before authorities dealing with criminal matters (*Preture e Procure*) was 2,618,883, of which about 60 per cent were *contravvenzioni* (minor offences) and about 40 per cent crimes. In Spain in 1965, the judicial statistics show that 528,050 criminal cases, of which nearly 37 per cent were *faltas* (minor offences), were dealt with by judges or courts of criminal jurisdiction. In the Federal Republic of Germany 3,444,314 prosecutions and charges were filed in criminal matters in 1965. In the United States, the diversity of judicial systems and the inability to organize national criminal statistics in many States prevented the President's Commission from presenting complete national court statistics. According to this Commission's *Task Force Report: The Courts* (1967), it is estimated that in 1962 over four million misdemeanour cases were brought to the lower courts, a figure which in my opinion is too conservative, also that the time between the preliminary hearing and the initial appearance before the court is less than three days for jailed defendants and seven days for released defendants; that the period between arrest and trial in felony cases is not more than four months, and the period between trial and appelate decision is within five months. No specific data are produced in support of these estimates which, as far as felony cases are concerned, seem to be somewhat optimistic. No information is available about the approximate number of felony cases dealt with by superior courts every year. According to the Bureau of Criminal Statistics of California, the work of which deserves praise, in that State in 1967 the number of cases of felony defendants brought before the superior courts was 42,489, of which 6,802 were disposed of without conviction. Certainly California cannot be regarded as an index of national felony cases brought to superior courts, yet as a point of reference in conjunction with other data of different States it might be concluded that no less than a million felony cases are handled by superior courts every year. Another possible point of reference is to consider that, as a rule, only 50 per cent of police felony cases are eventually referred to these courts as felony complaints. Since, according to FBI data, which do not cover the whole country, over 3.8 million serious offences were reported to the police in 1967, the tentative conclusion is that 1.7 million felony cases were filed in the superior courts of the United States in that year. For the number of persons kept in prison pending trial no data are available. Although the number of police felony arrests and police disposition of them may give a glimpse of the possible number of accused persons kept in this condition in the United States, the truth is that no information is available on this important aspect of criminal justice. Official data for New York City in 1965 show that the average length of time spent in detention pending trial in uncomplicated cases varies in each borough and type of court. At the Criminal Court of Richmond, the average is a little less than eight days, while at the Supreme Court of Kings County—which is not Supreme in the usual meaning of the term but simply a court dealing with criminal and other matters—it is two and a half months. Since the number of cases is given in thousands and the averages of the boroughs differ considerably, these two extreme averages do not reflect the fact that in a substantial number of cases the period of detention awaiting trial may be between four and eight months, and occasionally more than eight months. This unsatisfactory situation, which was aggravated by the no less unsatisfactory bail conditions, prompted the magnificent pioneer work of Herbert Sturz and his colleagues for the improvement of the bail system, which led first to the organization of The

Vera Foundation and later of The Vera Institute of Justice, the activities of which are already effective in many areas of the United States. Although obviously the improvement of bail systems may alleviate the condition of those sent into custody pending trial, as a problem on its own very little is known in the United States about the number of persons kept in such conditions every year.

In France on 1 January 1968 out of 34,083 prisoners almost 39 per cent were detainees awaiting trial. In 1965 almost 60,000 persons were kept in *détention préventive* pending a judicial decision. Of these, almost 50 per cent were kept awaiting trial for periods varying from one day to eight months, the majority of them from one to six months. Six thousand and ten were eventually sentenced to imprisonment *avec sursis* or suspended sentence, of these, 47 per cent had already spent no less than a month and almost 500 over four months in prison. The statistical data allow the conclusion that in all probability 50 per cent of the 31,885 detainees, eventually sentenced in most cases to short term imprisonment, had already spent the time as detainees. In some cases the detention period was obviously longer. Finally, 552 detainees eventually sentenced to pay a fine had spent periods varying from one day to eight months in prison. One of them spent more than eight months waiting to be fined. In Italy, the number of detainees on 31 December 1965 kept in prison at the disposition of a judicial authority pending trial or an appeal decision was 14,296, while the number of definitely sentenced prisoners was 18,588. In Spain on 31 December 1967, there were 5,438 sentenced prisoners and 3,886 detainees awaiting trial. In the Federal Republic of Germany apparently only the *Länder* of Bavaria and Nordrhein-Westfalen publish statistics of persons kept in custody pending trial or *Untersuchungshaft* and the length of time. These and other available data allow the conclusion that, in general, less than 15 per cent of accused persons are kept in custody awaiting trial, that in 40 per cent of the cases the time so spent is between one and three months, in 20 per cent over three and less than six months, and for the remaining 40 per cent less than one month. This tentative distribution does not preclude the fact that in certain cases detainees are kept for longer than six months. In Finland on 16 July 1968, there were 5,608 sentenced prisoners and only 438 detainees awaiting trial. As a rule, only persons accused of serious felonies are kept in prison awaiting trial. The length of this period varies according to the circumstances of the case and no statistical data were available to the writer. In minor felony cases, if the accused fails to appear before the court when summoned, he may be ordered to appear under penalty of a fine; if he still fails to appear, the court will order that he be brought before it by the police. In Norway in 1965, out of 5,057 persons sent to penal

institutions, 62 per cent were guilty of misdemeanours and therefore in most cases the sentences were for short periods. Seventy-
eight per cent of misdemeanants were traffic offenders and 20 per
cent vagrants; the remaining 2 per cent of offences are described
as other offences. The number of offenders for drunkenness in 1964,
1965 and 1966 was 31,783, 33,797 and 33,733 respectively; for illegal
distillation of spirits, smuggling, etc., 1,585, 1,786 and 1,418
respectively. The total number of persons sentenced for misdemeanours other than drunkenness in 1964 and 1965 were 15,447
and 15,878. From these figures one might conclude that vagrants,
sometimes an accommodating term, are less favoured than
drunkards in a country where welfare policies are widespread and
well organized. Certainly there are differences between the two
conditions, and I am not advocating that anyone should be sent to
prison for drunkenness, but the inequality shows up the role played
in the administration of criminal justice by individual and collective attitudes. The number of detainees or persons remanded
awaiting trial as a proportion of the daily average prison population
in 1964, 1965 and 1966 was 21, 20 and 22 per cent respectively.

In Yugoslavia, data on detainees are not included in the criminal
statistics published. During my visits to the more significant penal
institutions of some of the autonomous republics, I got the
impression that the number of detainees is comparatively small, and
that except in special circumstances the period of detention awaiting
trial does not usually exceed three months. With respect to the
USSR, no statistical data are available to the writer. Suffice it to
say here that, according to Art. 97 of the 1960 RSFSR Criminal
Procedure Code, the period of detention pending investigation and
trial may last through a series of extensions up to nine months.
Obviously the extensions are granted mostly in cases of serious
offences, among which those regarded as opposing the Soviet regime,
policies and ideology are the most frequent. In Japan in 1966 the
courts dealt with 4,248,089 defendants, of which 99.7 per cent
were convicted and 97·7 of these sentenced to pay a fine only. These
percentages invite reflection; do they mean that police and
prosecutor's evidence is so thorough that conviction becomes almost
automatic, or that for exemplary or self-justifying reasons judges
are inclined to convict even if in the vast majority of cases only a
fine is imposed? Whatever the answer, Japan is one of the few
countries where the gap between cases filed and convictions is so
small as to be practically non-existent. Can this insignificant margin
be regarded as an ideal expression of the administration of criminal
justice? Without detracting in any way from the highly respected
Administration of Justice of Japan, the answer is no. This is because
the margin is too representative of perfection to be considered as

an expression of what is required by a less formal approach to crime and delinquent conditions and circumstances. In other words, while the minute margin may be the expression of a perfect administration of justice as it is still conceived and practised not only in Japan but in all, particularly the socialist, countries, it cannot be regarded as an index of a social criminal justice. Furthermore, if account is taken of the enormous proportion of fines as the only penal sanction, here again the inflated character of criminal law is as obvious as in any other country. As a separate item the number of traffic violations in 1966 was 4,480,451; to these must be added 353,605 traffic accident cases (negligent homicide and bodily injury), as well as 14,832 hit-and-run cases. Obviously, only these and the accidents may be regarded as possible criminal offences. As for the daily average of prisoners awaiting trial, there were 9,910 in 1966, while prisoners serving imprisonment sentences numbered 53,736. No information is given about the average length of the detention period. In the United Arab Republic on 31 December 1964, the total number of prisoners was 24,022, of which 3,244 or 14 per cent were awaiting trial. Although encouraging, the picture is marred when the total turnover of prisoners during the year is considered; there were 39,692 and 17,822 respectively. As for detention pending trial, out of 4,641 brought before the *Cours d'Assises* in 1964, 908 were acquitted and 3,733 convicted, of which 2,618 waited for periods up to six months, 854 from six months to one year, 203 from one year to one and a half years, 30 up to two years, 15 up to three years and 13 over three years. In Syria in November 1965 there were 1,630 persons awaiting trial and 2,400 convicted prisoners. As for the time spent in detention awaiting trial, official data are not available. After repeated visits to the country and most of the prisons, my experience is that in too many cases persons waited for longer periods than those eventually passed on them by the court. This happened in 1962 not only in prisons as far away as Deir-ez-Zor on the Euphrates but also in Damascus, Aleppo, Homs, Hama, and Latakia. In Iran on 21 January, 1965, according to official data, there were 8,065 prisoners and 10,645 persons in detention awaiting trial. As for the length of time waiting to be tried, my own data from Iranian prisons show that an appreciable number of detainees wait more than a year before being brought to court. The fact that in some cases the imprisonment imposed was shorter than the time spent waiting for it was admitted, but no official data were available. In 1965 in Rezaieh, there were 2,000 prisoners, some of whom had been waiting for more than eight years. In Jordan in January 1965, according to official data, out of 1,414 prisoners 878 were convicted and 536 were persons awaiting trial. As for the length of the waiting periods, it was officially stated to be from one to two weeks in the case of petty offences and from one month to four months in the case of felonies. Here again from personal experience I know that the periods for the latter are considerably longer in some cases. In Turkey at the end of 1969 there were 27,379 prisoners awaiting trial and 23,375 sentenced prisoners. Although these figures are comparatively lower than those for the years 1960–65 and may show the salutary influence of penitentiary law No. 467/1965, still the proportion awaiting trial is too high. In Greece on 1 January 1965, the prison population was made up of 2,590 sentenced prisoners and 520 persons awaiting trial.

In the Latin American countries, judicial statistics are few and far between and in most cases not very reliable. My experience, based on repeated and often long visits to sixteen of these countries, is that the number of persons kept in prison awaiting trial, sometimes for very long periods, is usually higher than the number of convicted prisoners. When, during my visits, I raised the question of persons eventually sentenced to shorter periods than those spent in detention awaiting trial, the fact was admitted without exception. Here and there, reports were submitted showing the desperate conditions of many detainees and the slow working of an obsolete system of criminal justice. As a typical example, in Colombia a report submitted to the House of Representatives in 1966 stated that in 1964, besides 28,465 prisoners under police arrest, there were 68,564 persons in detention awaiting trial and 6,466 sentenced prisoners. The report of the Prison Administration for the same year says that out of 32,000 prisoners only 6,700 were sentenced, and that many of those awaiting trial had been waiting for years, and in many cases they had already spent more time as detainees than the possible length of imprisonment they might get if convicted. In Chile at the end of 1964, there were 5,452 persons in detention awaiting trial and 5,305 convicted prisoners.

In India, the proportion of persons in detention awaiting trial is often very high. On my last visit in October 1967 to Tihar, the Central Prison of New Delhi, out of 1,795 prisoners 805 or 44 per cent were awaiting trial. The situation is similar if not worse in other states such as Uttar Pradesh, Madhya Pradesh, Maharasthra, Bihar and West Bengal. In Ceylon, the number of convicted prisoners at the end of the fiscal year 1965–1966 was 9,945, plus 193 in training schools, and there were 23,5000 unconvicted prisoners. The time spent awaiting trial varies according to the different jurisdictions dealing with the case. The vast majority of detainees waiting for periods up to six months are Magistrates' Courts prisoners; sometimes they have to wait between six and eighteen months. For Thailand, the Annual Prison Administration

Report for 1966 makes a series of distinctions between convicted prisoners and persons awaiting final judicial decision, awaiting investigation, awaiting trial and detained persons. When I was in Thailand in 1967, I gathered that about 33 per cent of the prison population is made up of the last four categories and the balance by convicted prisoners. For the Philippines, reliable official data are not available, but it seems that in certain areas the number of persons kept in detention awaiting trial approaches 40 per cent of the total prison population.

In England and Wales in 1967 242,208 persons were found guilty of indictable offences, of which 25,585 or slightly over ten per cent by Higher Courts and 216,623 by Magistrates' Courts. On the other hand, the number of indictable offences cleared up was 497,902, and the number of persons cautioned by the police as an alternative to taking proceedings in court was 31,008. Although figures for offences and offenders cannot be compared unless the necessary adjustments are made, the gap is large enough to be worth studying. The answer would be partly provided if not only persons but also the number of cases brought to courts for indictable offences were known. This is important inasmuch as it would indicate the diversity of criteria of police and judicial authorities about the value of *prima facie* evidence, as well as their different attitudes *vis-à-vis* certain offences and offenders. On the other hand, the number of persons dealt with summarily for non-indictable offences in 1967—some committed prior to that year— was 1,611,865, of which well over a million were motoring offences, the vast majority of which appear as criminal without actually being so. Their exclusion, with many others, from criminal statistics would not only allow a more accurate and realistic knowledge of actual crime which is of primary importance for policy-making purposes, but would also avoid emotional interpretations about the 'alarming' increase of crime. The number of persons kept in custody pending trial in 1967 is not yet known; the data for 1964, published in 1966, show that the total number of receptions in penal institutions of untried persons (mostly from Magistrates' Courts) or pending inquiry or awaiting trial was 33,717 and 15,243 respectively. Of the former, 57 per cent were subsequently returned to prison duly convicted, and of the latter, 47 per cent. Although the daily average of these detainees constitutes only 8 per cent of the total prison population in 1964 and compares very favourably with the percentages of any other country, it is disquieting to see that even those detainees who were eventually fined had, like those acquitted, been deprived of freedom for some time. Furthermore, in a country like Britain in which prison overcrowding is chronic, the thousands of untried persons sent every year to prison—in 1964 over 22,500—aggravate an already difficult problem. A valuable study by the Home Office Research Unit, *Time spent awaiting Trial* (1960), shows that in 1957 in the case of Higher Courts, persons committed to custody and acquitted constituted 1.5 per cent of the total number of persons committed for trial—about 300. The average time they spent in custody was 31 days. Those committed to custody who were convicted but not sentenced to some form of custody constituted 8 per cent—about 2,000; for them the average time in custody was 29 days. In the case of Magistrates' Courts, 90 per cent of persons committed for trial were previously remanded; 42 per cent of committals were in custody, and most of the persons so committed had also been remanded in custody. The average total time between the first appearance at the Magistrates' Court and the first day of trial for those committed to custody was estimated at 42 days in 'breaking and entering cases' and 50 days in others, for those committed on bail it was 50 and 62 days respectively. As for those tried summarily for indictable offences, 31 per cent were remanded before or during the hearing, and about 7 per cent remanded for medical, probation or Borstal reports after the hearing or before sentence, including 2 per cent who had already been remanded during the hearing. Persons tried summarily for non-indictable offences were seldom remanded, except for certain offences under the Vagrancy Acts. For those not committed for sentence, the average total period on remand was ten days for those in custody, a fortnight for those on bail, and three and a half weeks for those in custody for part of the time and on bail for the remainder. Sixty-four per cent were on bail throughout, 30 per cent in custody throughout and a further 6 per cent in custody for at least one remand; of those remanded in custody, 38 per cent were sentenced to imprisonment. Although all these percentages and averages compare favourably in some respects with those of other countries, some of them are disturbing. Among them, that about 2,000 persons were kept in custody but not sentenced to deprivation of freedom subsequently; that 90 per cent of those committed for trial were previously remanded; that only 38 per cent of those remanded in custody by the Magistrates' Courts were afterwards sentenced to imprisonment, and that apparently more often than not those tried summarily as vagrants were remanded. Even if charity prompted these vagrancy remands, the decision seems somewhat puzzling in a Welfare State. The impression is that the police point of view is decisive in granting bail or sending a person on remand. Certainly the role of public prosecutor that the police in England perform, against which there is no objection, inasmuch as it is more efficiently and more independently done than by many investigators or public prosecutors in other countries, may explain the acceptance of the views of the police in more than 95 per cent of cases. On the other hand, the high percentages of persons who, after having been in custody, are not subsequently sent to prison, and the problems that their presence creates in overcrowded and not always well equipped and staffed prisons, seems to point to the need for a less pronounced 'remanding' policy.

Prison statistics. These refer to prisoners, their treatment and the main activities of the Administration dealing with both. Prison statistics deal more with persons as cases than with cases as crimes. The persons are convicted prisoners and those awaiting trial. As already shown, in the developing countries the latter are often as numerically important as the convicted prisoners, a situation which demands from the Prison Administration time, activities and resources which could more profitably be used for the benefit of convicted prisoners.

More than police and judicial statistics, prison statistics stress the well-known facts that the vast majority of offenders are male, that generally they belong to the lower classes, and that a substantial proportion of them are recidivists, even if their recidivism is mostly 'petty' recidivism against property and sexual mores. With some exceptions, prisoners are not particularly bright, well-prepared or skilled, their educational level is usually low, they are beset with family and economic problems of many sorts, are not particularly interested in changing their patterns of life, and a significant proportion of them are more or less mentally disturbed and some mentally ill. This does not mean that they should be regarded either bio-psychologically or sociologically as a species, inasmuch as many more like them do not commit criminal offences or, if they do, they manage to keep out of prison. Two elements may help to explain why this happens: one is risk and the other chance. Risk is part of everyday life, and the offender always runs the risk of being caught and sent to prison. Owing to their living conditions the lower classes are more inclined to take chances than other persons, and even for professional offenders repetition increases the risk of being caught. Since this is not the moment to discuss the role of risk and chance in crime, it may just be said that by and large prison populations are 'bad luck' populations. This simply means that their living conditions rely in some respects on repeating the 'chances'. Most of the careers of 'petty' recidivists are typical in this respect.

Thus for various reasons and with obvious exceptions, the prison population is handicapped in more than one respect, and their rehabilitation is extremely difficult, time-consuming and expensive. This means that it cannot be accomplished in short periods, and that when undertaken in large, walled prisons, too long periods of time do not help much either. My experience is that at a certain moment the point is reached beyond which there is no return. This does not necessarily discredit institutional treatment but rather the way in which it is at present understood and practised.

In principle, prison statistics should contain enough data for the study of these and other aspects of institutional treatment. Unfortunately most of them are still prepared according to patterns imposed by what I call the *system*, i.e. the machinery of the administration of justice of which prison administration is a part.[17] In many cases, prison statistics are reduced to a bare minimum on the number of prisoners, their transfers, releases, escapes and deaths. Another serious shortcoming is the lack of uniformity in presenting them. Not that total uniformity is required, but at least on the gathering and presentation of the essential aspects of institutional treatment, management and related problems. The convenience of this was discussed at some length as long ago as 1890 at the Fourth International Penal and Penitentiary Congress of Saint Petersburg (Leningrad). Prison Annual Reports double as prison statistics in many countries. Unfortunately, under the impact of the 'public relations approach', the glossy presentation of these reports is gaining ground over their substantial content. What they offer is a capsulized description of what should be dealt with in more detail. Pictures may no doubt be occasionally justified, but since prison administrations are not expected to make prison life attractive, their inclusion should be restricted and in any case combined with an account of salient facts and problems, what has been done and what should have been done in order to carry out and improve the institutional and semi-institutional treatment of offenders.

As for international penitentiary statistics, their fate is similar to that of international criminal statistics. At the International Statistical Congress of Paris in 1855, it was pointed out that they were necessary, and since then at subsequent statistical congresses they have hardly been mentioned. The matter was revived at the First International Penal and Penitentiary Congress held in London in 1872. As a result, Beltrani-Scalia, Director General of the Italian Prison Administration, submitted in 1874 a remarkable report and project which still deserves attention.[18] It is to be regretted that the programme of work of the International Penal and Penitentiary Foundation is not invigorated by the research on the essentials of prison statistics, so as to lay the foundations for a certain amount of uniformity and a system of international penitentiary statistics.

The study of the annual reports of the Prison Department, formerly the Prison Commission, shows that the English prison system, in spite of the progress made, is afflicted by the growth of the prison population, overcrowding, difficulties in carrying out the frequently imaginative programmes, insufficient and underpaid personnel, unsatisfactory prison labour conditions and more recently, markedly security approaches in dealing with policies and programmes.

Overcrowding has been endemic for many years. It already existed more than twenty years ago, according to the appendix on accommodation to the report for 1946. At the end of 1951, out of a total population of 24,000, over 4,500 or nearly 19 per cent were sleeping three to a cell. At the end of 1961, out of 30,000 prisoners, over 8,000 or 26 per cent were accommodated three in a cell. Their number fell from 6,296 in December 1963 to 5,337 in January 1965; it rose to 7,206 in December 1966, which is well over 21 per cent of the whole prison population. The number of persons sleeping two in a cell increased from 364 to 1,494 in the same period; the reasons against this are well-known. The actual population on 31 December 1967 was 33,460 compared with 33,776 in 1966, 30,134 in 1965 and 29,342 in 1964. At the end of December 1967 6,342 or about 20 per cent of the total prison population were sleeping three in a cell. In sum, in this respect the situation is no better than it was seventeen years ago. No information on the number of prisoners sleeping two in a cell is given by the 1967 Prison Report. As the 1966 and 1967 Reports state, overcrowding jeopardizes all aspects of the treatment of prisoners and creates unnecessary tensions and difficulties. The fact is that living space and privacy, which are necessary in the prison community, are being gradually reduced; the same applies to workshop space. The situation was aggravated in 1967 and 1968 by the tightening of security precautions and the unfortunate policy of dispersing maximum security prisoners in several prisons. About this, the 1967 Report as well as some of the testimony given before the Estimates Committee of The House of Commons 1966–67 Session are quite clear, and I myself saw the serious shortcomings created by this policy in my visits to Dartmoor, Wormwood Scrubs and Leicester in July and August 1968. In fact, the maximum security dispersion policy has originated a new form of inequality. The following example may suffice: in Leicester, while maximum security prisoners, a small minority of the population of the institution, have an open recreation yard, the other prisoners have none. My impression was that the open recreation area originally assigned to maximum security prisoners was considered unsafe. The open recreation yard of the general prison population was given to the already privileged maximum security prisoners, with the result that the open area left vacant by them, which is unsuitable for the general population, has since remained unused.

Out of 127 prisons, remand centres, Borstal and detention centres listed in the 1967 Report, sixty were overcrowded (seven only slightly) and fifty below normal capacity. To the latter belong most of the open, special, Borstal and detention institutions for boys and girls. On the other hand, the vast majority of remand centres for men, boys and girls are overcrowded, mostly as a result of the 'remanding policy' previously criticized. It is important to note that in quite a number of cases the remand centre is the first contact that an adult or minor has with the administration of justice. In all probability, the overcrowding in these centres will be aggravated by the policy of the Criminal Justice Act 1967, according to which sentenced prisoners and persons in custody over 21 years of age may benefit from the specialist facilities available in a remand centre, and sentenced offenders may be used in these centres for domestic and maintenance work. Although well-intentioned, the new policy will not easily compensate for the general scarcity of specialist facilities which, with few exceptions, exists in all institutions. One may ask if the prevailing 'security psychosis' will not prevent the maximum security prisoners from taking advantage of this modest remedy which, on the other hand, means more work and the eventual acceptance of more routine approaches and methods. Another possible ill effect is that temporary remedies often become permanent, and as such, prevent the introduction of more general and effective services.

As in many other countries and following what may be called 'prison numerical attraction' the largest institutions are, as a rule, the most seriously overcrowded. The following examples may be cited for 31 December 1967:

	Normal capacity	Average number of inmates
Liverpool	1,050	1,415
Manchester	779	1,114
Pentonville	896	1,328
Wandsworth	1,075	1,526
Wormwood Scrubs	946	1,082

The figures are deceptive in that they are compared with those of a normal capacity about which I have some doubts; I would not be surprised if at least in some cases 'normal' is understood according to obsolete criteria. Furthermore, since all these are multi-purpose prisons, the overcrowding is usually uneven inasmuch as while some sections or blocks are seriously overcrowded, others are not. Such is the case with sentenced prisoners, particularly long-termers, who as a rule occupy single cells. Obviously there are reasons for this; on the other hand the other sections or wings are overcrowded, especially those used for remand and allocation. It may even happen that in the sentenced prisoners block some cells are vacant, while in other areas prisoners suffer from serious over-crowding aggravated by the undignified and unsanitary traditional 'slopping out' ritual of most British institutions.

In 1967 the combined average prison population of the five above-mentioned institutions plus those of Durham and Leeds—each of them near the one thousand mark—constituted 55 per cent of the total average male population distributed in twenty-four local or closed prisons; 40 per cent of the total adult male population on 31 December 1967, and 24 per cent of the total average men and boys institutional population. No wonder they are the most important source of problems and shortcomings and of specula-tions for the future.

As a contrast, the average men and boys population in open institutions in 1967 constituted only 17 per cent of the total average male population. Although this percentage is slightly higher than that of past years, the situation is unsatisfactory, especially if it is kept in mind that out of 23 open institutions 20 are occupied below capacity. The lack of a good observation and classification system in spite of some improvements, e.g. Manchester, and the present 'security psychosis' are the main reasons for this. Every-body from the top to the bottom seems to be anxious to avoid 'trouble'. The truth is that, within reasonable limits, trouble is a normal contingency of prison services and programmes.

Will the prison building plan, most of it unfortunately devoted to closed institutions, and the implementation of certain provisions of the Criminal Justice Act 1967 reduce overcrowding and the steady rise of the prison population? Hopes were expressed before the Estimates Committee as well as guarded scepticism; the odds are that the prison population will increase. First because of the increase in the general population and the greater volume of the age groups which contribute most to crime, and secondly because crime always increases faster than the population, particularly habitual, professional and organized crime. Inevitably this means that unless a radical transformation of the penal system takes place, more people will be sent to prison. The increase will not necessarily be created by a greater use of long or short term sentences, but by medium term sentences as a 'compromise' between progressive penal ideas and judicial and public reaction to crime. These are subtly and deeply connected through a process which the misguided policy of 'uniform sentencing practice' will never break down.

With respect to prison labour, the situation remains unsatisfac-tory. Here again the 'security psychosis' and the policy of dispersing maximum security prisoners has been felt. Yet it is gratifying to see that the amount of prison labour for private firms is steadily increasing. The remuneration of prisoners is very low and sometimes not even comparable with that paid in some developing countries. The different rates in operation represent a weekly average varying between six and seven shillings. Some prisoners may make as much as ten or eleven shillings, and in the few cases in which work is really organized on a commercial basis it may be more. The reasoning that 'an immediate increase in prisoners' pay —to the rate for the job—would in fact result in *ex gratia* payments for quantities and standards of work which were not reached, since at present neither the general standards of labour nor the machinery are conducive to the achievement of rates of productivity similar to those reached in outside industry', seems to be more an expression of an exculpatory philosophy for a chronic state of things than a realistic appraisal of facts and purposes. To begin with, unless the general quality of free unskilled labour is magnified, much unskilled prison labour is not inferior; secondly, no administration will ever be able to provide the machinery required to compete with private industry; and finally, as the Estimates Committee says elsewhere, when the production is organized on a commercial basis the remuneration is far higher. The question then is to organize prison labour as far as possible on a commercial basis. In 1951, the average earnings were three shillings and, exceptionally, four. It has taken 17 years to increase it by three or four shillings; at this rate it will take between 65 and 70 years to reach a pound a week. In this connection, it has been estimated that during 1966, each prisoner employed in prison industry produced on average to the notional value of approximately £316 and that the cost of maintaining a prisoner, except for building and maintenance costs and headquarters salaries, is £757 per year. My own calculation on 250 working days a year and with respect to the total working population in 1966 and all the value of goods and services supplied, was £150. Since the figure of £316 refers only to those employed in prison industry, in all probability there is no serious discrepancy between the two figures, the first having a restricted and the second a general average meaning. Actually, both figures allow the conclusion that a better and more commercial organization of prison labour at least for the majority of prisoners would, besides the socio-psychological effects involved, appreciably contribute to the reduction of their living expenses and permit some financial help to the families by the prisoners themselves. Unfortunately, although the prisoners employed in 1967 amounted to nearly 90 per cent of the total available population, almost 53 per cent were occupied in making and repairing mailbags, metal recovery, domestic service and the obscure and not very attractive 'miscellaneous'. The fact is that in 1967 the total prisoners' earnings of £475,542 constituted only 1.5 per cent of the total expenditure of prisons, Borstals, etc. In 1961 it was 1.2 and in 1951 1.1 per cent. On the other hand the Estimates Committee's report on security states:

> The effect in 1966–67 on staff costs for such matters as overtime and hire of dogs is about £80,000. On the capital side, about £300,000 is estimated to be the cost in 1966–67 of such measures as perimeter security systems and similar devices. Looking further ahead £525,000 will be required in 1967–68 for expenditure on building work to enhance security.

According to a footnote, 'The revised provision for 1967–68 attributable to increased security requirements is £719,000.' Certainly security is necessary: the question is what limits are to be set, and whether it would not have been more effective, more humanitarian, and even cheaper, to centralize maximum security offenders.

According to the 1967 Prison Department Report, the average weekly cost per inmate in all establishments is £15 6s. 1d. In view of this modest *per capita* expenditure, nobody should expect very much in the way of care and rehabilitation of prisoners. In fact we can admire the work done by the Prison Service with such small financial resources.

The following percentages of the length of prison sentences during 1948 and 1967 are interesting:

Imprisonment	Percentages	
	1948	1967
Under six months	71	72
Under one year	85	83
From one to six years	15	16
Over six years	0.5	0.6

The small discrepancies are due to the rounding off of figures. Pending further research, the similarity of the percentages cannot be regarded as a constant feature of the intervening years; on the other hand, neither can it be dismissed as coincidence. The fact is that the sentencing trends between 1948 and 1967 are practically identical. Does this similarity mean that in spite of all intervening changes, including those of criminal legislation, judges' and magistrates' attitudes, as well as public opinion, so closely related, remain very much the same? What then has been the effect of all the socio-psychological explanations of human behaviour, criminal policies and programmes and training if, twenty years later, short-term imprisonment is as much used as ever it was? Can it be that in spite of some variations imposed by significant or 'exemplary' cases, the trends of medium and long term imprisonment are almost identical? It may be argued that the classification of the periods selected here is arbitrary, but six months and one year are generally admitted to represent the two current lengths of short-term imprisonment. As for the other two, they refer to lengths the representative character of which can hardly be matched by any other classification.

In the United States, the downward trend of the prison population confined in State and Federal institutions for adult felony offences has been declining in the last few years. On 31 December 1965, there were 211,151 sentenced prisoners. According to the President's Commission report on *Corrections* in the same year, the grand total of offenders dealt with was 1,282,386, of which 348,204 (institutions 62,773, community 285,431) were juveniles; 591,494 (institutions 221,597, community 369,897) adult felon corrections, and 342,688 (institutions 141,303, community 201,385) misdemeanant corrections. About 95 per cent of all offenders are male, most of them between 15 and 30 years of age. According to comparative national census figures, in 1960 well over half the adult felony inmates had had no schooling and the proportion of unskilled persons among them was higher than in the civilian labour force, and many had family problems. The report adds that there are about 400 institutions for adult felons, some of them grossly understaffed and under-equipped, that overcrowding and idleness are the salient features of some, brutality and corruption of a few others, and that 61 prisons opened before 1900 are still in use. Regarding the last point, my own findings, based on an analysis of the annual *Directory* issued by The American Correctional Association, is that in June 1967 no less than 80 institutions built in the nineteenth century—eleven in the first half—were still in operation, the vast majority of which are large and extra large, with over 1,000 or 2,000 prisoners respectively. According to my findings, in 1967 82 of these enormous prisons, not all built in the nineteenth century, accounted for about 132,000 prisoners—a disproportionate figure which raises many questions about the American penal system, especially considering that many of these institutions are—to borrow a term used by Fourier—little more than *falanstères,* i.e. living quarters of a particular social group, in this case convicted offenders. The following are typical examples:

	Average daily population in 1966	Normal capacity
Joliet-Stateville State Penitentiary (1858–1919)	4,070	5,800
Louisiana State Penitentiary (1866)	3,650	3,478
Ohio State Penitentiary (1834)	4,133	2,500
State Prison of Southern Michigan, Jackson (1839)	3,835	3,050
California State Prison, San Quentin (1852)	3,761	2,818

Partly for economic reasons and partly in the belief that new big complexes or compounds are essentially different from these old prisons, huge institutions are still favoured in the United States and elsewhere. In this respect California is leading the 'new trend' with

	Average daily population in 1966	Normal capacity
California Institution for Men, Chino (1941)	1,804	1,661
Deuel Vocational Institution (1946)	1,708	1,514
California Men's Colony (1954)	3,645 including 76 in forestry camps	3,834
Sierra Conservation Center (1965)	1,590 including 574 in forestry camps	1,820

Chino was never an open but a semi-open institution, the excellencies of which have unfortunately been marred by its enormous size. For juvenile and young adult offenders, the base of the central facility of Northern California Youth Center is a complex of institutions with approximately 400 beds each, that will ultimately reach a total of 12 institutions. The first two, one already operating and the other nearing completion, are O.H. Close School for Boys and Karl Holton School for Boys. In Texas the Coffield Unit, with a normal capacity of 2,000, is under construction.

The services and amenities provided in these huge modern institutions do not counteract their eroding environment. It is true that both services and amenities help, and even in some individual cases are decisive, but the huge institution, old or modern, seldom yields the results expected. Nobody visiting Joliet-Stateville and San Quentin, which I last visited in December 1967, will believe that their return in social rehabilitation compensates for what is spent on them in time, energy, efforts and money. The same applies to the huge semi-open or open institutions for young or juvenile offenders.

The situation with regard to county jails is even less satisfactory. There are well over 3,000 in the United States, all free from Federal and State supervision. Their average population in 1965 was 141,303; the total number of commitments for the year 1,016,748; the total operating expenditure $147,794,214, and few of them are equipped to carry out reasonable rehabilitation programmes. Generally the term of commitment is from one day to one year, which means that most of the prisoners are short-termers for less than six months—which is too short to undertake any effective programme, unless it is intensified. Even for those staying longer— in some counties in Pennsylvania the commitments may be up to five or ten years and occasionally life—the personnel in charge is seldom professionally equipped to introduce rehabilitation programmes. Nevertheless in some States the situation has improved. Some of these county jails are as big as State penitentiaries, as will be seen from the following averages for 1966: Detroit House of Correction, 1,500; Baltimore City Jail, 1,500; City House of Correction, Chicago, 1,918; and apparently the largest of all, Los Angeles County Jail, 10,400, of which on average 3,500 are in a camp.

The total operating cost for corrections in the United States in 1965 was about one billion dollars, excluding new construction, amortization, the cost of some services shared with other agencies and paid for out of other budgets, and many other items. The bulk of $435 million was spent on feeding, clothing and guarding adult offenders. The average annual cost of institutional treatment for the felon and misdemeanant offender was $1,966 and $1,046 respectively, and for the juvenile offender $3,613. If these figures are compared with the £15 6s. 1d. per week or $1,910 per annum, spent in the United Kingdom as an average, and account is taken of the difference in the cost of living in the two countries, it will be seen that the expenditure in the United States is low indeed.

In the five houses of detention in New York City, overcrowding is chronic; in 1966 with a combined normal capacity of 2,963, they actually lodged 5,136 detainees. The sentence institutions including the Reception Classification Center, were also grossly overcrowded.

According to the *Basic Data Book, 1967*, the Federal prison population shows a downward trend since 1962. At the end of 1967, the grand total was 19,133 distributed among thirty-one institutions of different types and eight community treatment centers (with 217 inmates). Four of the institutions are of the large type with more than 1,000 prisoners, and two have over 2,000; with only two exceptions, Leavenworth (1895) and McNeil Island (1867), all were built after 1902; most of those recently built vary in capacity from 500 to well over 600. While the *Directory* of the American Correctional Association shows that the large prisons of Atlanta and Leavenworth are overcrowded, the *Basic Data Book, 1967* shows all federal institutions operating in accordance with planned optimum capacity; possibly this means that although the physical capacity has been exceeded, the way in which things are planned compensates for the excess.

In the Federal Prison System, industrial labour is organized by the Federal Prison Industries, an autonomous body within the prison system. According to the report of the Board of Directors for 1967, out of 19,543 prisoners, 5,348 or 27 per cent were employed. This low percentage cannot be explained by the expanding of the programmes of work release, the existence of community centers (lodging no more than 271) or by the growth of inmate training. Certainly all three play a role, but too insignificant to offer a general explanation. The compensation is, in most cases, a disguised gratuity; it varies between 14 and 35 U.S. cents per hour and the annual average is $494.

In the State area, the situation is no better. More or less disguised idleness affects 75 to 80 per cent of the inmates. Anyone interested in knowing how prison labour data are padded with over-assignment should, after having visited the institution, ask for the labour sheets and compare them with what he has seen. He should note the number of prisoners doing productive, semi-productive, purely domestic or maintenance work, as well as those trying to give the impression that they are doing something, and those strolling or lying around in yards and corridors. The labour sheets show impressive figures for 'occupation', but doubts arise not only about the figures but annual reports as well. The last time I did this was in San Quentin in December 1967, and the number of those doing really productive work was not above 20 per cent of the population. Certainly, a larger percentage were doing something, but not real work. Substantially, the remuneration of prison labour remains what it was many years ago; the average compensation varies between 10 and 25 U.S. cents per day.

Overcrowding does not exist in North Dakota, Rhode Island or Wyoming where, furthermore, the institutions are smaller. In New Mexico, the Penitentiary, normal capacity 1,000, average 900, is the only large establishment, and none of the others is overcrowded. Wisconsin deserves special mention not only for having introduced the Huber Law in 1913, now adopted in different forms by 25 states, but also for the modernization of its institutions. As an example, there is the Correctional Institution of Fox Lake opened in 1962, normal capacity 600, average 484, which was well organized and run when I visited it in 1967.

In France the Prison Administration is afflicted by the growth of the prison population, overcrowding, lack of personnel, impossibility of developing adequately imaginative programmes, idleness and rising expenses. On 1 January 1968, out of 34,083 prisoners, 20,861 were convicts and 13,222 or almost 39 per cent, detainees awaiting trial. Overcrowding is widespread, particularly in the *maisons d'arrêt*, which are forced to keep sentenced persons who, in normal circumstances, would be sent to central prisons; Versailles with 49 cells and 170 prisoners. Pontoise with 88 and 361, and Corbeil with 40 and 160 respectively are examples. This lack of space was also seen at the National Observation Center of Fresnes where, in 1965, a substantial number of the cells were still used for custody of prisoners who had nothing to do with the Center. Although the situation improved in 1966, it deteriorated again in the second part of 1967.

As in England and the United States, the main problem for the French Administration is the building of new prisons and how they should be built. While sound policy principles advocate small, preferably open and semi-open institutions, financial and security considerations eventually impose the construction of large closed institutions at present called 'complexes' or 'ensembles'. The French Prison Administration, like many others, is the victim of a series of circumstances beyond its control. The case of the central prison of Muret, opened in 1966, is typical. Although an improvement *vis-à-vis* the existing situation, the fact that besides the type of prisoners originally envisaged others have to be sent, jeopardizes the treatment given to all of them. One wonders if its 680 capacity plus the general overcrowded conditions has anything to do with the change of the original treatment programme. In my experience, the greater the capacity of a prison, the greater the number and mixture of prisoners sent to it. Therefore, the aim assigned to small institutions has better chances of survival than that assigned to big institutions. Experience also shows that the implementation of different treatments for different groups of prisoners in a single institution is always seriously handicapped. The case of the complex of Fleury-Merogis is typical in this respect. Located at 30 km from Paris with a total capacity of 4,008 places—3,112 for men, 380 for women, and 516 for young offenders between 18 and 21 years of age—it was originally envisaged as a *maison d'arrêt* to relieve if not replace those of *La Santé* and *La Roquette* in Paris. Apparently, it is already partly used as a central prison. Furthermore, lawyers object to being forced to go so far to discuss matters with their clients. The

C.—G

objection is important, because usually the pressure exercised by Bar associations is powerful enough to compel any prison administration to change the purpose of a particular institution, if that purpose conflicts with the interests of the members of the Bar. This leads to the question whether criminal courts, except perhaps appeal courts, should not operate in the detention houses instead of in separate buildings in other areas of the city, and the nineteenth century tradition of the *Palais de Justice* or Courts Buildings be abandoned. If the judicial function is understood as a social and not as a professional function, the answer is yes.

The French prison population is kept in closed institutions many of which are too large to carry out adequately the rehabilitation programmes assigned to them. In 1967, the only open institution was Casabianda with a population of 193; if those enjoying the regime of *semi-liberté* are added, the total will not exceed 800. This means that less than five per cent of the prison population are kept in other than closed or semi-closed institutions. Furthermore, out of 20,528 sentenced prisoners on 1 January, 1968, 8,281 or 40 per cent had been sentenced to less than one year.

On average, between 60 and 65 per cent of prisoners were occupied; on the other hand, if occupation means productive and gainful work, between 40 and 45 per cent of the daily average population were so employed. The perseverance of the French Prison Administration in securing the collaboration of private industry instead of sticking to an obsolete conception of the State system of prison labour has made possible the above figures. Yet in spite of the progress made, the report for 1967 frankly admits the necessity for improving the existing situation not only concerning prison labour but in all other aspects as well. The general average remuneration is F6.32 per working day; it is only F5.74 in the *maisons d'arrêt* and between F11 and F12 in the *maisons centrales*. The average annual cost per prisoner in 1967 was F5,844 in the *maisons d'arrêt*, F7,749 in the *maisons centrales* and Penitentiary Centres and F9,472 in the special institutions. The annual average for all institutions was F6,125.

In Belgium on 1 August 1968, out of a total of 6,155 prisoners, about 11 per cent were mental cases kept and treated apart in accordance with the Social Defence Act 1964, 54 per cent were sentenced prisoners, almost 19 per cent awaiting trial or a final decision, and the remaining 16 per cent are described as transfers, transients, etc. with no further indication about their legal condition. The largest institution, which serves as *maison de depôt*, social defence institution and prison, is Merksplas with well over 1,000 male prisoners. With the exception of St Gilles with more than 500 male prisoners, all other institutions are well under the 500 mark,

which is the maximum capacity suggested by the United Nations
Standard Minimum Rules. No information about overcrowding is
given, and I saw none during my last visit to Belgian institutions.
In 1966 the gratuities paid for prison labour were as follows:
domestic work from F2 to F5 per hour according to the category
of the prisoner, and F2 to F6.60 per hour in maintenance, agricultural and industrial work. For private industry work, the
remuneration is from F8.25 to F11 per hour according to whether
it is skilled or unskilled. Prisoners unable to work but following
training or professional courses receive a gratuity of F2.25 to F2.50.
In Switzerland in 1966, out of 19,254 persons sentenced, 11,870 or
61 per cent were sentenced to imprisonment. Of these, 81 per cent
were for less than six months; in fact, 45 per cent were for periods
ranging from one to thirty days. In Yugoslavia in 1965, out of
113,877 sentenced persons, about 56 per cent were sentenced to
imprisonment, including what is called *reclusion,* and of these 81
per cent were for periods from one day to six months. However,
67 per cent of the latter benefited from *sursis* or suspended sentence.

In Sweden, the general picture differs considerably from that
of the United States, the United Kingdom and France. The institutions are small or medium-sized. In 1967 the average institutional
population was 5,136, of which 1,580 or 30 per cent were kept in
open institutions. Overcrowding is not mentioned in the report, and
certainly I have never seen it on my visits to Swedish institutions.
Prison labour policy has improved, and at 30 June 1967 the employment programme had 202 places of work and 5,108 jobs, of which
4,043 were in factories and workshops and 1,065 in agriculture at
57 places of work. The hourly pay for other than piecework varies
between Sw.kr.0.45 and 1.05 according to the character of the work
and the skill of the worker. In the fiscal year 1966/67, the average
hourly wage paid was Sw.kr.0.89 in factories and Sw.kr.1.20 in
agriculture. Wages, or as they are called, *work premiums,* are paid
to inmates engaged in supervised theoretical studies during working
hours. Inmates unable to work either because of illness or any other
reason receive a daily payment of Sw.kr.2.00. It is of particular
interest that since 1962 the National Labour Market Board has
reserved a number of jobs for released prisoners in forestry and
roadbuilding, with housing accommodation near the place of work;
356 men were placed in 1967. Finally in November 1967, out of a
total institutional population of 5,682, only 729 were awaiting trial,
and of these 163 were under psychiatric observation.

In Finland according to information provided by the Institute of
Criminology of Helsinki, on 16 July 1968 there were 5,608 sentenced
prisoners and 438 detainees awaiting trial. Of the sentenced
prisoners, about 15 per cent were in open institutions. The

remuneration of prison labour varies between U.S. $0.12 and 0.25 per day in the closed institutions; in the open institutions, the wages are those normally paid on the free labour market.

In the Netherlands, the capacity of the largest prison is 190; over-crowding is rare and always temporary. At the end of August 1968 the prison population was distributed as follows: 1,560 prisoners awaiting trial, 1,596 sentenced to imprisonment and 945 committed to *asylum* in Government and private mental institutions. During my last visit in 1966 I was impressed by the progressive character of the Dutch prison system based on two laws, one of 1951 which laid down the Basic Principles of the Prison System and the other of 1953 dealing with the General Prison Regulations. The construction of open and semi-open institutions for small numbers of prisoners with large grounds at their disposal is favoured. In this respect the four institutions of Veenhuizen are good, in spite of the fact that in the Esserheem section some old individual cages are still used. The explanations regarding the use of these penitentiary *reliquiae* were unconvincing. It is hoped that the new 'complex' to be built at Veenhuizen—similar to that of Gouda—will not ruin the pleasant physical and psychological conditions of the present institutions. Out of 50 institutions 26 are for less than 100 prisoners; Almelo, one of the newest, is for only 41. Prison labour is available all the year round for the vast majority of prisoners, very often of a high technical character and almost exclusively provided by private firms. The remuneration varies between D.fl.0.60 and D.fl.1.10 per day, and bonuses are from D.fl.0.20 to D.fl.0.55. A new form of remuneration has recently been introduced in the semi-open institution 'De Fleddervoort' as an experiment. According to this, prisoners receive a basic wage of D.fl.1.10 per day, plus the equivalent of 40 per cent of the minimum wage paid for similar work in free labour. The total amounts to about D.fl.60.00 per week. In some cases, prisoners are allowed to work outside and earn normal wages. Efforts are made to bring prison labour remuneration as near as possible to the level of these wages by providing private work for the prisons with the co-operation of trade unions and employers' associations, and according to the Administration the degree of co-operation is surprisingly effective.

In Spain on 31 December 1967, out of 9,324 detainees, more than 41 per cent were awaiting trial. The largest prison populations were in the men's prisons of Madrid and Barcelona with 1,049 and 1,307 respectively. With the exception of Valencia prison for men, with 554 prisoners, none of the other institutions had a population higher than 375. Of the 52 main prisons listed, 34 had less than 100 prisoners as an annual average. No mention is made of over-crowding in the annual report. For a total sentenced population of

5,438 on the same date, there were 3,384 jobs available. Taking account of other statistical data, it seems that about 62 per cent of the sentenced population were working productively in industrial and agricultural activities. Prisoners are classified as foremen, qualified workers, assistants and trainees and receive remuneration according to their work and condition. The average daily remuneration is equivalent to U.S. $1.60, 0.75, 0.60 and 0.20 respectively, which compares favourably with that paid in other more developed countries.

In the Federal Republic of Germany the gathering of data is not easy. New institutions have been built in several Länder; in those of Baden-Würtemberg and Hesse I saw no overcrowding during my visits. The workshops were well-organized and provided work for the majority of the prisoners. At the end of 1963 the data on these two Länder showed that 20 per cent and 60 per cent of the prisoners worked in domestic-maintenance and industrial-agricultural activities respectively. Industrial work was done mostly for private industry under the direct supervision of the prison authorities. In fact, only sick prisoners and those awaiting trial were not working. The remuneration varied between DM 0.50 (Baden-Würtemberg) and DM 0.40 (Hesse) and DM 1.00. In both, special bonuses up to DM 20.00 per month were given to prisoners according to the amount, quality and presentation of the work done. As a rule the same types of remuneration are in force in all Länder.

In Yugoslavia, none of the prisons I have visited was overcrowded. The institutions of Croatia appear to be more rapidly modernized and more receptive to new experiments and programmes. Open and semi-open institutions are encouraged and receive constant attention. Even Mitrovica, probably the largest prison in the country, with a normal capacity of 1,500, average 1,000, has an open and a semi-open institution as annexes. The open institution is devoted to agricultural work, the semi-open and the closed to industrial work. The workshops are large and well-organized with adequate machinery. There were no individual cells; the men sleep in dormitories. Good educational and technical teaching are available. Recidivists are kept in a separate wing with plenty of work. In fact, the whole life of the closed institution area revolves around the workshops, some of which work two shifts daily. The greatest shortcoming is the lack of privacy. In the 1,000-acre farm the daily average population was around 275 prisoners, most of them first or short-term offenders, about 50 per cent of whom are sent directly to the farm without any previous stay in the closed or semi-open part of the institution. Inmates may also teach, and I met a doctor who was practising his profession, a fact which no doubt many people will frown upon. Home leave is granted, and for those who are not entitled to leave there is a rest house with some individual rooms and others for two or three persons, where they may spend two weeks at leisure and still receive their share in the profits of the prison work. According to the general economic pattern of the country the remuneration for work is not set up according to a salary system. In fact, the word 'wages' is not used. From the gross income obtained in each institution a series of complicated deductions for the State, business fund, maintenance—which takes the greatest amount—improvement and premiums fund, etc., are made before the benefit percentage is distributed among the workers in accordance with the work done by each. In sum, although the execution of criminal sanctions and of sentences of deprivation of liberty are regulated by two national laws, both promulgated in 1961, the Prison Administration of each Republic is free to organize its penitentiary system as it sees fit within the limits set up by these laws. Each Prison Administration has enough autonomy to seek orders, even abroad, and distribute the benefits obtained.

Whether or not this system could be applied elsewhere cannot be discussed here. It is not necessarily a socialist system, although a socialist country has introduced it with satisfactory results. In accordance with the Federal Constitution and the Constitutions of the Republics, work is the right of everyone, and since prison work is no different from free work and is moreover part of the national, regional and local economy, it is no wonder that Yugoslavia has organized it.

In Turkey most of the closed prisons are overcrowded, and productive prison labour is available only for a limited number of prisoners. On the other hand, Turkey has far more open and semi-open institutions than some developed countries. In 1965 there were twelve such institutions which had been in operation for many years, none of them overcrowded, with work all the year round—either industrial or agricultural, and with the exception of Imrali (an island), average population 700, the average of the others seldom exceeds 300. The remuneration for skilled workers is equivalent to U.S. $0.70, for the unskilled 0.50 and for trainees 0.35. In the closed institutions the remuneration is somewhat lower, but comparatively higher than the gratuities of some prominent developed countries. It should be noted that Ankara Yeni Cezaevi (New Ankara prison) is, for all practical purposes, an open institution located in the middle of one of the most populous areas of Ankara, with a completely open front garden where prisoners often spend their free time. Escapes are rare in this and other open and semi-open institutions. It is unfortunate that in other respects Turkish progressive penitentiary reforms have been marred by the new closed prison of Saǧinalcilar near Istanbul, representative of a policy which I tried to discourage when I was consulted in 1963. The new prison, with a capacity of 2,150, and which cost 36 million lira—about U.S. $4 million—has nevertheless been praised by the Press as the largest and most modern closed prison in Europe and Asia.

As far as large closed prisons in Asia are concerned, most are overcrowded, and prison labour is seldom available and poorly if ever remunerated. As a rule, prison authorities are not able to secure regular work; at best, some kind of occupation or agricultural undertaking is occasionally provided, or some prisoners are helped to work on their own. Overcrowding is still prevalent in the prisons of Karachi, Montgomery, Colombo, New Delhi, Bombay, Calcutta, Benares, Nang-Kwang, near Bangkok, and many others. The situation was better in the Central Prison of Teheran, Bogambara in Kandy, Ceylon, with reasonably well-equipped industrial workshops, the main prison of Lahore and in Multan, a semi-open institution in West Pakistan which impressed me as the best organized in this part of the country. It was better in some respects in the prisons of Padu, near Kuala Lumpur (Malaysia), Lucknow (India) and most of the institutions of Singapore, although the compound of Pearls Hill prison needed urgent and extensive improvement in some sections. The Pulau Senang settlement was a mistake which ended tragically shortly after my visit. On the other hand, in most of these countries there are some open institutions which, although modest, are usually well organized, with work all the year round, mostly agricultural, and prison labour is modestly compensated. All of them perform a social function of great value and show the interest of the respective governments in improving existing policies. A few examples may suffice: the open institutions of Kundasale and Pallekele organized as camps, and the prison farms of Anuradhapara and Batticoloa in Ceylon; the mobile camps for public work in India; Burewala in Pakistan and the open institutions of Huay Pong and Aranyik in Thailand. The so-called Sampurnanand Camps in India, sometimes with 2,000 prisoners, go from one place to another, although they usually remain in one place for long periods of time, and are used in public works of different kinds. The living conditions are far better than those available to the majority of prisoners outside. Educational and training programmes are organized, and there is no exploitation. The Reformatory Camps of Bulaware for young adult prisoners in Pakistan constitute a remarkable institution organized in accordance with the Prisoners' Probational Act, 1926, according to which first offenders are sent as 'probationers' to the farms, where they receive, free of charge, a piece of land and tools and may be granted loans for the purchase of cattle, manure, etc. A system of co-operatives facilitates the acquisition of most of what is required for farming. When some years ago I visited the camp, 'probationers' were living with their families, who were also working on the land. Upon release, 'probationers' may take with them their earnings and possessions. Educational facilities were also available. As an even more refreshing experience, reference should be made to the well-organized prison system of Hong Kong, for many years under the able direction of Commissioner of Prisons C. James Norman. In normal circumstances the institutions were never overcrowded, and work was available all the year round, although modestly remunerated.

In Japan, overcrowding has been reduced partly by the extensive use of probation and parole and partly by opening sections in certain prisons where some types of offenders receive what is called open treatment. This consists in allowing prisoners to move about freely indoors by not locking doors, workshops, rooms, etc. These sections exist in the prisons of Toyohashi, Narashino and Kakogawa for adults. In December 1967 I still had the impression that the whole Japanese system relies too much on the closed institution. The number of prisoners kept in open institutions is small. Regarding overcrowding and open spaces within the prisons for the benefit of prisoners—particularly in the large prisons of Yokohama and Fuchu—it should be kept in mind that space is a rare commodity in Japan. This explains why the individual cell is less used than in other countries, and why large rooms with sleeping capacity for several prisoners, between five and 12, are the rule. Generally, prisoners' personal effects do not take much space, and furthermore, apart from sleeping, they spend very little time in their cells. Either they are working or attending courses or doing something useful. More open space may be found in smaller institutions such as Nara.

On average, 50,000 prisoners work every day at 73 different institutions in Japan. The work provided is varied and well-organized; modern machinery, often demanding great skill and training, is used. Every prisoner is working unless sick or otherwise unable. In fact, institutional life revolves first around work, of which there is plenty, and second, around educational and other activities, of which there is no scarcity. Whether this factory or production approach is bad is difficult to say; before passing judgment, it should be remembered that work is an inherent part of Japanese life. In my three visits to the country, I have never seen people idle, except for the very old and the sick, and the fact that prison life has the same pattern is not surprising. While in socialist countries work is regarded as a right which has been acquired and shops are being enlarged and improved, and as often as possible must be secured, in Japan work is a natural feature of everyday life. To tell the Japanese that work is a right would probably make no sense to them. This explains why the employment rate is near the 90 per cent mark among sentenced prisoners and 75 per cent among those awaiting trial. Prison labour is partly organized according to the State use system and partly according to the piecework and contract systems for private contractors, which apparently yield better results. There is no exploitation of prisoners, and according to my own observation, there is no padded employment, and the number of prisoners assigned to domestic chores and maintenance is kept to a minimum. Remuneration is modest; in industrialized prisons like Fuchu the monthly average is about Y700. There is a scale of compensation in case of accidents—the maximum indemnity being Y200,000.

Whether prison conditions in the Arab countries have improved since 1965 is difficult to ascertain, but up to that time they were seldom satisfactory. Probably political and economic conditions have not helped much. Overcrowding, even in the small prisons, was the general rule; work was seldom available except for a minority of prisoners in the large prisons; for remuneration some sort of compensation was occasionally given, either during imprisonment or upon release. In the Lebanon, Syria and Jordan, the gendarmerie or the military are still in charge of the prisons, a task which young officers often dislike. The fact that in the Lebanon the first Prison Administration was created in 1964 has not altered the situation, inasmuch as a commandant was appointed director and no prison service has as yet been organized. The large and dilapidated central prison of Alramel (the Sands) in Beirut, average population 1,000, is still waiting to be replaced by a huge complex—opposed by many people in the Lebanon and the Social Defence Advisory Services of the United Nations—which was still unfinished in 1968. In Syria, the prison conditions of Damascus, Homs, Hama, Aleppo, Latakia, Suweida, Deir-ez-Zor and others were, in 1965, unsatisfactory in spite of some efforts to improve them. At Hama, the new prison outside the city was finished in 1963, but there was no space for workshops. Conditions were always better in the institutions for juveniles, particularly in Homs, Hama and Damascus. In the United Arab Republic, although of a para-military character, there is a well-organized career prison service which, since 1952, has been improving the penal system as much as possible, in spite of the scarcity of financial resources. Overcrowding is still a feature in the prisons of Cairo, Alexandria, Port Said, Barrage, Tanta and others. Nearly all are large institutions where labour is not available to all prisoners. Work-some sort of compensation is paid to some of the prisoners for their work. As for Algeria, the prison situation in 1968 cannot be regarded as satisfactory.

In Latin America, prison conditions vary from country to country but are generally unsatisfactory or really bad. The most progressive policies and programmes were carried out in Brazil in the States of Rio Grande do Sul and São Paulo a few years ago, in the former, by replacing the old central prison and most of the local prisons. In São Paulo, the development of large open agricultural institutions, some of them with accommodation for the families of prisoners, received considerable impetus with the organization of institutions such as Itapitininga, Bauru and Ouro Preto. Unfortunately, poor selection of offenders and of the personnel in charge of them as well as political changes have prevented the continuation of a policy which was an improvement on the present one, in spite of its obvious shortcomings. In Argentina, a distinction should be made between the provincial and national systems. According to the Constitution, the different provinces are autonomous in the organization of their prison systems, but not all of them, either because the number of prisoners is small or for other reasons, have organized them and therefore by special agreements the national (federal) system takes care of prisoners, including those awaiting trial in some provinces. Of the two systems, the national has always been the more progressive, especially when it was run by R. Pettinato. Afterwards, the demolition of the old Penitentiary of Buenos Aires, which up to now has not been replaced, the bloody riots of Villa Devoto in which the guards were at least as brutal as the inmates, and the protracted construction of the ill-advised complex of Ezeiza and of the skyscraper House of Detention in Buenos Aires have marred the policy of the past. On the other hand, there are encouraging signs, like the enlarging and improving of already existing open institutions, and the organization of new ones such as General Pico in La Pampa, with a capacity of 50 prisoners able to work outside if necessary, and other improvements in working conditions and medicopsychological treatment. All this is largely due to the persistence of J. C. Garcia Basalo as Inspector General of Prisons. As in most developing countries, the Argentine penitentiary progress is seriously handicapped by the enormous number of people sent to prison to await trial—this, besides absorbing personnel and services which could be used for the better treatment of sentenced prisoners, means considerable public expenditure. Thus on 31 December 1967, out of a total of 19,903 prisoners, only 7,322 were provincial and federal sentenced prisoners and the rest, up to 64 per cent of the total, prisoners awaiting trial. On average, a felony case takes a year before sentence is passed by the court of first instance. Chile, Mexico and Venezuela have introduced penitentiary reforms in the last few years. The last two by building large penitentiaries, but adequate staff and services as well as enough prison work are still scarce. This is particularly the case with the Penitentiary of the Federal District of Mexico City, which was supposed to replace the old prison of Lecumberri still in use. Curiously enough, no regulations have as yet been enacted for the organization and running of the Penitentiary, in spite of the years which have elapsed since it was opened. This is contrary to the United Nations Standard Minimum Rules for the Treatment of Prisoners, according to which, 'Every prisoner on admission shall be provided with written information about the regulations governing the treatment of prisoners of his category, the disciplinary requirements of the institution, the authorized methods of seeking information and making complaints and all such other matters as are necessary to enable him to understand both his rights and his obligations and to adapt himself to the life of the institution.' On the positive side, the discreet way in which conjugal visits are organized should be stressed.

In Venezuela, the large Penitentiary of San Juan de los Morros is one of the most telling cases of failure.. The only exception was the psychiatric unit which, when I revisited the institution a few years ago, was doing an excellent research job and giving some treatment. The same comment applies to the more modern Penitentiary of Maracaibo, the women's section of which was the worst in every way. As for the Carcel Pública of Caracas (Detention House) with a capacity of 360, it contained 1,300 prisoners in 1963, most of them awaiting trial. According to my inquiries, conducted in the presence of the warden, a number of untried prisoners had been waiting for more than two years, and two for more than four. All were kept idle. In the Valencia prison, with a capacity of 150, 415 were kept idle. The information received since then shows that although here and there improvements have been made, overcrowding, aggravated by the increasing number of detainees and prisoners sentenced for subversive activities, idleness and scarcity of staff and services were still the prevailing characteristics of the penal system at the end of 1967. In Chile, although the Prison Service is doing its best within the limited financial resources allotted to it, the situation is far from satisfactory. The Penitentiary of Santiago and the prisons of Antofagasta, Iquique, Concepción, Tacna, Temuco and Valparaiso show how much has still to be done, before it can be said that the United Nations Standard Minimum Rules are applied.

In Colombia, prison conditions are appalling, in spite of the fact that the directors of the Prison Administration have repeatedly drawn the attention of the Government to these conditions. The same may be said about Panama. The situation is better in Costa Rica, where the Government has been trying for years to replace the old Penitentiary and organize a Prison Service. In Guatemala, the Central Prison of Guatemala City and those in most of the other cities are still reminiscent of the prisons of more than a century ago. In Guatemala City Prison, I never found the traditional separation between persons awaiting trial and sentenced prisoners. The dormitories are poor and the Administration unable to procure either work or clothing. The central yard, fortunately large enough, brings back old scenes of prisoners left to their own devices to earn money for survival by selling 'souvenirs', cooking or working for other prisoners, and repairing that which often seems to be beyond repair. Peru is one of the few countries in which, once in a while, prisoners collectively complain about lack of food. The colony of Sepa was still severely criticized in 1967 by prominent Peruvian professionals. The prisons of El Frontón, El Sexto, Lurigancho and the small prisons of Callao and Lima are actually run by the prisoners themselves. Lurigancho penitentiary, near Lima, visited by the writer in August 1969, is a flagrant denial of penitentiary progress. It should be added that the new military regime of Peru has abolished the Ministry of Justice and that the prisons are run by the Ministry of Interior. The conditions were depressing in the prisons of Cerro de Pasco, Trujillo, Cajamarca, Tingo Maria, Cuzco and Arequipa, visited some years ago. Yet Peru has had a Prison Administration for a long time, and some years ago under the leadership of Altmann Smyth as director, it was oriented to a progressive policy. This has been changed by his successors, some of whom were unfit for the task in every respect. As for Ecuador, suffice it to say that more than once I succeeded in going in and out of the Panopticon, the large 'security' prison of Quito, without being stopped. In Guayaquil, the new Penitentiary of Siteral, also visited in 1969, is a fiasco in every respect. In Ecuador, there is no Prison Service or Administration; the prisons are run by the police or municipal authorities according to the circumstances.

In Bolivia there is no Prison Administration proper, but a section in the Ministry of Justice and the Interior which has been trying for many years to improve the fragile structure of a prison organization which, as in many other countries, is frequently totally dislocated by political turmoil. The Panopticon of La Paz is little more than a prison where prisoners of every sort are kept with no attempt to apply any other treatment than that of custody. No prison labour is provided beyond giving facilities to some prisoners to work on their own. With few variations, the situation was the same until recently in the prisons of Oruro, Sucre, Potosí, Cochabamba, Santa Cruz de la Sierra, Trinidad and others. Prisons are usually run by the military or uniformed police. In Uruguay, which in the past played a leading role in prison reform, the general situation has deteriorated. Many years ago the construction of a large closed prison was decided on and started; it is still unfinished for lack of funds, and its musty cement structure has become a memorial to a mistaken prison policy.

For African countries, prison data are frequently non-existent, incomplete or out of date. When nearly four-fifths of Africa's population was under European rule, the extent and gravity of crime were only known in a few areas, and here and there some statistical data were available. Although not particularly illuminating, the report of the Conference on the Treatment of Offenders held at Dar-es-Salaam in 1953 drew attention to a series of problems; now that nearly four-fifths of the population have become independent, it is doubtful if they receive more attention than before or are better known. This implies no criticism of independence, which in every aspect of life, individual or otherwise, I have always actively supported, but if the transition period has improved many aspects of national and individual life, it has not as yet made similar progress in the penitentiary field. Certainly here and there some improvements are made and others claimed, but the fact remains that reliable information is seldom available. It should be added that political turmoil and the kind of regimes prevailing in some African countries are not the most conducive to the improvement of penitentiary policies and programmes.

The scarce data on Nigeria, Ghana, Dahomey, Togo and Senegal can only be regarded as reflecting generally unsatisfactory conditions. In the Congo, Leopoldville, on 3 May 1965 at Makala, one of the largest prisons, out of 1,903 male prisoners 1,240 were awaiting trial, many of them for over six months and others for more than a year. The situation is occasionally less unsatisfactory in Kenya and Tanzania. Yet it was in Dar-es-Salaam, the capital of Tanzania, that in July 1968 the High Court sentenced two officials to ten years' imprisonment for their part in a mass suffocation tragedy in which 13 out of 42 people died when crammed into two small cells. In a United Nations report on juvenile delinquency in Zambia published in 1967, the most recent statistical data refer to 1963; Zambia became independent in 1964. In 1966 at the XVIth International Course of Criminology held at Abidjan, the most significant facts about the treatment of prisoners in the Ivory Coast were: that the food had considerably improved; that although administratively part of the Ministry of Justice, most of the functions assigned to a non-existent Prison Administration were performed by the police and prefectural authoritites; and that, in spite of the increasing number of prisoners, the budget had not been changed for the last six years. The Ivory Coast became independent in 1960. As for countries like Sudan, Mauritania, Mali, Chad and Volta, nothing is known about prison conditions from official or semi-official documents. With respect to the Republic of South Africa, according to the report for the period 1963–66, as at 30 June 1965 there were 72,580 persons in custody, 60,477 of whom had been convicted. During the year ended 30 June 1966, 339,143 sentenced prisoners and 204,773 unsentenced prisoners were admitted to prison, of whom 80,329 or about 39 per cent were readmitted to prison as sentenced prisoners. Of the 339,143—male and female—only 1.8 per cent are listed as white. The proportion of white in the general population is about 19 per cent. Sentenced prisoners are classified as white, Bantu, Asiatic and coloured; by far the greatest proportion is Bantu followed by coloured and Asiatics. Of the above total, 91 per cent were sentenced to periods of up to six months. Out of 281 prisoners sentenced to corporal punishment only (caning) 204 were Bantu, 52 white, 23 coloured and 2 Asiatic. While the proportion between sentenced white women and men was roughly 20 to one, those of Bantu and coloured was 6 to one, and that of Asiatics 45 to one. The report makes the point that, in order to avoid a misapprehension, the category of prisoners apparently regarded as political detainees, with a single exception, are persons tried in open court, convicted and sentenced for offences against public security. Such persons fall under the respective group of ordinary sentenced prisoners, and on no occasion were more than 1,825 in custody, and on 30 June 1966 there were only 1,395. On the other hand, apart from referring to these persons as saboteurs and perpetrators of violence, no reference is made to the special legislation declaring them as such, or to relevant circumstances in which it is applied. No specific data are given about the different types of treatment applied to each of the four groups of prisoners, type of institutions and personnel in charge. As for prison labour, nothing specific is said about remuneration, beyond the general assertion that the gratuity scales for internal employment have recently been considerably improved and extended. The whole prison system is run in accordance with the antidemocratic apartheid policy of the country.

For Australia, the most complete data concern Victoria. In the year ending 30 June 1967, the average prison population was 2,111 (51 female), of which 1,214 were kept at Pentridge, apparently the most important multipurpose institution of the State. The others were fortunately distributed in a series of small prisons, some closed and others reafforestation or farm prisons. Existing data show some unemployment among prisoners. The total earnings amounted to $38,996 which, if compared with the total turnover of prisoners and the net profit from prison industry, means that what is paid for prison labour is barely a gratuity.

The most recent official and semi-official information for Israel refers to 1962 and is not complete enough to allow any analysis, either of the number of prisons, their classification, overcrowding conditions or prison labour. Some years ago when I visited them, most of the prisons were too old, and there was some overcrowding. At that time the directorate was introducing a series of reforms, some of them well oriented. According to statistical data published by the Institute of Criminology of Jerusalem in 1962, out of 1,179 prison inmates, only 67 were awaiting trial. In 1961, 61 per cent of the prison sentences were up to three months, 25 per cent from three months to one year and only 14 per cent over one year. The impression given is that fine and probation are less used than they should be, either because judges and magistrates do not favour them, the type of offenders do not permit it, or because obsolete penal and criminal legislation prevent their wider use. As in many other countries, this great proportion of short-termers and the corresponding turnover all the year round means that the treatment of these offenders is little more than a custodial task.

2   Crime as a social problem

It has been shown that together unknown and known but unreported crime are more extensive and serious than reported crime. Therefore criminal statistics are not the only source of knowledge about crime; officials, authorities and highly placed persons, although unpunished, are frequently offenders; and, in the main, those responsible for reported crime are a socially, economically and psychologically well-defined group.

The extent of crime and the variety of social groups involved refute the thesis that it can be explained by causal generalizations, or that as a problem it can be dealt with as part of socio-economic planning. In order to be understood, it must be viewed in the light of such an ensemble as socio-economic change, the structure of the general population, political organization and stability, and politico-social values.

The persistence and widespread increase of crime, in spite of all efforts to reduce it, raise a series of questions about the necessity for a new approach to the prevention of crime and the treatment of offenders; the effectiveness of criminal justice and the need to review the system of values it protects; as well as the validity of the distinction between crime and delinquency.

All these questions show clearly the socio-political character of crime, both as a general and as an individual event; it is essentially a policy problem and should be dealt with as such. Scientific findings should be used within the limits imposed by political and policy considerations, among which respect for human rights is of primary importance. Owing to its complexity, crime defies scientific integration if this is understood as putting together all the parts in order to form a scientific whole.

This puts crime in a different perspective which has not, up to now, been contemplated. Only recently has it been fully realized that the unknown territory of crime requires attention from a political and scientific point of view. It means that the criminal justice system should be organized so as to reduce the non-reported areas of crime, and that some of the pillars of contemporary research have to be abandoned and new ones built up.

The connection between crime and politics has always existed but rarely been taken into account by criminology and penology, which are almost exclusively devoted to preventive-treatment policies and programmes covering only a part of the complex problem of crime. In other words, up to now crime has been studied through the magnifying glass of a limited group of offenders. With the new dimension given to the problem, individual crime and clinical criminology can no longer be regarded as the departing points of criminological generalizations. It should be kept in mind that as an individual act, crime implies a twofold relationship; between the individual as author and the legitimate system of order under which he lives, and between him and the victim. When appraising criminal behaviour, these two aspects must be considered. The motives and aims of the offender are not the only factors to determine the kind of treatment he should receive: there is also the protection of the legitimate order. To conclude, crime and not the offender is the point of departure and return of criminal policy as well as of criminology and penology.

Partly following Weber, I should add that legitimate order does not mean either total conformity to it or an authoritarian conception of criminal law.[19] The manifestations of non-conformity, even in a rebellious form, may not constitute a criminal offence or may, in certain cases, underline the need to reform the criminal system. A number of crimes, particularly those related to corrupt practices and *mores*, are often expressions of social adjustment. On the other hand, a person opposing discrimination in a discriminatory society may be considered maladjusted and even criminal, when he is actually perfectly adjusted to a system of higher social and political values.

The internal mechanism of crime may be better understood when it is pointed out that the legitimacy of a given order is due to the free sharing of common beliefs, values and rules, the preservation of which is entrusted to a legal system enforced by a legitimate authority. Preservation does not exclude change, even sudden change, if it is in accordance with currently accepted procedure. The sharing and acceptance do not mean universal conformity with everything the legitimate order stands for, and even less that the fundamental norms of that order have to be incorporated into the individual personalities of the members of the group or assimilated by the entire community. What is important is that the legitimate order is democratically established and maintained. Consequently, conflicts between individuals and the legitimate order are to be expected and should not necessarily be taken as expressions of cultural conflicts or socio-pathological or abnormal manifestations. Only in cases of extreme disruption called crimes, and because they have first been disapproved by general consensus, does the legitimate order react by imposing a penal sanction. It follows that they should be as few and well-founded as possible, as they are to be treated in accordance with the social disapproval that penal treatment implies. I repeat, the personal motivations, conditions and aims of the offender may be taken into account but can never be decisive in determining what should be done with him. The decisive factor is the purpose assigned to the legitimate order, the protection of a fundamental system of values, the *ratio essendi* of which is social justice.

Certainly the legitimate order of a given society is conventional, but this does not mean that its content and purpose have a permanent character. Changes are introduced according to social and political evolution or revolution and under the impact of scientific progress. The important thing is that changes be accepted through a democratic process and that the individual and social guarantees that every legitimate order should offer are not taken from it. Part of the legitimate order is the enumeration and definition of criminal offences. Their perpetration cannot be considered as individual acts divested of social significance, which by itself is above the possible explanations of the causation of the crimes committed or of crime as a general phenomenon. These explanations, even if scientifically correct, have no socio-political meaning. This presupposes that in order to be used in the formulation of criminal policies, the scientific explanations of criminal behaviour should be as correct as possible; socio-politically feasible and acceptable for social and political considerations.

Thus the ultimate decision when dealing with the crime problem as well as with the individual criminal offence belongs not to a causation process but to an evaluation process in accordance with the fundamental values incorporated in the legitimate order. There are several reasons for this: first, that as far as criminology is concerned the causal theories of crime have not as yet been able to offer a sound scientific explanation of crime, either as an individual act or as a general phenomenon; second, the neutral character of science, which often overlooks the fact that no scientific findings should be applied without due respect for human rights; the case of juvenile delinquency speaks for itself; and third, that taken as a whole, the system of fundamental values, which is not immutable, has been proven historically more reliable than the scientific criminological findings and theories. This lack of scientific reliability is usually explained by the fact that criminology is young. But the study of crime, the criminal and the criminal justice system have been going on for centuries, and some of the findings of the past are still valid, and much of what is offered as scientifically new was known a long time ago.

1 Theories of crime

Social disorganization. The thesis that crime is the outcome of social disorganization has its most distinguished representative in Sutherland. In his exposé of the differential association he said: 'The origin and the persistence of culture conflicts relating to the values expressed in the law and of differential association which is based on the cultural conflicts are due to social disorganization. Cultural conflict is a specific aspect of social disorganization and in that sense the two concepts are names for smaller and larger aspects of the same thing.' He concludes that his theory may be summarized as follows: 'Systematic criminal behaviour is due immediately to differential association in a situation in which cultural conflicts exist and ultimately to the social disorganization in that situation.'[20]

Unlike others who refer to social disorganization without saying anything about the type of organization which would prevent or reduce crime, Sutherland suggested as the most promising the substitution of communism for the individualistic system. Apparently in 1939 he regarded Soviet policy as an experiment which might produce disasters greater than the criminality of the individualistic society—a prophecy which has come true—but he added that the significant thing about the Soviet system was probably not communism but the common purpose and enthusiasm for communism, and that it resolved the conflict between self-interest and social welfare for a considerable number of people and developed a social organization in which integration rather than disintegration is the characteristic thing. Sutherland's remarks are still extremely significant, since after so many years of communist integration and disorganization, crime in the U.S.S.R. is as serious as elsewhere, particularly political and economic crimes. The enthusiasm of the past and the present rigidity of the regime imposed have not suppressed conflicts between self-interest and social welfare or the overt lack of conformity with communist ideology imposed in the U.S.S.R. and its satellites. The preservation of an ideological dogmatism has originated not only the legal formulation of a series of crimes but also the multiplication of crimes committed under cover of official position.

The thesis of social disorganization still widely referred to by criminologists, ignores the fact that no social structure or system will ever be free from contradictions, inequalities and conflicts, whatever the politico-social and economic regime. Evolution and renewal imply social discarding and disorganization and therefore crime. In turn the new organization may eradicate some sources of crime but will inevitably create others. As for reorganization and organization, what Taft said years ago is unacceptable: 'Perhaps the most basic change needed in the interest of crime prevention would be the incorporation in our culture of a genuinely scientific point of view which sees criminals as products. Such a society would not hold the individual criminal responsible though it would continue to hold him in every way accountable for his behaviour.' Here one may ask if the consideration of offenders as products would imply more human preventive and treatment policies or the opposite. As history has shown, a 'genuinely scientific point of view' can lead to brutal preventive policies which, while they may be explained on scientific grounds, can never be justified. In any case, to regard criminals as products is not only dangerous for them but for society as well.

The thesis of social disorganization attracts many developing countries which assume that as soon as the socio-economic organization takes root, crime will be eradicated or considerably reduced. Most of them have introduced some sort of socialist system which is regarded as the most effective for the prevention of crime. This is perhaps correct, provided it is freely accepted and maintained, but it must be remembered that, like any other socio-political system, it breeds its own forms of criminality.

Social pathology and crime. The consideration of crime as a social pathological phenomenon is the result of regarding as such any act or condition which, owing to its frequency and harmful effects on the social system, requires immediate or continuous official counteraction. The same criterion is occasionally still applied to prostitution, illegitimacy, vagrancy, alcoholism, and even poverty and divorce.[21] Nowadays, this approach to social problems or conditions is changing rapidly, and what was assigned to social pathology has been taken over by social welfare, social medicine, social hygiene, social psychology, better social legislation and corresponding programmes and services. At its best, social pathology was a label imposed either by a wishful conception of how society should be, or by borrowing from biology an organic idea of society, or both. The fact that occasionally individual crime is the result of individual pathological conditions or that many offenders live in poverty, come from broken homes with or without divorce, or are illegitimate, does not make crime a social pathological product, neither does the fact that large expenditures of public money are required to deal with it, inasmuch as this is not inherent in crime but in the implementation of a public policy. The same applies to prostitution, vagrancy, illegitimacy, alcoholism, etc.

Culture, subculture and crime. Closely related to social disorganization is the thesis that crime is the outcome of a cultural conflict. The connection between culture and crime, the latter being regarded as the infraction of what was loosely termed 'norm of culture', was studied by the jurists before the sociologists took any interest in the matter. It was Max Ernst Mayer who, in the first edition of his *Der Allgemeine Teil des Deutschen Strafrechts,* (1915) formulated the *Kulturnormen* theory of crime and criminal law.[22] Briefly, it is that culture creates a series of norms of varying importance, many of which entail prohibitions or commands of different types which may or may not be observed by members of society. Because of their social importance, some of these norms are incorporated into criminal law. In Germany, Mayer's theory was severely criticized on two counts: the vagueness of the term 'culture' and the difficulty of separating norm from criminal law. This does not mean that the relationship between culture and crime has been denied in Germany or for that matter elsewhere, but the number of variables involved and above all the lack of specificity of the term 'culture' prevented it from being considered as an all-embracing source of crime. This relationship was recognized by Sauer, who also pointed out the important fact that, while crime follows culture, the latter never follows the former. In other words, crime does not create culture. According to him, while culture may offer some form of diagnosis of crime, it cannot explain it in its entirety. In Exner and Mezger, culture conflict as a general explanation of crime is not mentioned. Following the traditional distinction between *Anlage* and *Umwelt* ('tendency' and 'environment' would be the approximate translation of these words), both authors examine the factors of crime, among which cultural conflicts may here and there play a role. Like them, Seelig does not regard crime in general as the outcome of cultural conflicts.

In the United States Thorsten Sellin is the most prominent advocate of crime as an expression of a culture conflict. According to him, crime is the sequel of an external conflict of conduct norms. These are the crystallization of social rules, the violation of which arouses a group reaction. As an instrument to secure conformity, criminal law should be regarded as an important body of rules which Sellin calls crime norms, the function of which is to protect certain interests. The conflict between individual reaction and conduct norms—apparently crime norms—may be avoided by acculturation, i.e. by the absorption of ideas with meanings which, as cultural elements embodied in the mind, become personality elements or, more conveniently and broadly, personality. According to Sellin 'personality is a social product' and 'whether the manner in which a person responds in a life situation is the result of habit or of deliberation, his reaction may be regarded as an expression of his personality'. The decisive factor is whether or not the conduct norm has become an element of his personality. If not, whatever the significance of the norm to the group, it has none to the person concerned. According to the degree of absorption, Sellin evolves a series of types and suggests sociological research for preventive and treatment purposes.

Sellin's criminological theory calls for some comments:

a The content of culture as an ensemble of ideas which embody meanings attached to customs, beliefs, artifacts and relationships with fellow men and social institutions is too broad and unsystematic as a basis for theory building and research. Culture cannot be reduced to a series of personal relationships and meanings;

b The terms conduct norm, criminal law norm, conduct code, group rules and crime norms are repeatedly used, but no attempt has been made to differentiate between them or to explain their respective roles in the personality assimilation process which is considered as the decisive element of the theory; and

c Personality is regarded as a social product, which is in opposition to the generally admitted thesis that it is a structure constituted by bio-psychological as well as by environmental components.

Sellin's thesis may be regarded as the outgrowth of cultural conflicts which in a few cases may help to explain offences committed by immigrants. Experience shows that the fact of sharing identical norms or absorbing new ones does not prevent people from committing offences. Although presented in a different way, the culture conflict explanation of crime is a variant of the multiform theory of maladjustment. Furthermore, the task of determining how the absorption process takes place raises insurmountable research difficulties. In this respect Reckless's remark that 'Sellin's framework is very hard to substantiate in research and practically no-one has tried to substantiate it directly' is fully justified.[23]

From the concept of culture as an ensemble of ideas, beliefs, etc. to that of subculture with the same content but usually assigned to lower class groups, minorities and the like, there was only a step, which was readily taken because of the prevailing empirical approach to the study of social problems. The step was prompted by the role played in the formulation of sociological theories with self-satisfying national images, particularly in the United States.

Hence the proliferation of subcultural theories which try to explain as *sub something* what is actually an integral part of it. More recently a new step has been taken by regarding some aspects of family relations as subcultural. Accordingly, the subculture of parental-male relations is presented as an explanatory thesis in connection with juvenile delinquency. By the same token, the subculture of parental-female relations should be included, and since the family is involved, it would not be surprising if the subculture of mother-in-law relations is eventually brought forward too.

These empirical approaches explain why, while some propound the thesis of a delinquent subculture, others, talking about the same things, use that of delinquent culture or use the terms indiscriminately. A perusal of American literature shows that subculture is generally understood as a subdivision of the national culture, which is sometimes regarded as an ensemble of capabilities, ideas, etc. and sometimes as social status, ethnic background, rural or urban settings, etc. Although related, these and similar elements are not necessarily culture. No wonder then that Milton Yinger, after having noted the confusion created by the term subculture, coined that of *contraculture* in his 'Contraculture and Subculture', in *American Sociological Review*, October 1960, which is as confusing as the term subculture. Are violence, illicit sexual relations and murder, to cite a few cases, contracultural, anticultural, subcultural, cultural or acultural? Whatever answer is given, it will be misleading as long as culture is understood as it is by most American sociologists. More often than not they stress the connection between culture and production-consumption to explain either a cultural or a subcultural thesis. There is indeed a connection, but by stressing it they show that their style of thought or *eidos* is not as broad as it should be. As Charles Madge, *Society in the Mind* (1964) says, 'social membership has a pervasive effect on all thinking and social eidos therefore tends to spread over into eidos as a whole'. The same happens although the content of *eidos* is different, with socialist writers dealing with social problems. The production-consumption approach to culture is maintained, among many others, by Jessie Bernard in her essay 'Teen-Age Culture: An overview', in *The Annals of the Academy of Political and Social Science*, November 1961, devoted to a series of essays on *Teen-Age Culture*. According to her,

Teen-age culture is a product of affluence: we can afford
to keep a large population in school through high school.
The teen-age culture of younger adolescents is
characteristically lower class. The material traits of

teen-age culture include certain kinds of clothes, automobiles
and the paraphernalia of sports and recreation. Teen-agers
constitute an important market; advertisers are in
coalition with them if parents protest. The nonmaterial
cultural traits include a special language. There also is great
emphasis on fun and popularity. Popular songs reflect
the preoccupation of teen-agers with love in its various stages.

The other essays, some interesting, some superficial, are variations
of the same conception of culture as an ensemble of ideas, usages,
antisocial acts, etc. of particular groups, again showing the existing
confusion of the terms culture and subculture among American
professionals.[24]

The generally accepted ingredients of delinquent subculture are
truancy, profanity, illicit sex relations, theft and drunkenness.
Violence, especially vandalism, running away from home or school
and wandering are also mentioned. The condemning of some of
these acts has a moral and puritanical flavour which, although respectable, should not transform into delinquent or subcultural what
actually is not. In fact the condition of subcultural is not a
juvenile creation but a label assigned to the young by adult ways
of thinking, which in turn are not cultural at all. Apart from the
silliness of considering truancy as a delinquent act in the second
part of the twentieth century, by itself it has nothing to do with
culture or subculture, and incidentally quite a number of persons
who were persistent truants made remarkable cultural and scientific contributions to mankind in later life. Certainly profanity is
more distasteful in young people than in adults, but profanity and
restrained language are very insecure indexes of subculture or
culture. My personal observation is that at present juveniles are
becoming less inclined to profanity than in the past for two reasons:
one, because they are less interested in the beliefs or values indirectly
denied by profanity; and two, because, as part of the process of
breaking apart from many social and family patterns, they are less
inclined to imitate their parents. As for illicit sex relations, it
would be difficult to maintain that because they are more frequent
among juveniles they become subcultural, when among adults
they were never so regarded. The point here is whether the term
illicit should be applied. The question is not rhetorical, since if it
were, the present increase of illegitimate children would be a
subcultural pattern. Perhaps it was in the past, but not nowadays.
Curiously enough, in these and other cases, sociologists, and for
that matter criminologists, supporting subcultural theories, do not
realize that they are still operating with ideas and attitudes which

are not subcultural according to contemporary thinking. Theft has always existed among both adults and juveniles; the fact that they are at present more inclined to it than in the past does not make them more subcultural, nor does it make theft a subcultural pattern. Drunkenness, which in some societies is widespread, is certainly becoming more frequent among some juvenile groups. The question is why a misdemeanour committed by adults becomes a subcultural pattern among juveniles.

The conceptual confusion about culture, values and norms has recently led to elaboration of the theory of the subculture of violence. Close scrutiny shows it is little more than theoretical glorification of a particular kind of homicide. The fact that in certain groups violent response is frequent, and that this response is facilitated by the ready access to weapons, does not justify the thesis. In the United States, homicide among Negroes is more frequent than among whites. In 1967, Negroes made up 59 per cent of the arrests for homicide and 54 per cent of the victims. The question, however, is whether this type of violence has not been taken from the general violence which has always impregnated American life. It would be worth while to know when Negroes in the United States started to use guns and other weapons to kill each other in greater proportion than the white population and whether, before being brought as slaves to the United States, violence and homicide were as frequent among them. What has actually happened is that violence was passed to them partly as the result of poor living conditions and discrimination and partly through an imitation process. The conclusion is that violence is not a subcultural but a cultural pattern, the extent of which depends not upon the availability of weapons but of the value assigned to human life. If the value is low, as a rule the number of homicides is high. In 1967, 8,218 murders were committed in the United States, of which 63 per cent was by firearms. During the recent discussions about the licensing of guns, it was said that well over a million were owned in the United States without any kind of permit. The number reflects more the cheapness of life than the lack of restrictions to acquire arms. Actually, their easy acquisition is the logical consequence of the low value assigned to life. This also explains the constitutional right of Americans to keep and bear arms. Life is also cheap in Mexico where an attempt is now being made to reduce constitutionally the right to carry arms. Proportionally, the number of murders in Mexico is greater than in the United States. Life was cheap in Mexico long before the Spaniards arrived. According to Octavio Paz, Mexican pre-colonial history was always conditioned by violence and cruelty, particularly under the Aztecs. Life is also cheap in India, where the annual number of murders is higher than in the United States. Yet since the population is more than twice that of the United States, Indian culture is less violent than American culture. Life is also cheap in the Arab countries and Turkey, and therefore the annual number of murders is exceedingly high; it is not cheap in the Scandinavian countries, the United Kingdom or in Germany, hence the ratio of murders is far below that of the United States. Life is relatively cheap—but not as cheap as in the United States or Mexico—in France, Spain and Italy, hence their intermediate position as far as homicide is concerned. The different importance assigned to life reflects a general attitude of the country as a whole and not of the segmented subcultural parts of it.

Briefly, there is no culture without violence whether legitimate or not, neither is there any culture without crime. Culture embraces exalted as well as lowly expressions of creativeness and inventiveness in the moral, juridical, scientific and other fields. It also brings forward and tries to preserve knowledge, art, literature, etc. It contributes in many ways, including violence, to the organization, continuity and expansion of high types of life—as something different from high standards of living—for the greater enjoyment and sense of accomplishment of mankind. At present, more rapidly than in the past, culture—not to be confused with technological or scientific progress—in spite of serious setbacks, is becoming more uniform throughout the world. This would be an advantage if certain materialistic patterns were less prevalent. Although implying individual as well as collective participation, the content and aims of culture are more than this, inasmuch as they represent a process of objectivization of what is historically regarded as essential for the continuity of human life in a dignified and free way. In a figurative way, as Ortega y Gasset aptly put it, culture is the continuous natatory exercise of man in the bottomless sea of his existence, it is the plank on which the radical and constitutive insecurity of human existence may temporarily become firm and secure. In the last instance, culture is the only way through which man can be rescued, but salvation is always possible if the essential only is aimed at.[25]

If this is so, culture is something very different from what is propounded by empirical sociologists. Only a correct concept of culture allows, with some reservations, the use of the term subculture as the ensemble of cultural patterns of a cohesive community with some anthropological characteristics, when compared to those of another community culturally more advanced. In fact culture, norm and value, although in some respects interdependent, each possesses its own sphere of action. Thus there are many aspects of life, some of them important, which have nothing to do with culture, norm or value. The thesis that culture or subculture may be found in a candy store or in a particular gang is the unavoidable consequence of assigning a superficial meaning to fundamental concepts. It is true that in the past and still occasionally in some developing countries, culture is imparted at the market or in the public square. But those who impart it are not members of any gang, vandals or juveniles. Therefore the fact that man is born into culture does not mean that he exudes culture, or that everyone participates in the culture process, or that the latter reaches everyone. Public servants, employees, labourers and many others may engage for various reasons in some fraudulent practices; juveniles talk in a certain way, have their own loyalties, abscond, organize themselves, quarrel with other groups and destroy things, attack minors, elderly or derelict people and commit other criminal offences; prostitutes and pimps devise new methods to lure clients or satisfy them better, etc. These and many other forms of behaviour may or may not be part of daily life, but certainly they are neither cultural nor subcultural. The fact remains that crime, prostitution, homosexuality, vagrancy, etc. are patterns of society but not necessarily features of its culture. In fact, culture is independent of society not only because it may contradict some prevailing social patterns in a given society but also because sometimes it survives the society in which it was created. The Greek and Roman cultures are examples: they also show how the conditions above enumerated may sometimes be related to culture but not identified with it.

As far as crime is concerned norm means a mandate formulated in a negative way: not to do this or that. The mandate is objectivized by criminal law in a positive way by saying that whoever commits this or that is liable to a particular penal sanction. Exceptionally, the norm may be formulated in a positive way by asking that this or that be done, which in turn is negatively expressed by criminal law. This happens when the norm requires that everyone give assistance, which is transformed by criminal law by defining as criminal offences the failure to give assistance when no personal risk is involved. Incidentally, it is here that the main difference between criminal offence by commission and omission lies. This concept of norm as a general and fundamental mandate differs from that of norm in a sociological sense as an ensemble of usages, mores, etc. more or less general, always of a more flexible character, which do not imply a command but an acceptance which, if refused, may entail some social consequences but not those established by the legitimate order, in our case criminal law. In some, juridical and sociological norms may here and there coincide and some of the former may embody some social conduct norms but they are not identical or interchangeable.

Everything has a value, but this does not make values as a category identical to the value that things may have. As far as crime is concerned, value is the objectivization of a process of evaluation of something that, owing to its political, social or other significance, is juridically protected by criminal law. Such is the case with loyalty to the country, the security of the state, human life, etc. As values they are neither real nor ideal, and their existence does not depend upon individual or group preferences. They condense social needs for the continuity or survival of society; they are neither qualitative nor quantitative. Their selection is made through a process usually entrusted to political machinery which may be influenced by ideologies or interests of many sorts. Not all essential values are embodied in norms, and those embodied are not necessarily incorporated into criminal law. In fact, it may happen that for various reasons the legitimate order fails to embody what should be part of it. Values are not necessarily permanent, although some of the juridical values have virtually acquired this condition. Such is the case with life as value, but even here some changes have taken place, inasmuch as the legality of abortion in some countries has reduced its extent as far as criminal law is concerned.

There are other fundamental values, such as beauty, which are important enough to govern without compulsory acceptance certain areas of human activity. Finally, there is a lower concept of value often identified with goal and approval or used as an expression of the beliefs and demands of a particular group. By empirical sociologists these values are also loosely identified with cultural or social norms, conduct norms and the like. In no case, however, should this kind of value be identified with the categorical rank of fundamental values incorporated in the legitimate order of a given society. These are relatively few, cannot be quantitatively measured and must be effectively protected, inasmuch as no society can survive without having its own system of fundamental values. While the disregard of some values is tolerated and at the utmost entails some sort of social disapproval or exclusion, the disregard of fundamental values is not tolerated, conveys serious social disapproval and entails the imposition of a penal sanction. Normally fundamental values may be replaced through the existing political machinery or by force when they are imposed by an oppressive authority or regime.[26]

Social change and crime. With the theory of social change as a general explanation of crime we face what may be regarded as the most embracing criminological theory of our time. Its main ingredients are industrialization, urbanization, population growth, system transformation, social forces, migration, social mobility and modernization. The latter is sometimes so ambitiously conceived that it covers up the entire theory of social change.[27]

Lack of time and space prevents the consideration of all these ingredients; suffice it to say that in different forms and degrees industrialization and urbanization, whether planned or not, have been going on for centuries; that short of a total and brutal dictatorship they cannot be stopped or totally planned; and that experience shows that as contributing or explanatory factors of crime they are ambivalent in the sense that they may create new forms of crime, but reduce and eradicate others.

With respect to lack of 'traditional security', I confess that I have failed to understand what it means. History shows that the Parthian, Greek and Roman enjoyed far less security than the average man of our time. If we want to come nearer, the same can be said of the Victorian era, where individual status, freedom and work as well as the effectiveness of human and social rights were far less assured than they are at present with social welfare policies and services, insurance schemes, labour organization and greater guarantees. It is doubtful if agriculture and handicrafts, which are becoming the subject of what may be called romantic sociology, offered greater individual and collective security and provoked less personal frustration and crime. A perusal of living conditions in the eighteenth and nineteenth centuries will show that the security available was mostly based on the submissive acceptance of the existing political and social order. As for the guilds of the more remote past, they were based on privilege, servitude and rigid organization. In sum, security existed, but only in a fragmentary way, and it was far more widespread among the upper and middle classes than in the lower classes. As for the separation between occupation and family responsibilities so much stressed by contemporary sociology, this too existed in the past. Such was often the case among business, professional and army men, who were often away from home and country, and such was also the case of servants, labourers and employees. In all cases, distance and poor transportation and communications increased the gap between occupation and family roles and responsibilities. Political power and democracy have certainly changed élites, but new élites have been created, as inaccessible as those of the past. The question may be raised if the present social mobility, regarded as a tenet of contemporary society and by criminologists as a source of crime, will not be replaced in the near future by a more rigid social structure under the growing impact of scientific and professional knowledge in the moulding of social classes. If so, the possibility exists that the present socio-economic mobility may be replaced by a scientific-technological and functional structure of society, rigidly organized and run by scientific and technological élites. The 'old' occupational and professional social security of the past will return, although by quite a different road.

The term 'anomy', so often used by the theoreticians of social change, is so rapidly expanding that it is becoming more and more difficult to ascertain exactly what it means. Sometimes it is used as alienation with no explanation from what the alienation takes place; sometimes as lack of access to means with no further clarification; and sometimes it implies achievement, apparently individual, social or both, or success often interpreted first as financial success then as social and even political, but seldom as intellectual or professional success.

This terminological confusion serves the all-embracing meaning of social change. One may ask whether the term 'social evolution' would not be preferable. Social evolution means continuity and discontinuity of old patterns, and the introduction of new ones which may or may not conflict with them. As a process determined by many factors, it certainly implies changes, some cumulative and others disruptive or destructive; these changes, however, do not reach every corner of the social structure and system. Patterns or segments of them may be modified or replaced, but unless a revolution takes place others remain very much as they were or transform themselves very slowly, sometimes so much so that they are replaced by what was originally a new but has become in turn a traditional pattern. On the other hand, technological change, which should not be identified with social evolution or, for that matter with social change, may give quite a different impression. Behind the façade of technological change or modernization in material aspects of living, traditional attitudes are still alive and from a social and political point of view sometimes more important than what I call 'technological attitude'. My own experience in many developing countries is that traditional attitudes and technological change co-exist, and that the impact of the latter on firmly rooted attitudes is not very great. Whether or not these attitudes will eventually disappear is open to conjecture, but certainly not under the sole impact of technological change. The distinction is important for criminal policy purposes because, contrary to what is criminologically affirmed by the theory of social change, fundamentally crime has remained the same after many centuries of social change. Here again the confusion between new forms or modalities of a particular crime and perennial types of crime should be avoided.

Social evolution necessarily implies conflict, violence and change, each playing a beneficial as well as a disorganizing role according to the circumstances. On the other hand, the complexity of society prevents all its parts being affected by social evolution, and those reached by it are not affected in the same way and to the same degree.

Sometimes, reading the descriptions of social change, one gets the impression that either the description reflects the image of an imaginary society, or that social change is conceived as a sort of social earthquake. As a rule, images are either incomplete or distorted. As for social earthquakes, suffice it to say that most of what is rebuilt afterwards is only outwardly different from the past. In sum, while social evolution implies among other things change, the prevailing descriptions of social change do not imply evolution but social breakdown, conflict, disintegration and the like. The fact is that developing as well as developed countries are always changing in one way or another. The result is that the expression 'crime in a changing society' except for its dramatic appeal has little if any meaning, since, as stated, every society is always changing. Still, one may ask what is the kind of social change which more directly may affect crime in all its aspects. As far as crime and criminal policy are concerned, the eighteenth century was in many respects more significant than the present one. As Paul Hazard explained in his remarkable book *La Pensée Européenne au XVIIIe siècle* (Paris 1946), it was then that by bringing nature and reason to the fore Christianity was put on trial, and morals, politics, law, education and other fundamental aspects of the social structure and system were given new foundations. These were so solidly established that they are still with us, especially as far as crime and administration of criminal justice are concerned; the technological change of our time has only been able to modify techniques and instrumentalities.

Intellectually, as something providing a *raison d'être*, the eighteenth century provoked a change, the concepts and aims of which are still accepted by the technological and scientific social change of our time so much revered but unable to provide a better *raison d'être*.

Briefly, the individual is only one of the protagonists of social evolution or social change. Its various aspects are the subject matter of policies and programmes which have their own existence and impact, i.e. although individuals may within modest limits change or influence them, by themselves their impact goes far beyond the individual.

It follows that the primary role assigned in current theories of social change to self-identification, social mobility, success, achievement and the like play only a limited role. Hence crime cannot be explained as the result of a change so individualistically conceived.

The relationship between social change and crime has been

discussed at two United Nations Congresses: first, at the London Congress in 1960, where prevention of types of criminality resulting from social changes and accompanying development in less developed countries offered good grounds for profitable conclusions, and second, at the Stockholm Congress in 1965, where such broad items as social change and criminality and social forces and the prevention of criminality opened the door to all possible generalizations.[28] At the London Congress, the following points were made:

a The conclusion that social change be identified as cause or as general explanation of criminality is unwarranted. At most, it is associated with or related to crime, but in this case it should be noted that social change has even contributed to the decrease of certain forms of it;

b The disruptive action of social change is increased when it takes place in a disorganized way;

c Social change is subject to a certain degree of control and should be the subject of social planning;

d By itself migration is not conducive to criminality. The same applies to urbanization and industrialization;

e The unfavourable results of rural migration to urban areas may be reduced by providing these areas with appropriate social and economic advantages, and by preparing the migrants for the experience as well as the urban community to receive them;

f Programmes for the prevention of criminality should be closely coordinated, if possible by an agency organized for this purpose and constituted by persons highly qualified. It is recommended that this agency operates as an integral part of a coordinated scheme for national social and economic planning;

g In considering the question of criminality and social change, emphasis is generally laid upon the urban centre; this may be warranted, but it is advisable to assess the impact of social change on rural areas as well, since this may uncover the roots of crime which later manifests itself in the urban setting;

h The penal code must be in harmony with and reflect social change; and

i Research is required. Statistical techniques and procedures should be improved; case studies, field observations and pilot projects are justified.

Although these recommendations are open to some criticism, they reflect an appraisal of facts, experience and aims far more in accordance with conceptual precision, knowledge and ways and means than that currently found among the theoreticians and professional researchers of social change.

Psychology, mental health and crime. For a long time now psychologists, psychiatrists and psychoanalysts have tried to provide a theory of crime by devoting their efforts to the study of criminal behaviour.[29]

To De Greeff, what is essential is to know how the idea of crime generates in the offender. Many elements, especially the feeling of justice or of being unjustly treated, may originate the idea and with it an internal process in which the personality is directly involved. This process, called criminogenesis, develops a criminogenic attitude which does not necessarily lead to the commission of the offence unless other stages are passed through. Many honest persons remain honest although their criminogenic attitude is at least internally manifest. Thus there is a distinction and eventually a passing from criminogenic proneness to actual criminal behaviour, the latter manifesting itself in the commission of the offence. The evolution from criminogenic to criminal implies several stages such as the habituation to the idea of crime, consenting to it and finally its acceptance and putting into effect. Sometimes the passage from one stage to another is rapid and sometimes slow. The longer the period of resistance the greater the chances that the offence will not be committed. A number of persons contemplate the idea of crime—even toy with it—but eventually reject it. The type of personality, its degree of stability, moral and other circumstances may prompt, retard or prevent the rejection or acceptance of the idea of crime.

As an intersubjective psychological theory of crime, De Greeff's construction may well be correct in a number of cases. Particularly attractive is the role played by the idea of justice which I have found clearly expressed or latent in many cases, especially among offenders for vendetta or feud reasons. In a latent form, it exists in homicides in Mexico and historically in Mafia retaliations. On the other hand, it is doubtful if the process always takes place in the regular way described by De Greeff. Many crimes do not seem to follow this intersubjective process, and in some its stages are not clear. Such is the case of crimes in which gain, sexual desire or sheer impulsiveness play a definite role. De Greeff makes a distinction between effective and ineffective consent, between the resistance of the self and personality reactions, external and internal attitude, etc., which are hard to disprove and no less hard to accept. What is particularly important is his conclusion, with which I fully agree, that the human being can never be understood by the consideration of one single act. Single acts reflect only part of the personality; the main reason is that the internal attitude of the individual which leads to the act does not necessarily correspond to the act committed. For preventive purposes De Greeff's theory is as impracticable as the culture conflict theory, although for different reasons. It would be extremely difficult to determine outwardly the criminogenic condition of a person, and whether or not if the condition is established he would go ahead through the other stages of the intersubjective process. What are the characteristics that may reasonably be regarded as safe enough to differentiate a criminogenic from a non-criminogenic person? If, as De Greeff says, the offender seldom regards himself as a failure or as a frustrated person, it would seem that his treatment as well as his rehabilitation would be extremely difficult.

Di Tullio's bio-psychological theory regards crime as the outcome of a criminogenic process which in turn leads to a conflict between the individual and the social self. According to him, *la science de la personne humaine* ('the science of the human being') demonstrates that when man enjoys physical, mental and social health good enough to maintain a harmonious condition between the different elements of his personality he is normal, but he becomes abnormal when this harmony is disturbed or altered by morbid processes, disfunctions of many kinds, physio-psychic unbalanced conditions and conflicts between the individual and social self. In other words, as long as man is able to control his egoistical and aggressive impulses and rationalizes them in an acceptable social way and is able to adapt individual natural demands to those of social life and above all to adapt himself to the codified moral norms, he will not commit a criminal offence. Further, he adds that all this means that the genesis of criminal behaviour, political crimes excepted, is the result of a contradiction between the individual and social self, or between individual and social interests, or more specifically that every time the individual self prevails over the social self antisocial actions take place. He concludes that criminal phenomena are the result of immaturity or more specifically of biological inferiority.

Di Tullio's theory is formulated in such general terms that discussion and analysis are very difficult. From a terminological and systematic point of view it is open to serious criticism. Although he contends that biological and psychological elements are combined, and that his conception eliminates the contradiction between biological and sociological conceptions of crime, the fact is that he considers that biological inferiority is the cause of proneness to crime. Furthermore, sometimes it is difficult to determine whether the conflict between the individual and the social self is merely a contributing element or the result of all active elements. Yet Di Tullio's thesis has met with some acceptance, especially among endocrinologists and psychologists.

As might be expected, the multiplicity of factors involved in

117

the preservation of the bio-psychological equilibrium of Di Tullio's normal man calls for a prophylaxis of crime which, according to him, should fight all the 'causes' whatever their form, which may disturb the development of human personality. To this he adds a series of special prophylaxis. He maintains that in order to make effective the prevention of crime, modern police should dispose of all necessary ways and means to maintain a constant and rigorous supervision of all persons who, because of their activities, may be regarded as socially dangerous. Among them are vagrants and prostitutes; the police should be equipped to achieve their social rehabilitation.

To Eysenck the psycho-physiological trilogy, conscience, conditioning and crime may explain criminal behaviour. His main claims are that conscience is simply a conditioned reflex; that it is the person who fails to develop conditioned moral and social responses, due to his low conditionability and his extroversion, who tends to become the psychopath and the criminal; that the absence of conscience in criminal and psychopathic persons may be due to the fact that they form conditioned responses very poorly, if at all, and that even when these responses are formed they extinguish quickly; that neurotics and criminals are predominantly extroverted; that both types of persons tend to have a strong emotional component; and finally that, like the neurotic paradox, the criminal paradox may be solved by what he calls the law of temporal sequence, according to which '. . . if a given action is followed by two consequences, one of which is agreeable or positive, while the other is disagreeable or negative, then the probability of a person's undertaking this action will be proportional not only to the respective size of the positive and negative reactions, but also to their temporal sequence'.

Following traditional patterns among deterministic psychologists, Eysenck's statements are based on a series of laboratory experiments conducted on rats, puppies, etc., inconclusive findings among groups of offenders, mostly prisoners, and above all on his thesis of conscience as a conditioned reflex, a condition which is not demonstrated. To be fair, Eysenck's findings on the use of drugs may be useful in the treatment of offenders, provided human rights are observed. The same may be said about his conclusions on prompt punishment as a way to increase the deterrent effect of penal sanctions, a matter dealt with by many authors. On the other hand, his basic conclusions are scientifically and criminologically extremely vulnerable. To begin with, his reduction of conscience to 'simply a conditioned reflex and that it originates in the same way as do phobic and neurotic responses' may be useful in connection with caged animals, but it is very doubtful as far as free human beings are concerned. The question is not that something which may be found in animals is excluded from application to persons and *vice versa*, but simply that concerning crime the thesis is too simple to be acceptable. The 'crime' committed by a rat in doing what it should not have done is no foundation to draw a parallelism with crimes committed by human beings. For reasons which must be obvious to everyone, rodent and human criminality are not comparable. Although rats live with men their society is not governed by the same rules. Actually, laboratory conditions do not reflect the natural conditions of animals, and what they do in a cage is not necessarily what they would do if they were free. The claim that human behaviour is learned, or that without learning only the most disorganized reflex behaviour would be possible, is also untenable inasmuch as man invents, creates and acts with no previous learning. If criminality were, as Eysenck says, 'a continuous trait of the same kind as intelligence or height and weight' certainly the problem of crime would be easy to solve. Unfortunately, he compares things which, according to scientific methodology, are not comparable. Furthermore, it is not clear what he has in mind when he refers to crime; all crimes, only serious crimes, or only some of them and which. Experience shows that it would be difficult to explain all of them according to inherited proneness or reflex conditioning. Moreover, there are many other crimes which are not 'natural' but 'artificial', which nevertheless are particularly important if only for the survival and orderly functioning of society, such as those against the security of the State, international relations, national territorial integrity, national economic and public order. None of these has anything to do with Eysenck's conception of values of human contentment and happiness. Although some crimes may have certain connections with inherent or hereditary conditions, many of them have a purely conventional character which may be changed for purely political, social or other reasons with which, unless grossly distorted, human contentment or happiness have very little to do.

The thesis of criminal behaviour as equivalent to mental disease or as the consequence of feeble-mindedness has been abandoned. Occasionally, the correlation between mental illness and crime is raised by references to the mentally ill or disturbed being as high as 70 per cent in some prisons. The assertion is denied by those who point out percentages below one. As Guttmacher said some years ago, careful inquiries have demonstrated that in the United States the percentage of insane prisoners is far below that of abnormal people. A perusal of more recent data shows that Guttmacher's conclusion is still valid. My experience in many countries is that the varying percentages are mostly due first to the meaning given to the term 'mental illness', secondly to the concept of mental illness prevailing in forensic practice and accepted by judicial authorities, and finally to the scarcity of mental institutions in the country or region concerned.

The numerical comparison between persons mentally ill or disturbed and criminal offenders to see whether there is a correlation is difficult not only because of the incertitude of psychiatric concepts, but also because of the lack of chronological correspondence between mental and criminal statistics, and the difficulty of establishing equivalences between those admitted to hospital and hospital population on one side and those cautioned by the police, indicted and sentenced to prison on the other.

In Britain in 1964, the mental hospital population was 128,700; in the same year the number of persons found guilty was 1,327,649. If traffic offences dealt with summarily are excluded, the number is reduced to 470,897. In the same year, the national psychiatric admission rate per 100,000 population was 347; the rate of persons found guilty of indictable offences was 393 for men, 51 for women and 222 for both, that of persons cautioned by the police was 110, 25 and 68 respectively.

As regards age groups the difficulties increase, because as a rule criminal statistics give no breakdown after the group aged 21 and over. This is almost meaningless, since in all probability this group embraces no less than 50 per cent of the total population. The available data show that in 1960 the lowest number of admissions and resident population in psychiatric institutions was in the group under 24 years of age, while the number of persons under 21 years of age found guilty of indictable offences was almost equal to those of 21 and over found guilty. For males, those under 21 indicted were far more than those of 21 years of age and over. For females, it is the opposite; the age group 25–64 years is by far the largest for admissions and resident population. As for offenders, available data suggest that the largest number over the age of 21 is probably found in the 25–34 group. It should be noted that the number of persons over 64 in need of mental care is very high, while there are very few offenders. In fact the number of offenders over 50 decreases considerably.

While admittedly inheritance plays a marked role in the causation of or predisposition to mental disease, this is not so with crime; while women are far more vulnerable to mental disease than men, they are far less frequently criminal offenders, and this in spite of their growing participation in professional and occupational life; the mean age of admission to mental hospitals and prisons differs considerably, and finally the term recidive has quite a different meaning in mental and criminological matters.

The reasonable conclusion is that there is no general or direct correlation between mental illness and crime, either with respect to causation or predisposition. Therefore Penrose's claim, unfortunately still repeated, that there is an inverse relationship between the number of mental hospital beds occupied and the prison cells provided, has no more meaning than the older one that the greater the number of schools opened the greater the number of prisons closed. Furthermore, since in the mental health and prison fields the out-patient and non-institutional treatment have been gaining ground, the relationship between hospital beds and prison cells is far less impressive than it was thirty years ago.

In an extremely valuable study prepared for the United Nations, Gibbens put forward the following considerations: the comparative rate of relapse between mental illness and crime is not certain but is probably higher in mental illness; mental illness is a widespread and serious problem, crime, although equally widespread is a much less serious problem which is dealt with very effectively by criminal law; it is often overlooked that the relation between mental abnormality and crime is a dynamic and constantly changing one; the fact must be frankly faced that psychiatry has not yet evolved satisfactory objective measures of personality factors; there is no close relationship between the type and the severity of the offence and the abnormality of the offender; it is universally appreciated that a higher proportion of abnormality is found among offenders against the person, but this has tended to obscure the fact that in absolute numbers the smaller proportion of abnormal property-offenders far exceeds the number who commit the relatively uncommon sexual offences; though mental illness predisposes to social maladjustment, there is little to suggest that it predisposes to crime; crime itself and probably even recidivism, does not imply mental abnormality, nor do many well-marked eccentricities in other respects, and in England some one per cent of offenders are certified as insane or mentally defective after sentence. Experienced prison medical officers have agreed that there are 5 to 10 per cent showing other abnormalities who would best be regarded as medical cases, and there is a further and less definite number in whose treatment psychiatrists can help. '. . . some 80% of offenders can be regarded as within the broad range of the normal. . . . What is more relevant . . . is to recognize that the provision of services for up to 20% of offenders represents a vast undertaking.' More specifically, with respect to the young offender, West says that mental diseases like manic-depressive psychosis and schizophrenia are hardly worth mentioning in connection with young offenders since their incidence is so small.[30]

The contribution of psychiatry to criminal policy in general and criminal law and criminology in particular is plagued by the following difficulties:

a The uncertain character of psychiatry as a science. Admittedly, psychiatry is the medical branch of knowledge which deals with the study, diagnosis, treatment and to some extent prevention of mental diseases and disturbances. Certainly there are other more ambitious but more vague definitions, such as the science of human behaviour which, with due respect, makes no sense. If anything, it shows the disturbed condition of the study of mental disturbances. In her penetrating analysis of the term 'mental health', Lady Wootton concludes that either the condition does not exist or mental illness, at any rate in its milder forms, is no less elusive. The same applies to the more vague term 'mental disorder' so frequently used as a substitute for mental illness. The references to normality of behaviour, feeling of well-being, unity of personality, correct perception of reality, etc., show the inability of the discipline to determine what its own subject matter is:

b Closely related to the term mental health are normality and abnormality. Since human behaviour is not a purely psychological manifestation of an individual psychological mechanism, the terms normality and abnormality imply an evaluation process, the aim of which is approval or disapproval in accordance with a system of fundamental values. Therefore, individually considered, the concept of normality is not uniform and does not pervade the whole personality; on the contrary, it fluctuates and its different levels are determined by personal as well as external factors, so that every person is variably normal and may become variably abnormal. Only when the variations are extreme and disruptive and in marked contrast to what is generally accepted can it be maintained that the person is abnormal; and

c While at first, like any other discipline, psychiatry tried and to some extent succeeded in organizing the subject matter of its study by introducing a reasonable although not necessarily permanent classification of nosological entities, this scientific trend has given way to the thesis of a unitary concept of mental illness. According to K. Menninger, since there is an essential unity of sickness and health, the trend towards a unitary concept of mental illness is clearly apparent in psychiatric history and follows modern trends in other fields of science. With due respect, following the same criterion, good and bad, honest and dishonest, moral and immoral should also be unified. When some years ago I criticized Menninger's point of view, I said that if sickness and health constituted essentially a unity, why not go a step further and include in the unitary concept of mental health and sickness physical health and illness? I was told that it should be done, and that the unification would show the relationship between mental illness and crime on the one hand and mental illness and somatic disorder on the other. If the unification of health and illness is made, I fail to see how the relationships can be established with respect to mental illness. The fact is that science requires a certain amount of classification in order to understand a particular subject, and although the expression 'mental illness' as a unitary concept may be used in a certain context as a subject of psychiatry, it is as incongruous as to maintain that the subject of medicine is physical illness.

These and other conceptual and systematic shortcomings and the growing inflation of the more equivocal term 'mental disorder' explain the predicament of psychiatry as a science which, before reaching this condition, is already telling other disciplines how to solve some of their fundamental problems. It is not known to what extent this attitude, fortunately not adopted by all psychiatrists, is damaging psychiatric theories, especially in the forensic field. The truth is that psychiatry and, for that matter, psychology, are not natural sciences but something between these and the normative or cultural sciences.

Psychoanalysis and crime. Psychoanalysis has led to the creation of three different confessions and also, within a short period of time, to a proliferation of trends, the value of which is sometimes doubtful.[31]

The basic tenets of Freud were the empirical formulation of the id, ego and superego and the theory of instincts, both conceived in accordance with a strict deterministic point of view. Adler's theory is essentially teleological, in the sense that although man's actions may be related to causes, they are actually dictated by goals, and finally Jung's theory—the most versatile of the three—is basically built on the existence and impact of the collective unconscious which is far more important than the individual one. As Benjamin B. Wolman has aptly put it, Freud was deterministic, Adler purposivist and Jung eventually decided that man lives by aims as well as by causes.

None of these theories, either in their original or modified forms, provides a general explanation of human behaviour and hence of crime. Certainly Freud's theories of the id, ego and superego, of the different instincts, of neurosis and of guilt are extremely valuable in some respects and decisive in certain cases to explain a particular form of human behaviour, but as general explanations they have failed. The reason is not methodological in the sense that Freud's psychoanalysis is not based on experiment but that a biological approach does not by itself offer solid theoretical foundations. Karen Horney has criticized most of Freud's biological tenets, often rather radically; she discarded the libido as a sexually charged and omnipotent factor, the fixed development of personality according to instinctual and invariable forces, and the general validity of the Oedipus complex as the foundation of neurosis, which she explained in terms of 'basic anxiety' instead of mostly environmental caused by the lack of security that society is supposed to provide. More objective is her criticism of a universal psychology, inasmuch as the behaviour regarded as neurotic in one culture may be quite normal elsewhere. Her criticism that Freud's biological orientation was determined by the philosophical beliefs prevailing in the nineteenth century seems unfair, since those of the future were not available.

Freud's biological fixity of human nature was badly shaken by Ruth Benedict and Margaret Mead who, in different ways, stressed the role of culture in the shaping of personality. To Benedict, it is the total cultural situation that plays a definite role, while to Mead the primary importance belongs to the child-rearing cultural pattern. Here again the thesis of culture so much favoured by Americans emerges, although in a more reasonable way, inasmuch as the cultures here concerned are those of small primitive communities which, for many reasons, are nearer to the individual than American culture to Americans; the larger the country the smaller the effect of culture on individuals. Yet culture as a term of reference is elusive. As Roheim, quoted by J. A. C. Brown, said, all talk of culture (whether in the form of technology, environment, economic factors or child rearing) creating personality, boils down to the old problem: does the hen (culture) come from the egg (childhood situation) or the egg from the hen? 'Do people develop in a particular way because of what happened to them in their childhood (psycho-analytical viewpoint) or do the parents behave in a particular way to their children because "society" or "culture" makes them do just those things (sociological view)?' Kardiner's solution was to consider both answers correct which, according to Roheim, is tantamount to saying that half a hen lays an egg and from that egg we get the other half of the hen. The sociological approach was further expanded by Sullivan, mostly on the basis of his experience with psychotics. He postulated two basic purposes in human activities—satisfaction and security. The first refers to the satisfaction of hunger, thirst, etc., and the second to the pursuit of cultural activities. This reductionism, so typical among psycho-analysts and deterministic psychologists, is little more than an oversimplification of causes, processes and results. Sullivan's thesis is of two different areas of personality, one accessible through interpersonal relations and the other inaccessible and incommunicable; culture can only reach the accessible side of personality.

If true, this would considerably reduce the possibility of success in the rehabilitation of offenders as well as the validity of culture and subculture theories of crime.

Fromm is probably the most sociological representative, inasmuch as he maintains that man's nature, his passions and anxieties are a cultural product. As Wolman elegantly puts it, this is indeed a far-reaching statement. In fact, putting aside the wide meaning given to culture, he admits within limits the role of the instincts. On the other hand, he rightly rejects, probably not only because of his socialist leanings, Freud's thesis that man is biologically fully equipped to enter into social relations with others. More radical is his claim that the fundamental problem of psychology has nothing to do with the satisfaction or frustration of any instinct *per se*. If account is taken of Fromm's thesis that the freedom gained by Western man is rather a 'freedom from' than a 'freedom to', has he not been trying unsuccessfully to be free from instinct? His assertions that no therapy is possible unless the therapist takes a stand on moral issues, that man is not fundamentally antisocial, that a certain insecurity is normal, and that history is important in the understanding of psychological problems not necessarily viewed from an individualistic point of view, are of interest to the criminologist and policy-maker. They constitute a blend of experience and scientific reasoning and show that the need for individual security so much emphasized with respect to juvenile offenders who are, indeed, often referred to as insecure offenders, should not be inflated. His statement that the failure of man is due to his lack of interest in his real self because he is too much concerned with his self-interest may be used as a guiding principle in the treatment of offenders.

The attachment of Anna Freud and Melanie Klein to classical Freudian conceptions even if modified, are still too much centred on childhood disappointments, frustrations and acculturation conflicts to be of particular interest to criminology and criminal policy. To be sure, their thesis may explain some specific cases of criminal behaviour, but their marked biological instinctual determinism makes its acceptance difficult, even as a partial explanation of juvenile delinquency.

Adler's purposive or teleological conception of all psychic activities as the basic principle is attractive in the sense that it tries to avoid the constant riddle of causation. According to him every psychic phenomenon, if it is to give us any understanding of a person, can only be grasped and understood if regarded as preparation for some goal. The final goal or guiding principle is the advancement of self-esteem, the overcoming of inferiority feelings, the striving for superiority. This purposive pattern of life may manifest itself in many ways, either as an ideal or as seeking a more immediate attainment in life such as work, sex, art, etc. As a psychoanalytical school of thought, Adler's has little value. Yet its influence has been and still is considerable, so that some criminological considerations are justified. The thesis that every action should be understood in connection with the goal it aims at is not new and in principle it may be agreed that every action has a conscious or unconscious goal. The question is that with regard to criminal offences committed by negligence, which are punished by many criminal codes, the goal is not visible even if unconscious. One may argue that the goal is of the parallel action, i.e. of the action which took place instead of that expected. Yet since criminal law is primarily concerned with the criminal result, the conclusion is that no goal or purposiveness exists, and even less when no parallel action has taken place but the person concerned has simply been inactive. This leads to the case of offences committed when the action required by law is not performed, such as giving assistance without personal risk to somebody in serious danger. Here again no goal exists. The situation would be different and therefore purposiveness present if the demand for a particular action had been provoked by the person who is supposed to act. Such is the case of the mother who deliberately stops feeding the baby so that it dies. As Wolman has pointed out, Adler's purpositivistic approach creates innumerable difficulties, inasmuch as of the three possible theses—that the goal of life is immanent in each individual, is set by external forces or is chosen by the individual—he decided in favour of the last, which seems to be denied even by common-sense. Without subscribing to Wolman's thesis that the universe—an ample term—seems to function in a well-organized and ordered manner, it is obvious that the gap left by the rejection of causality cannot be filled by the teleological or purpositivistic approach. To me, determinism cannot be denied; the problem is whether or not with respect to human action a satisfactory general causal-deterministic explanation is possible, or whether we should content ourselves with a reasonable causal-deterministic explanation of every specific criminal offence, and whether this explanation is enough to pass judgment about the social significance of the individual action. While causal explanations of specific offences are possible, the judgment of individual actions lies far beyond that explanation; to explain and to justify are two different things.

Jung keeps the term 'libido' but divested of the Freudian sexual content. It means a life energy which underlies self-preservation as the preservation of species as well as the pursuance of cultural, social and other purposes. In other words, to Jung the libido is life itself, and as such, as Munroe has pointed out, similar to

Bergson's concept of the *élan vital*. Although deterministic, Jung's thesis is that more than the past the future counts, and that the importance of the latter is determined by which of the two possible directions man may take when relating himself to the world: one towards oneself, called introversion, or the other towards the outside world, called extroversion. This dichotomy, together with his theory of functions—sensation, intuition, feeling and thinking —constitute the basis of Jung's personality types, which criminologically have no greater importance than other typology. What may have far greater criminological significance is Jung's thesis of the collective unconscious to which belong the archetypal images— not to be regarded as expressions of a typology, but rather of certain human situations. The collective unconscious is more important than the personal unconscious and may be considered as the deposit of ancestral experience, the echo of prehistoric world events added by each century, which as an ensemble of traits and cultural patterns is transmitted by heredity. Hidden in it are the primordial images or archetypes. In sum, these ancestral patterns and representations constitute a force which, although lying in the deep layers of the mentality of the members of a particular race, act on the individual. According to Wolman, Jung, who apparently had a friendly attitude towards racist philosophies, found in German patients 'archetypes stemming from the pre-Christian era; the symbol of the ancient German god Wotan which expresses violence and cruelty was found in the unconscious of German people'. Certainly the existence and transmission of the collective unconscious and of its archetypes cannot be experimentally proved but, like other mental traits, are inherited. This does not mean that all and every individual inherits it, or that eventually the content of a collective unconscious cannot be replaced at least in part and more rapidly than the 'untold millions of years' mentioned by Jung. To what extent this collective unconscious is related to the *Volkgeist* with which the German *Völkerpsychologie* was so much concerned at the end of the past century and the beginning of the present is a matter for conjecture. The question is, can the collective unconscious of certain peoples explain why the number of crimes ideologically committed under cover of official position is so large and frequent and regarded as a matter of course? Two peoples come to mind: The German and the Russian. Nazi atrocities cannot be conceived as the sequel of an imposed ideology without the accompanying collective unconscious with particular archetypes. This may also explain why many Germans who were not Nazis performed their brutal duties to the entire satisfaction of the Party. As for the Russians, their historical past is full of oppression and persecution, the examples of which at present are too numerous to mention.

Certainly one may argue that other peoples can be cited, but I doubt if any of them is as typical as the two mentioned here.[32]

All this shows how difficult it is to talk in general terms of a psychoanalytical conception of crime. Unfortunately, it is done by referring mostly if not exclusively to Freudian orthodox conceptions which even Freud modified to some extent. His statements that murder and incest were the only two crimes which troubled primitive society, and that both originated out of the sense of guilt of the son and correspond to the two repressed wishes of the Oedipus complex, are still brought up as possible explanations of what cannot be explained by a totemic approach. Incest has never been universally prohibited; the ancient Egyptians apparently allowed it, not just among the royal family and nobility. Probably adultery, originally considered as an attack against property and dignity, was prohibited before incest. Be that as it may, the fact is that the origin and evolution of crimes require far more than psychoanalytical explanations. As for the feeling of guilt which leads a person to the commission of an offence in order to find relief in the punishment imposed, the possibility of such cases cannot be denied, and their detection is important for treatment purposes. Unfortunately, the thesis has been unduly expanded.

Rank's sexual symbolization of practically everything, Alexander and Staub's assertions, Reiwald's generalizations about the vindictive character of criminal law, Reik's thesis on the theory of guilt, the psychoanalytical symbolization of political crime, of robbery as an expression of rape, etc., have discredited rather than helped towards the possible use of psychoanalysis in criminal matters. The dogmatic point of departure of Alexander and Staub that 'The human being enters the world as a criminal, i.e. socially not adjusted', besides the regrettable confusion between crime and lack of adjustment, assumes as fact a human condition which is not confirmed by scientific knowledge and experience. It merely reflects Freud's pessimistic and biologically deterministic conception of human nature, which is neither angelic nor devilish. Curiously enough, Alexander and Staub's claim is used by Sheldon and Eleanor Glueck as the point of departure of chapter XX of their *Unraveling Juvenile Delinquency* (1950) in which the foundations of their prediction thesis are laid down. Reiwald criticizes the resistance of lawyers to psychology—a fact which cannot be denied but could be at least partly justified in view of psychology's vagaries. His statement that criminal law has developed counter-aggression is only a repetition of one of the best-known psychological platitudes. Instead of this legalized aggression, he suggests non-violence and self-government and ends by saying that the future of criminal law lies in its abrogation, that is, in the removal of all right to punish. Certainly this possibility cannot be excluded, but I doubt whether medico psychological systems would render better results.

As for the sense of guilt demanding punishment, it may well happen, as Melitta Schmideberg has said, that criminals do not have an over-strict conscience which may demand punishment, but that they are more likely to have an insufficiently developed conscience. The use of the father figure to explain political crimes, public disorders, strikes, etc. is often little more than psychoanalytical verbalization. In this respect Eysenck is right when he says in his *Uses and Abuses of Psychology* (1953), that psychoanalysts apply their putative principles to general social phenomena without proof of their applicability. He mentions that in a serious document intended for official consumption, it was stated that part of the unrest in the coalfields was due to the unconscious conflicts aroused in the miner by having to use his pick-axe (a phallic symbol) on the earth (a mother symbol). I still remember the case of a distinguished director of a prison administration who, in order to ensure a good prison policy, not only underwent psychoanalytical treatment himself but asked his immediate assistants to do the same. Those who were not good subjects psychoanalytically speaking, were replaced. Shortly afterwards the whole system collapsed and the director was replaced by a police official.

The foregoing does not mean that psychoanalysis has not made significant contributions to a better understanding of human nature and hence of criminals. Perhaps its contributions would have been greater if psychoanalysts were more accessible to dialogue and discussion, but as Lady Wootton has pointed out, and my own experience has confirmed, constructive controversy with them will be difficult as long as they deny the capacity of those who have not been analysed, or are more interested in identifying the unconscious motives which prevent their critics from accepting their doctrines. With respect to the prevention of crime, the contribution of psychoanalysis will be extremely limited as long as generalizations are the rule. For treatment purposes it may be significant in some specific cases. The length of the treatment, between one and two years with almost daily interviews, excludes its general application. Ferenczi and others tried to reduce it to a few months by imposing on the patient a series of conditions, one of which was abstention from sexual relations, which may easily be complied with by prisoners if homosexual practices and onanism were not so frequent among them. Another question is whether or not the tension created by the imposition of conditions will not be increased by prison living conditions.

Biological theories of crime. The connection between biological factors and crime has a past which goes much further back than criminology itself. As Bernaldo de Quirós pointed out in *Las Nuevas Teorías de la Criminalidad,* 1908, it has its origin in the old belief of the correspondence between body and soul, or more broadly, between matter and spirit. Accordingly the nature of man may be anticipated by his physical characteristics. This sort of anthropological predestination has its parallel, if not its precedent, in the no less ancient belief of a link between astrological signs and criminal behaviour which Gustav Radbruch examined years ago in his essay *Planetarische Kriminalantropologie* which, with six others, makes up his *Elegantiae Juris Criminalis,* 1938 and a valuable collection of notes and lectures on penal and criminological matters for students, hence the term *Elegantiae.* Since biology is the study of the enormous complexity of the phenomenon of life, in our case human life, manifesting itself in many forms and processes, biological theories of crime are extremely varied and in some respects the most promising as far as criminology is concerned.

The thesis of a series of criminal physical characteristics has a prominent pioneer in Esteban Pujasol who, in the seventeenth century, described among other typological traits those more frequent among murderers and other offenders.[33] Yet Lombroso was the creator of the anthropological school of thought which, as has been said more than once, was fatally wounded at the Congress of Rome in 1885, died at the Congress of Paris in 1889, and was buried at the Congress of Brussels in 1892. Anthropological traces may be found in di Tullio's conception of criminology and the Institute of Criminal Anthropology of Rebibbia, Rome, recently rebaptized Institute of Criminology; in Max G. Schlapp and Edward H. Smith with their glandular conception of *The New Criminology,* 1928; E. A. Hooton with his *Crime and the Man,* 1939, so much criticized but not always in the right way, and all others who raise the always evocative question of crime and destiny. Perhaps one of the most objective criticisms of the so-called criminal stigmas was made by J. Dallemagne in his *Théories de la Criminalité*, Vol. 1, and *Stigmates Biologiques et Sociologiques de la Criminalité* (no year). He seems to have guessed something of what is at present being put forward about the possible connection between genetics and crime. Among the numerous factors which, according to him, were waiting for criminological investigation, he mentioned the biological X as being more recalcitrant—by implication the most important—than the X factor of integral calculus. Yet, like many of his contemporaries, Dallemagne thought that the key to the crime problem lay in a better psycho-physiological study of the criminal. There are many others at present who forget that, after all, crime is a human creation and not the sequel of any biological or psycho-physiological individual purpose.

The biological conception of crime and hence of criminal typologies prevailed in Germany up to the 1940s—Nazi criminology is here ignored—which explains the frequent use of the term *Kriminalbiologie* sometimes, however, used to express a far broader content.[34] An extreme biological stand may be assigned to Gruhle and Wetzel with their *Verbrechentypen*, 1913–14, in thre volumes. Less stressed but still bio-typologically oriented was Adolf Lenz, *Grundriss der Kriminalbiologie,* 1927, who, with German thorough-ness, tried to establish a distinction between criminal biology, psychology and sociology. The first was supposed to deal with the offender as a physical individual, *als Körperliche Person,* as the subject matter of an *Individuelle Kriminalbiologie,* one of the main problems of which was the formulation of a theory of the personality and another the establishment of the relationship between per-sonality and criminal act. Criminal psychology was supposed to study the psychical, *seelische,* aspect of the personality, and criminal sociology the different criminogenic aspects of human relations. This tripartition, which still prevails in many countries and lingers in others, is at present of limited value. As for criminal typology, although Lenz's biological foundations are more diluted than those of other German authors, it is still biological enough to justify the title of his book. Following Kretschmer,—for many years the typo-logical emperor inside and outside Germany—he stated that his types should not be considered as classes, and that the elements of one may be found in others, yet he set up a series of biotypo-logical structures with their own tendencies and personalities which, although useful in some respects, do not justify the proposed criminal typology. Actually, Lenz went so far as to make a distinc-tion between endogen and exogen crime.

More scientifically and more reasonably systematic, Mezger considers criminal psychology as part of criminal biology, a term which is broadly understood by him; on the other hand he regards criminal sociology as something apart. What is significant is that his book was called *Kriminalpolitik auf Kriminologischer Grund-lage,* 1934—criminal policy upon criminological foundations—and not 'criminology' as it was in the Spanish translation. Mezger's aim was to establish a firm link between criminal law and criminology by a well-formulated criminal policy. After an analysis of the anthropological, psychopathological, biological and sociological conceptions of crime, he formulated a dynamic conception of crime as the basis of the dynamic combat against crime. According to him, the individual genotype plays a definite role in the develop-ment of psychic as well as physical features, in turn influenced or determined by the milieu. The interplay between *Anlage* and *Milieu* originates what he called latent criminality as something having a potential character, the importance of which is larger than is usually admitted. This potentiality is not the condition of a particular man but of all men. As an example of general human impurity, baseness and wickedness, in short criminality, Mezger quotes Goethe's well-known phrase: 'When I read in the newspapers about crimes I have the feeling that I would be capable of committing any of them.' Unfortunately, his scientific approach to the problem of crime was marred at the end by his uncalled for references to *Volk und Rasse*.[35]

To Exner the concept of Kriminalbiologie never meant a unilateral biological conception of crime but a biological as well as anthropological, psychological and sociological consideration of it.[36] Exner denied that owing to inherent characteristics a person will inevitably become a criminal offender, and that there are psychosomatic criminal characteristics. On the other hand, he maintained that in some individuals there is what may be regarded as a hereditary or genetic directional development towards crime which may or may not be counteracted or facilitated by environmental factors. In his thorough analysis of the etiology of crime he made a series of considerations which I would summarize as follows:

a There is no such thing as disposition to crime. On the other hand, owing to hereditary or genetic characteristics, a directional development, latent or manifest, towards what is regarded as crime may exist from the very beginning in some persons. This directional development implies a possibility, the degrees of which vary, and not a predisposition to crime and even less a crime-destiny connection;

b The possibility may be reduced or increased by the action of internal as well as external factors or circumstances. This means that by themselves neither the directional development nor the surrounding world but both acting upon each other in different ways and degrees may lead a person to crime;

c Many persons become criminal offenders without having in them any directional development towards crime; and

d In any case it should be kept in mind that crime is a juridical concept which varies according to time and place. Therefore, what biologically may be regarded as directionally probable in one case is not so in others. Such would be the case with homosexuality in Germany and Italy respectively.

In sum, to Exner biological characteristics or processes, hereditary, genetic or otherwise, may play a role, the significance of which as far as crime is concerned varies not only according to the biological elements involved but also to the action played on them by the surrounding world. Even if one speaks of proclivity to crime, this should be understood with some reservations because, owing to their inadequacy, words sometimes go beyond the meaning the mind wants to convey. Books like J. Lange's *Verbrechen als Schicksal,* 1929 are misleading in the sense that the title promises more than the contents offer. Between the thesis of a crime-destiny and a directional disposition to crime there is an enormous field in which individual as well as environmental factors act in many different ways. On the other hand, the biological criminological findings concerning monozigotic and dizigotic twins, although vulnerable, cannot be dismissed on merely sociological considerations.

To Ernst Seelig in *Lehrbuch der Kriminologie,* second edition, 1951 although the surrounding world plays a decisive role in setting off the offence, this does not mean that external factors answer the causal question, since the deep causes are in the individual 'preparedness' of the person concerned in his criminogenic disposition. This different operating action reflects the fundamental distinction made by Seelig between the 'provocation' and the 'dispositional' problem in the causation of crime.

I hesitate to regard Armand Mergen's *Die Kriminologie,* 1967 as biologically oriented. Nevertheless, in view of the role he assigns to organic elements as the foundation of what may eventually happen, his assertion that the individual constitution possesses the 'preparedness' to reject or accept criminogenic impulses, and finally his conclusion that there is a criminal receptiveness, I am inclined to include him here rather than elsewhere. This does not mean, as he says, that the *Anlage-Umwelt* problem is solved. To him, conflict situations are 'criminally charged' in the sense that there is scarcely a crime which directly or indirectly is not rooted in an internal or external conflict. To me, although in many respects valid, the assertion is too general, inasmuch as many crimes do not reflect conflicts of any sort. Only an excessive broadening of the term conflict, which incidentally is one of the characteristics of contemporary psychology and psychiatry and hence criminology, can explain the overall role assigned to it.

Recent biological discoveries, among them the genetic mechanics of human life, have opened new horizons in biology as well as in criminology, and with it the danger of a greater manipulation of man in general and of the offender in particular.

What seems certain is that some forms of genetic control as well as hormonal treatment will make possible the reduction of certain crimes while others, as a consequence of different patterns of life and new fundamental politico-social values in need of penal protection will emerge.

133

Recent genetic findings among male prisoners in Britain, the United States and other countries, again raise the question of a limited criminal constitution in certain individual cases. Unfortunately, this possibility has already brought back the idea of the *criminal nato* as a general proposition by the Press and other mass media.[37]

Briefly stated, it seems that in some male prisoners chromosomal surveys have revealed abnormal karyotypes XYY or XXY. The men are usually taller than average, and there are other more or less widespread physio-physical characteristics; most of them are mentally ill or disturbed or of below average intelligence and are the authors of crimes usually involving violence against persons or property. In the survey conducted in Britain by Bartlett, Hurley, Brand and Poole in Grendon prison for the psychiatric treatment of offenders, 204 male inmates were examined, of whom five had abnormal karyotypes. Estimates of the incidence of the XYY sex chromosome constitution have suggested a figure of one in 1,500 to one in 2,000. Surveys conducted in other countries also point to a high percentage of abnormal karyotypes, generally among unusually tall offenders frequently affected by mental disturbances, but the percentages as well as the types of offence are too varied to draw definite conclusions. In his informative paper, Dr, Escoffier-Lambiotte gives details about the relatively high percentages established by Jacobs and Casey in Britain, Telfer in Pennsylvania and several others.

These findings should not be regarded as proof of a criminal constitution even if further research shows higher percentages among certain offenders. Pending this, the following remarks are deemed necessary:

a The findings apply only to men with some prevailing physical as well as mental characteristics;

b Although violent offences are the most frequent, the range of those committed is too wide to establish a definitive correlation. Some of them, like homicide, arson and certain sexual offences are serious, while others like frauds, damages and indecency are far less serious; this is particularly the case with car offences and drunkenness. As for homosexuality, the trend is to abolish its criminal character. More than a general genetic relationship, this variety indicates that, although directional in character, genetic factors are modified or even overcome by other biological and surrounding world factors;

c Existing findings show that among non-offenders abnormal sex chromosomes may be present, that the disequilibrium caused by its presence among offenders is not constant, and that this genetic condition is not hereditary;

d Prison percentages are always high, since they reflect a particular segment of the general as well as the criminal population;

e The fact that the members of the control group have no criminal records refer only to known, but not to unknown offences, which may be of a serious nature;

f Assuming that all male children could be examined in order to detect the presence of the extra chromosome, the question arises as to the kind of preventive and treatment measures which could be taken without impinging too much on human rights in view of the wide range of offences which may be committed; that the presence of the extra chromosome does not necessarily mean that a criminal offence will be committed, since its effects may be modified by biological as well as surrounding world elements; and that this complex interplay makes it difficult to predict when and what offence will be committed; and

g Pending further research, the findings stress the markedly male character of crime.

As for the present hormonal treatment of prisoners, results achieved in Wormwood Scrubs show a marked decline in the abnormal sexual tendencies of prisoners. Unfortunately, detailed information about what is meant by sexual tendencies is not easily available; as far as homosexuality in Britain and other countries is concerned, as it is not a criminal offence when committed without publicity and by consenting adults, the treatment cannot be regarded as aiming at the rehabilitation of the prisoner but at the cure of a condition which a consenting adult regards as desirable; and so as to keep order in the penitentiaries, hormonal treatment may be applied to those prisoners who seriously disturb it owing to their sexual tendencies.

Biological theories of crime have never been well received by American criminologists. Tappan said that the little attention given —except in a negative and critical way—was in large part due to the 'strongly environmentalist orientation of the sociological criminologists and because of the preoccupation of the dynamic psychiatrists with their postulated processes of psychogenesis'. To this may be added the all-pervading impact of the American image in sociology and psychology. Sociologically, life was epitomized in a conception of success in which initiative, opportunity and chance played the main roles. The fact that recently Negroes and other minorities have been admitted to this conception of life and success is not the recognition of the constitutional principle that all men are created equal but something imposed by socio-political transformation.[38] As for the psychologists, Watson's *behaviorist manifesto* from which all present behavioral sciences originated rejects everything which is not overt behaviour. On the other hand,

135

if account is taken of the pitiful example of the sterilization and sexual psychopath laws of the United States and the bio-psychiatric foundations which were used to pass them, one may sympathize to some extent with the sociologists' reaction to the biological approach to the causes of crime.

Other theories. There are other theories which I shall call neutral abstracts which, instead of operating with a factor or series of factors as causal terms of reference, such as culture, social change and the like, offer a general working causal mechanism within which an ensemble of factors also neutrally expressed play a role. The most significant theories of this group are the differential association introduced by Sutherland in 1939 and maintained with some substantial modifications in the last edition of Sutherland-Cressey's *Principles of Criminology*, 1966, and Reckless's containment theory. Both are popular in the United States; have supporters and detractors and pursue the same fruitless task of offering the 'grand criminological theory'.

Briefly, the general differential association theory of criminal behaviour 'refers to the process by which a particular person comes to engage in criminal behaviour'. The process is one of learning criminal behaviour through interaction with other persons in a process of communication which occurs within intimate personal groups by verbal and gesture expressions. Movies and newspapers are regarded as relatively unimportant. The learning includes techniques, motives, drives, rationalizations and attitudes.

Cressey is right when he says that a great part of the criticism against the theory is not criticism at all, since it is directed at the deletion of the term systematic from the original formulation, at the fact that free will is not duly considered, that biological factors are not taken into account, that no explanation is given as to why persons have the associations they have, that social processes are dogmatically shaped, etc. To me the theory is incorrect because it is based on assumptions which are incorrect. The first is that the problem of criminology is to explain the criminality of behaviour, but not behaviour as such. This is the most common misunderstanding of contemporary criminology. With respect to criminal behaviour two explanations are possible: one, why a particular form of behaviour has been 'promoted' to or sometimes 'demoted' from the condition of criminal, and the other why the behaviour performing a criminal offence has taken place. The first explanation is outside criminal law and criminology. The second refers to something that by itself is not intrinsically criminal. Therefore, what has to be explained is a behaviour like any other. As such, its motivation, rationalizations and techniques cannot be circumscribed to any particular group, although some of them may be more important than others; and the term 'learning' cannot be used in the restricted way advocated by Sutherland-Cressey. From a socio-psychological point of view, it means the ability to respond and act adequately to a situation which may or may not have been previously encountered. If this is so it is obvious that, although important, verbal expressions and gestures are not the only ways of interaction and communication; that the specific direction of motives and drives are learned from definitions of the legal codes as favourable or unfavourable; and finally, that no theory can take account of all the factual information regarding crime causation and organize all multiple factors in relation to each other, or more modestly abstract from all of them certain common elements. Contrary to what is assumed by Sutherland-Cressey, no criminological theory can be applied in the same way that the engineer applies the scientific theories of the physicist.

Like many others, Sutherland-Cressey's theory of differential association is an attempt to build up in an abstract way a general theory of crime on the assumption that criminal behaviour is *per se* something specific, which it is not. The misunderstanding is aggravated by regarding criminology as a natural science or as a discipline to which the methods or abstractions of natural sciences may be applied. If there is anything that will always successfully defy such a transposition it is human behaviour, of which criminal behaviour is one of the many forms.

Reckless's containment theory is the abstract formulation of all possible factors that either from outside or inside may act as containment against crime.[39] By considering the problem from the anti-criminogenic angle rather than from the criminogenic, Reckless is far more original than many of his colleagues. The theory attempts to supply a general explanation of crime by embracing all possible outer and inner containment factors. Outer containment means the holding power of the family, village, society and State to keep the individual within the bounds of the accepted norms and expectations, including customs, rules and laws. Inner containment represents the ability of the individual to follow the expected norms and to direct himself accordingly. It ranges from strong to weak control of self. As components in order to resist deflection favourable self-image, self-concept and self-perception are mentioned. Briefly, favourable self-concepts are decisive in keeping a person within accepted limits. He adds: 'Another identifiable component of inner containment consists of retention of, adherence to, defence of values, norms, laws, codes, institutions and customs. The negative side of these self-factors includes alienation from, emancipation from, withdrawal of legitimacy from, and neutralization of formerly internalized ethics, morals, laws and values'. Containment does not apply to persons with marked characteristics, disturbances or faulty personality development. According to Reckless's guess, this eliminates 20 per cent of the population; from the remaining 80 per cent should also be excluded those whose way of life is influenced by prevailing forms of criminal activity.

Here again, one may ask whether this outer-inner containment theory is more than another version of the millenary tension-relief continuum mentioned or discussed by philosophers, theologians and writers and more recently by psychologists and psycho-analysts. Actually, it is only a sociological form of reductionism which, like any other, is unsatisfactory. Anyone acquainted with criminals knows that favourable self-image and self-concept are more the rule than the exception among them, that quite often there is an identification with criminal law and social values, and that the internalization of models does not prevent people, especially those of the medium and upper classes, from committing serious crimes. In sum, whatever the number of identifications *with*, adherences *to* and defences *of*, which may be thought up, the containment theory is only an abstract framework promoted to a general theory. One may further ask what should be the extent of these identifications, adherences, etc., to act as containment, and what are the specific aspects to which they should be referred. The reason is that often criminals are excellent fathers, husbands or sons, respectable pillars of society, hard workers, competent professionals, excellent civil servants, entrenched defenders of criminal law, religion and morals, and nevertheless they commit crimes. As for the exclusions, since not all persons with faulty personality development commit crimes, one wonders whether this is due to an outer-inner containment of their own—a thesis which cannot lightly be dismissed—or because no containment theory of any sort is needed. According to Reckless, every fairly normal person has his own containment mechanism, but beyond the general and neutral references to self-respect, self-concept, identifications, adherences, etc., nothing is said of how the containment actually works. What should be its extent in order to be successful? What are the essential aspects of values, norms, institutions, etc., which should be taken into account by the outer-inner containment and non-containment continuum? Does he think that the conclusion that 'The connection with deviant, wayward, delinquent and criminal behaviour takes place when the person is released or releases himself from the moral bind of his formerly internalized principles' is a clear answer, particularly when so many different types of social behaviour are lumped together? What is the meaning of moral bind? Does it mean that the types of self he mentions as well as all adherences, identifications, etc., should be morally impregnated?

Similar to Reckless's theory are all those which, with different labels, are based on reductionist conceptions of human behaviour as something moving in a continuum between two extreme conditions or subjects. Only an oversimplification of socio-bio-psychological processes, to which behaviourism was inevitably destined, can maintain that human behaviour moves only between two opposing extremes. Certainly this may explain crime and delinquency in some cases, but not in all. In this respect Matza's *Delinquency and Drift*, 1964, is a typical case of reductionism. According to him, the majority of offenders fit the model as drifters, i.e. as persons drifting between law and crime 'responding in turn to the demands of each, flirting now with one, now the other, but postponing commitment, evading decision', thus drifting between 'criminal and conventional action'. Close scrutiny will show that Matza's theory, like many others, is only a variation of the juvenile delinquency subculture theory which, in turn, is a variation of the culture conflict theory and crime. This theoretical cascading is typical of contemporary American criminology, where every professional of significance is supposed to produce a theory or a variation of one already created, or at least a variation of a variation. One may ask what is the preventive and treatment value of the drift thesis. Everyone drifts, but not necessarily between two extremes or borders. Life and crime and delinquency also mean immobility, i.e. the fact of having taken a definite attitude, either consciously or unconsciously. To say that delinquency subculture is 'delicately balanced' between convention and crime has no more meaning than to say that the subculture of prostitution is delicately balanced between chastity and marital sexual intercourse. Reckless is again right when he says Matza's thesis is a reformalization of the neutralization theory and a reinterpretation of the delinquent subculture theory which, in my opinion, has already had too much reinterpretation.

2 The socialist approach to the causes of crime

The socialist approach to a theory of crime is based on the following premises:
a Marxist-Leninist philosophy, broadly stated philosophical materialism, which regards economic evolution as the determining factor, not only of the total social structure, but above all of its 'ideological super-structure'. Consequently not only material living conditions are determined by the ways of production but social,

political and spiritual processes as well. It is therefore not consciousness that determines what man is, but his social self that determines his consciousness. It was in the light of these tenets that Marx, Engels and Lenin referred occasionally to the problem of crime. To them crime was the outcome of competitive economic conditions and exploitation which would eventually disappear in a socialist structure of society. Eventually, because none of them nurtured the illusion that the abolition of crime was an easy matter. Perhaps the best way to express it would be to recall here what Lenin said: that a high degree of impatience with the enemies of the working people whose crimes are directed against the foundations of the Soviet system, should be combined with a degree of patience towards those who do not oppose the Soviet system. The question as yet not clearly elucidated is whether or not the conventional criminal opposes the Soviet system. According to dialectical materialism the socialist transformation implies as a prerequisite with respect to crime, important changes in other fields such as education, health and culture. Another important assertion is that by its own structure and aims the conflict between individual and social interests does not arise in socialist society. This is not true and experience has proved it repeatedly, but as a theoretical premise it is still much in use among socialist writers. This conception has led to that of a man whose wants and desires would always be in harmony with those of socialist society and it is here that Soviet psychology, widely accepted in socialist countries, with the exception of Yugoslavia, is supposed to play an important role.

b Marx was never in favour of mechanistic psychological conceptions and hence his thesis that men are producers of their concepts and particularly that it is not consciousness that determines life but life that determines consciousness—see *German Ideology* in *A Handbook of Marxism*, 1935. The thesis is important and in all probability constitutes the most distinctive feature of socialist criminology in the sense that it opposes social development to natural processes and therefore man participates actively in making his own history, a principle which is found in contemporary criminological writings. This means that man is responsible and consequently criminal responsibility, although it may be denied in certain cases, cannot be abolished as is sometimes claimed in the West. Another important sequel of the theory is that the concept of personality as it is understood in the West is denied, or if used, it is within the context of dialectical materialism, i.e. as something reflecting a purposive character, as man as an actor within a socialist framework, hence again the need for a concept of responsibility. Incidentally, *lichnost*, which corresponds to personality in Russian, can also be interpreted as person of character. In sum, Soviet psychology tried from the beginning to build up a man who could fit into socialism. This explains the efforts of Bekhterev to adjust his theories to Marxism. As Wolman puts it, after a prolonged period of trial and error Soviet psychologists adjusted their theories to Pavlov's findings. The adjustment is now less rigid and references have already been made to some aspects of psychoanalysis, but essentially the psychological conception of man as a functional being remains unaltered and it is more than doubtful that Freud's trilogy of ego, id, and superego, owing to their idealist character, will ever be accepted by socialist psychology; and

c Like any other kind of research, criminological research is under close supervision and scrutiny by the party and various agencies. Scientific 'deviations' are not permitted. In this respect V. N. Kudriavtsev, in his double role of Assistant Director of the All-Union Institute for the Study of the Causes and Prevention of Crime and criminologist at present very much in vogue, clearly stated in *The Plenum of the CPSU Central Committee on Certain Questions Concerning the Scientific Organization of the Struggle Against Crime*, in *Sovetskoe gosudarstvo i pravo* (Soviet Law and Government, No. 9, 1963) that 'the so-called innovations of bourgeois law are, on the whole, reactionary and unscientific in nature'. He significantly concludes, 'The decision of the June Plenum of the CPSU Central Committee constitutes an extensive programme of work'. Broadly speaking it is within this programme that Soviet criminology is developing with the addenda of self-imposed restrictions in order to avoid being accused of 'deviationism'. The subjection to party lines was more forcibly stressed by M. D. Shargovodski in his paper *The Causes and Prevention of Crime*, reproduced in the *Soviet Review*, Vol. V, 3, 1964, by repeating all the slogans of dialectical materialism on crime. Since then the situation has improved with the realization, as yet not publicly admitted, that as in capitalist countries, crime is here to stay and will even increase in a number of aspects. Yet the ritual performance of repeating the slogan of the disappearance of crime in a socialist society is still continued by such prominent authors as Professor J. Lekschas of the German Democratic Republic and Professor S. Walczak of Poland.[40]

With respect to Russia, before the Revolution criminology was mostly patterned on the German biological school of thought. This was rejected as soon as the Revolution started and the dialectical basis for a future theoretical conception of crime was established. It is interesting to note that in Lenin's time references were occasionally made not only to crime but also to the personality of the offender. Lenin died in 1924 and interest in the problem of crime faded quickly. According to Professor M. Milutinović of Yugoslavia, between 1926 and 1930 all traces of criminological interest disappeared from the current literature. Thus under Stalin's rule criminological research was in disfavour and no progress was made or permitted. As A. B. Saharov says, the dogmatic subsumption of criminal behaviour in the corresponding legal definition was enough to establish criminal responsibility in accordance with the orthodox thesis that between the individual and socialist society no conflict was possible and that crime was a remnant of capitalist society and should be eradicated as quickly as possible. Stalin died in 1953 after having used this thesis to execute more than a million people and send at least twelve million to the so-called labour camps according to the objective research made by Robert Conquest in *The Great Terror*, 1968, which criminologically is of great significance. Briefly, criminology was for almost thirty-five years non-existent. *Mutatis mutandis* the same happened in the German Democratic Republic and still happens in Bulgaria and Czechoslovakia.

The most significant publications are Saharov's *The Personality of the Offender and the Causes of Crime*, 1961; A. A. Gersenzon's *Introduction to Soviet Criminology*, 1966; *Soviet Criminology*, 1966 by A. A. Gersenzon, I. I. Karpets and V. N. Kudriavtsev, and *Causality and Criminology*, 1968 by V. N. Kudriavtsev, and a series of papers and essays. In some of them there is no clear distinction between criminology and criminalistics, in others the ideological approach is too heavy to permit a scientific appraisal. The most sober socialist definition of criminology was found in G. M. Minkowski's contribution *Questions on Research and the Prevention of Juvenile Delinquency* to the Symposium on *Jugendkriminalität und ihre Bekämpfung in der sozialistische-Gesellschaft*, 1965 edited by the *Institut für Strafrecht* of the Humboldt University of Berlin. According to him, Soviet criminology is a complex science which evaluates the results obtained by the implementation of criminal law, criminal procedure, criminalistics, psychology, demography and other social sciences in conformity with Marxist-Leninist methodology. Putting aside the reference to Marxist-Leninist methodology which, in the USSR, has been left far behind by the scientific and methodological progress, the 'evaluative' character assigned to criminology satisfies far better than the 'causative', contemporary penal needs in socialist as well as non-socialist countries. For many years past analytical criminology has been stressed by the writer as the most important type of criminology.

In the German Democratic Republic the blending of originality, a systematic approach to theoretical problems and dialectical foundations is far more noticeable than in the USSR. The most significant publication is *Sozialistische Kriminologie*, 1966 by John Lekschas, Erich Buchholz and Richard Hartmann, of a markedly theoretical character aiming at a dialectical interpretation of the causation of crime, criminal responsibility and the personality of the offender. Lekschas tries to close the gap between criminal law and criminology on the assumption that there is no opposition between the legal and social world inasmuch as crime is a normative matter as well as part of *eine Realität des Lebens*, a remark with which I fully agree, although not for dialectical reasons. In any case, the constant preoccupation with greater interdependence between criminal law and criminology, especially in Yugoslavia, reflects a realistic approach often lacking in the West, where criminal law and criminology are still thought of as two parallel disciplines. On the other hand the new criminology cultivated in East Germany is more theoretical than empirical, while the opposite is the case in Yugoslavia and even in Poland. Among many other essays Richard Hartmann's 'Die Bürgerliche Kriminologie am Scheidewege', in *Wissenschaftliche Zeitschrift der Humboldt University zu Berlin*, XVII, 5, 1968 deserves mention because his criticism, almost exclusively addressed to American criminology, is scientifically and objectively made and he barely uses the traditional dialectical slogans. On the other hand, his assertion that '*das Sein der Menschen ist ihr wirklicher Lebenprozess*', taken from Marx and Engels, and that it constitutes the basis of methodology, seems to contradict his other assertion that crime reflects the historical, economic, political and ideological conditions and relations in society, of which man is part. It is here that the writer sees a gap that up to now has not been filled by the new socialist criminology.

In Poland as far as I know, although criminological research was conducted during Stalin's hegemony in the socialist world, criminology as a discipline with a theoretical content has not received great impetus. Up to now only the voluminous manual, *Kryminologia*, 1950, by Pawel Horoszowoski has been published. On the other hand, several reviews particularly *Archiwum Kryminologii* are devoted to criminology and related matters. The thesis that crime would eventually disappear in a socialist society was maintained by Professor Walczak at the 1960 United Nations Congress and stated in more detailed form in the report submitted by the Polish delegation on *Les transformations sociales et la lutte contre la criminalité*, according to which what actually determines the situation in which the individual acts is the ensemble of economic and social conditions. Yet a concession was made to psychological circumstances by saying that they should not be minimized. As a reference it reflects what, since then, might be regarded as an intermediate position in criminological matters between the dogmatic approach of the USSR and the more pragmatic approach of Yugoslavia. Far more to the point was the essay submitted to the Congress by Professor St. Plawski on *Prevention de la recidive*, in which it is admitted that although crime in general is declining, recidivism is increasing, a fact which may explain the continuous interest of the Ministry of Justice in penological research. Since then Poland has also devoted considerable research to juvenile delinquency and now participates in a comparative study with the cooperation of the *Centre de Formation et de Recherche de l'Education Surveillée*, at Vaucresson in France.

In Hungary the criminological consideration of crime reappears at the beginning of the sixties, although sporadically essays had been published before. As in other countries, crime is explained according to traditional dialectical tenets. In this respect the most significant attempt was made by Dr. A. Szabo in his *Theoretische Probleme der Methodologie der sozialistische Kriminologie und Technischen Fragen der Kriminallogischen Forschung* in the Humboldt University's compilation already mentioned. His main points are the following:

a Crime is the product of social conditions;
b The essential characteristics of personality are determined by these conditions; in the personality objective social conditions are reflected in subjective form; and
c Man is not only an actor playing his own life but also a *Gestalter*, i.e. he originates possibilities as well as events and facts.

Although all three tenets involve more elements than those here summarized, Szabo's theoretical construction does not differ essentially from that submitted by other socialist writers. On the other hand, Szabo specifically refers to man as the 'evolving cause' of his behaviour in general and crime in particular. In this respect he stresses the need for criminal responsibility more systematically than is done on purely dialectical generalities. As in Hartmann and others I detect a certain contradiction between the actor or *Gestalter's* role of man and the assertion that the whole of the social conditions are reflected as in a mirror in a subjective form in man's personality. This mirror process is more theoretical than real. Moreover, the role assigned to man as *Gestalter* means that he creates a sphere of action which in some respects has nothing to do with the mirror process.

The independence of Yugoslavia from Stalin's hegemony facilitated the development of criminological research both in quantity and quality and governmental or party supervision is less noticeable than in other socialist countries. The Institutes of Criminology of Ljubljana and Belgrade were created in 1954 and

1961 respectively. The most significant publications are Milan Milutinović's *Uvod u Kriminologiju*—Introduction to Criminology —1963 and *Kriminologija*, 1969; *Kriminologija*, 1966 by Katja Vodopivec, Milos Kobal, Ljubo Bavcon and Vinko Skalar, and although not strictly criminological, *Socialna Patologija*, 1969 by Kobal, Vodopivec, Lev Milcinski and Boris Uderman. There are also a series of essays and projects, some of them published or referred to in the excellent *Revija za Kriminalistiko in Kriminologijo*, edited by the Institute of Criminology of Ljubljana.

The attempts to build up a general theory of crime in Yugoslavia are far less marked than in the other socialist countries. The pragmatic approach within a socialist framework prevails particularly in what may be called the Ljubljana group, in which psychology, psychiatry and other disciplines play a role in criminological research. The difficulties of the latter, partly due to the inadequacy of materials and the problems arising from theoretical-logical interpretation, were mentioned as a general warning by Vodopivec in her contribution *Zu methodologischen Problemen der Erforschung der Ursachen der Jugendkriminalität* included in the publication of the Humboldt University already mentioned. In Belgrade, Milutinović seems to lean more towards a sociological interpretation of crime by referring to processes of social disintegration and alienation closely related to social conditions and structure which may lead to crime.

The attempts made in socialist countries, particularly in the German Democratic Republic, to build up a theory of crime are, like those of non-socialist countries, doomed to failure in spite of the elastic way in which Marxist-Leninist quotations are used. Actually, although it will not be discussed here, Marxist-Leninism and socialism are two different things and by itself socialism cannot explain the complex socio-political character of crime or of any other socio-political problem. This does not mean that it cannot contribute to a better world and to a better criminology, but certainly not to a better theoretical construction of crime. Another obvious difficulty is that, with some exceptions, e.g. Yugoslavia, theories and research are under supervision for ideological reasons. So much so that full statistical data are often not provided to professionals. Yet the importance given by socialist authors to the historical and socio-political condition of crime, frequently ignored in the West, to the role played by the individual as actor and creator, the closeness of the relationship between criminal law and criminology, the criminological role of criminal procedure, not from an individualistic but from a socio-political point of view, and the need for a concept of criminal responsibility which cannot be construed only psychologically, deserve close attention inasmuch as they represent a more

145

realistic approach to crime than that of the West. The main question is whether a socialist theory of crime is needed. As with non-socialist countries the answer is no, because any theory implies the search for and subsequent abstraction of a series of causes of crime, the futility of which is already obvious.

3 The theory of juvenile delinquency

The theory of juvenile delinquency as something apart from crime, with its own etiology, characteristics and preventive and treatment policies and programmes, is still widely accepted for reasons that belong to the past. The theory has found firm support in administrative proliferation and professionalization as well as in welfare policies and lingering sentimental attitudes *vis-à-vis* juveniles.[41]

1 Origin and evolution

The concept of delinquency as different from crime evolved around a child who no longer exists even in the less developed countries, where children have never been exploited as they were in the developed countries of the eighteenth and nineteenth centuries. 'Child' with respect to juvenile delinquency is a fictional concept which does not correspond to reality. It refers to any person under 17 or 18, sometimes up to 21 years of age, who has committed a delinquent act, which in some countries may run from smoking without permission to murder.

Juvenile delinquency as something to be treated apart from crime asserted itself in 1889 when the first juvenile court was established in Chicago. This important event was one of the achievements of a long humanitarian movement with strong political overtones in favour of the family, more educational facilities, better working and living conditions and greater individual freedom. At that time there was a correlation between the meaning of the term child, his role in the family and society and the need for protective measures in his favour.

The inhuman treatment meted out to children both as workers and as offenders, particularly in certain European countries under-

THE THEORY OF JUVENILE DELINQUENCY

going rapid economic transformation, was one of the main factors
which led to a new way of thinking, to the intensification of
philanthropic activities, and eventually to public opposition to the
use of children as a cheap labour force for industrialization. In
Britain the Factory Act of 1802 limited child labour to twelve
hours a day without night work. Their situation improved in 1833
with a new Act which declared that no child under eleven for the
first year. under twelve for the second year and under thirteen for
the third year was to be employed for more than forty-eight hours
a week or nine hours a day. In the seventeenth century, the practice
existed of sending children 'running wild in the streets, sleeping
under stalls at night and begging during the day' to the American
colonies. The practice decreased with the admission of the working
class to the franchise in 1867. More effective was the Reformatory
Schools Act of 1893, by which it was no longer obligatory to send
a juvenile to prison before committing him to detention in a
reformatory. According to Teeters and Reinemann, in Colonial
America there seems to have been no provision for delinquent
children except incarceration in county jails. The unsegregated
treatment of 'lads of tender years' was protested against in 1821
by the Philadelphia Society for Alleviating the Miseries of Public
Prisons, organized in 1787. The situation was the same in New
York.[42]

In sum, the protective movement in favour of children gained
force, and the concept of juvenile delinquency was introduced;
with it a special jurisdiction and care emerged, but the theory of
juvenile delinquency came later. The protective attitude *vis-à-vis*
children found its more general expression in the Geneva Declaration of the Rights of the Child in 1928, revised in 1948 and
reformulated in 1959 by Resolution 1386, XIV, of the General
Assembly of the United Nations.

While the thesis of juvenile delinquency was the creation of a
large humanitarian movement and of a social and political evolution, the theory of juvenile delinquency is mainly the elaborated
product of medico-psychological or sociological assertions, the
influence of which has been facilitated by the expanding of social
and welfare policies. Under their combined impact, the thesis that
juvenile people were a group apart, living in a world of their own,
evolved gradually and successfully. The reason given was their
immaturity and inability to understand the basic distinction between
right and wrong, and even less the meaning of the fundamental
values of society. Accordingly, permissiveness was the rule governing that world, and criminal acts were regarded as expressions of
rejection, disturbed personality, maladjustment, etc. The operation
was conducted by transforming individual cases into general but

diversified theories propounded by professionals; they were all sub-mitted as scientific explanations of child behaviour. The impact of these theories was facilitated by the general improvement of living conditions, industrialization, urbanization, etc., which, in a subtle way, originated what was later to become the enormous gap between children and parents and the growing inability of the latter to fulfil their duties and responsibilities. The evolution was inevit-able and regrets are useless. Yet the gap was accelerated and in some cases aggravated by unwarranted social and medico-psycho-logical assertions which independently or jointly tried to explain juvenile delinquency and crime. Nowadays teenagers as consumers are also regarded as a class apart. The whole theoretical process has culminated in the United States, and to some extent in Britain, with the thesis of a teenage culture the content of which, owing to the way in which the term 'culture' is used, is not only confusing, but leads to the most contradictory conclusions. To Marvin E. Wolfgang, in his essay, *The Culture of Youth* (1967)—the inside title is 'The Subculture of Youth'—this subculture implies a cluster of values or a social-value system which is both apart from and part of the central-value system. He adds: 'If a subculture, like a culture, is composed of values, conduct norms, social situations, role definitions and performances, sharing, transmission, and learn-ing of values, then there is sufficient reason to speak of the sub-culture of youth in American society.' The main characteristics of youth, and on this I agree with him, is that they are richer and more privileged and that for some time have constituted an increasingly significant portion of American purchasing power. 'The statistics of consumption of lipsticks and brassières, even by 12- and 13-year-olds, are well known, as are those of records, used cars, popular magazines and transistor radios.' Suggestive of this trend is the credit-card slogan quoted by him: 'Grow up now and pay later.' Wolfgang points out two important facts not often mentioned in the United States: the increasing feminization of the general culture—also stressed by Ronald Segal's *America's Reced-ing Future* (1968)—and the identity of youth with the protestation process to which European authors attach more importance than to the consumer aspect.[43]

2 The concept of delinquency

By itself *delinquere* always had a broad meaning. It referred to any wrongdoing, unlawful act, crime, or what in Roman law was regarded as *delictum,* or private offence. Later the meaning was expanded to apply to any neglect of duty, default or misdeed. As such, the criminal connotation of the term was, if not lost, considerably diluted. Yet in Latin countries 'delinquent' and 'delinquency' still refer to the criminal adult and criminality. The concept became almost boundless when, under the impact of juvenile delinquency theories, it embraced any form of unusual juvenile behaviour or condition. This broad meaning was expressed by the report of the Juvenile Delinquency Committee, Melbourne, Victoria (1956), according to which: 'Delinquency consists in behaviour resulting from a failure of the individual to adapt himself to the demands of the society in which he lives.' The concept adopted by the Bureau of Delinquency Statistics and Research, The Children's Aid Society, Bombay (1956), was similar: 'that delinquency must be used to denote a certain behaviour pattern, or a series of behaviour patterns, of a juvenile below a certain age, and the behaviour pattern must be such as is generally viewed as non-conformist by a given community at a given time and place within or without the framework of law'. Fortunately, this approach has been ignored in India by some of the Children's Acts, which more sensibly make a distinction between the actual criminal juvenile offender and the juvenile in need of assistance. At the First Arab States Seminar on the Prevention of Crime (United Nations Publications, Sales No. 1954. IV. 17), it was stated that 'No distinction should be made between juvenile delinquents, juvenile vagrants and minors whose circumstances and behaviour call for protective or re-educational measures'. Fortunately, the findings of the Second Arab Seminar (ST/TAO/SER. C/42) stated: 'Maladjustment and delinquency are not interchangeable terms. Consequently, delinquent juveniles should be considered as constituting sociologically a separate problem from that raised by juveniles who are in need of assistance or protection.' Further, it was said 'that by juvenile delinquent should be understood the commission of an act which if committed by an adult would be considered a crime'. By adopting this conclusion, the Seminar was one year in advance of the 1960 United Nations Congress. Unfortunately, the Arab countries are not always able to follow the recommendations made, because they lack the ways and means; such is the case in the Lebanon, Syria and the United Arab Republic. In the latter, a juvenile offender is a person between seven and fifteen years of age who has committed a felony or misdemeanour according to the criminal code. On the other hand, vagrant children are often sent to institutions for juvenile offenders.

In the United States a definition of juvenile delinquency is not always available; in at least eight jurisdictions, juvenile delinquency is not defined by statute but determined by the jurisdictional powers of the court. In most jurisdictions, the delinquency statutes include truancy, incorrigibility, being beyond control, growing up in idleness, using obscene or common language, wandering around railroad yards, smoking cigarettes or using tobacco in any form, begging, attempting to marry without consent, being given to sexual irregularities, being a vagrant, loitering, patronizing a public pool-room, wandering in streets at night, etc. These and other forms of juvenile behaviour constitute a particular illegality area which is not applicable to adults. One may ask whether the provisions enforcing this kind of juvenile delinquency are still applied in the United States. Surprisingly enough, they are, although those concerning smoking and begging are less invoked. On the other hand, truancy, incorrigibility, absenteeism, promiscuity—among girls—and being beyond control are specifically mentioned in United States' statistics, or sometimes discreetly hidden under more general items or the mysterious one of 'miscellaneous'. In the Juvenile Court Statistics, 1966 (Children's Bureau Statistical Series No. 90), the term 'delinquency' embraces criminal offences as well as truancy, disobedience, being incorrigible, etc. However, no specific figures are given of the total or specific amount of these offences, as was done in previous statistics. In those for 1965 they were 26·4 per cent of the grand total, and in both 1964 and 1963 they amounted to 26·8 per cent. According to the *Interim Report on Juvenile Delinquency* (U.S. Subcommittee of the Committee on the Judiciary, 84th Congress, 1955), it was estimated that a minimum of 200,000 boys and girls become runaways annually, of whom a little less than 22,000 were brought before the juvenile courts. The recommendation was made that running away should not be considered an act of delinquency, but, like many other recommendations, it was ignored. This unsatisfactory situation for 'children' and society has been stressed by the President's Commission Report on Juvenile Delinquency and Youth Crime (1967), by pointing out the anomaly of regarding as illegal for 'children' what is legal for adults. Yet none of the recommendations made refers to the convenience of restricting the meaning of juvenile delinquency to the commission of acts defined as crimes by criminal law. On the contrary, it is said that 'the need that led to the creation of that broad and general jurisdiction was and remains a real one'. In support of this unrealistic reasoning it is added: 'A firm, objective way is needed to apply the truancy laws, fortify flagging parents and encourage substitution of healthful for self-destructive pursuits before it is too late.' One wonders if the present picture of American society in general and parents and 'children' in particular will be well served with such an obsolete approach, and if the flagging parents, let alone the 'children', will be fortified with such persistence. As attempts to solve the problem, two recent juvenile court Acts are mentioned, one the Illinois Juvenile Court Act, 1966, and the other the New York Family Court Act, 1963. The former has introduced the category of 'minor otherwise in need of supervision', which applies to non-delinquent acts. On the other hand, 'delinquency' is defined as violation or attempted violation of a Federal or state law, municipal ordinance or court order. As for the New York Family Court Act, it calls a 'non-criminal misbehaver' a person in need of supervision, and 'juvenile delinquent' means any person over 7 and less than 16 years of age who does any act which, if done by an adult, would constitute a crime. Apparently the main purpose of both Acts was to avoid the stigma attached to the term 'delinquency', a stigma created by assigning welfare functions to juvenile courts.

In Canada 'juvenile delinquent' means

> any child who violates any provision of the criminal code
> or any Dominion or provincial statute or of any by-law
> or ordinance of any municipality or who is guilty of
> sexual immorality or any similar form of vice or who is
> liable by reason of any other act to be committed to
> an industrial school or juvenile reformatory under the
> provisions of any Dominion or provincial statute (Juvenile
> Delinquents Act, 1952, in *Juvenile Delinquency in
> Canada*, Department of Justice, Committee on Juvenile
> Delinquency, 1965).

No wonder juvenile delinquency is increasing rapidly every year, and that the Committee has very sensibly recommended that the term 'juvenile delinquent' be abandoned and those of 'child offender' and 'young offender' be substituted, with the proviso that they apply to the commission of a violation defined by the criminal code or other Dominion or provincial statutes, and that any other offence be known as a 'violation'.

In Britain the welfare approach persists, although with its own characteristics. One of them, corporal punishment, still advocated by many, came to an end with the Criminal Justice Act, 1948; another is that juvenile courts in Britain have always offered more individual guarantees than American courts; and, finally, that the mixture welfare-criminal Act is less broad than the American mixture and sometimes permits a clearer distinction between children in need of care and criminal juveniles. The juvenile court jurisdiction applies to any person between 10 and 17 years of age, exceptionally up to 21. While the Children and Young Persons Act, 1933, maintains a terminological distinction between 'child' and 'young person', under the general term 'juvenile offenders' in the Children and Young Persons Act, 1963, the term 'children' applies to any person under the age of 18 in need of care, protection and control.

The welfare approach was stressed by the White Paper, *The Child, the Family and the Young Offender* (1965), the main purpose of which was to spare 'children' under 16 years of age, many of whom are actually as criminal as adults, the stigma of criminality. According to the paper, 'children' under that age would be taken over by local family councils of social workers and other selected persons, which were supposed to deal with each case as far as possible in consultation with the parents. No specific reference was made to whether these also included the victim's parents; if so, a return to the 'compositio' system was possible. If no agreement was reached, which confirms the idea of 'compositio', the case was referred to the family court—fortunately, made up of magistrates. The welfare concept of 'juvenile', irrespective of the criminal offence committed, embraced not only criminal cases, but also any person in need of care, control or protection, or who failed to attend school. To these was added the fact of being unruly or depraved. As envisaged, the family councils did not offer any kind of guarantee with respect to human rights if agreement between the parties concerned was reached. This and other obvious shortcomings explain why the paper was discreetly withdrawn. Yet, perhaps more boldly than before, the welfare approach has again made its appearance with another White Paper, *Children in Trouble* (1968). To begin with, it maintains the wide concept of juvenile delinquency by making the usual references to immaturity, deviant, damaged and abnormal personality and social circumstances of every sort. No less apodictically, it says that social control of harmful behaviour by the young designated as 'children', which admittedly may cause considerable damage and suffering to the community, and social measures to help and protect the young, i.e. 'children', are not distinct and separate processes. Accordingly, the present definition of the 1963 Act of 'child in need of care, protection and control' will be amended by extending it to all minors from 10 to under 14 years of age who have committed a criminal offence. The decisions will be taken by professional workers acting by consent. The prosecution of offenders in this age-group will cease, and action to deal with them will be taken where possible on a voluntary basis. If a child commits an offence and his parents are not providing adequate care, protection and guidance, or the offence indicates that he is beyond parental control, it will be possible to take him before a juvenile court as being in need of care, protection and control. As for those aged from 14 to under 17, they will also be dealt with as far as possible on a voluntary basis, without recourse to the courts. Prosecution will be possible only if one or

153

more prescribed criteria are satisfied, and on the authority of a magistrate. The care, protection and control procedure will apply up to the seventeenth birthday.

The most significant features of this welfare approach are, first, that the present age-limit of criminal responsibility is virtually raised from 10 to 16, and, second, that the present protection of individual guarantees is considerably reduced. Deprivation of freedom for a period of up to three years for treatment purposes may be decided on by administrative authorities. The fact that the places of internment will be called 'community homes' does not change the anti-democratic character of such proceedings. Here again the futility of changing labels, so typical of social workers' schemes, is obvious. Thirdly, while criminal juvenile offenders with parents who have ways and means of providing care will escape the so-called stigma of being regarded as delinquents by being brought before the juvenile court, the less fortunate majority will not. The most tangible result of this system is the creation of a privileged minority which is undemocratic. And fourthly, that acting by consent is not progress, but a regression. It opens the door wide to a system of composition between families and authorities which was repudiated centuries ago, with the risk of personal and political pressures in order to get an agreement.

According to the Criminal Statistics for 1967, the proportion of criminal offences against the person committed by minors between 14 and 17 years of age is half those committed by the age-group 21 and under 30. For sexual offences, the difference between the two groups is minimal. As for rapes, the 23 persons found guilty by magistrates courts were aged 14 and under 17. Although this seems to indicate that there is less voluntary promiscuity in this age-group than in the others, it also shows that when boys of this age do not get what they ask for they use violence. This is partly confirmed by the great number of indecent assaults on females committed by this age-group, which ranks second among the nine age-groups of the whole classification of offenders. As for unlawful sexual intercourse with girls between 13 and 16, out of 72 persons indicated, 68 were aged 14 and under 17. With respect to entering with intent to commit a felony, the second most important age group is boys of 14 and under 17, only slightly surpassed by those of 17 and under 21. For robbery dealt with by all courts, boys under 17 years of age found guilty are the third among the age-groups. With respect to sacrilege dealt with by magistrates courts—the number of cases at the other courts is very small—out of 233 persons, 202 were under 17 years of age. For housebreaking and shopbreaking, offences committed by young persons under 17 are not always surpassed by those committed by persons 17 and under

21, who usually constitute the most numerous group of persons indicted for these offences. The figures concerning larceny are still more significant, especially in the case of larcenies from shops and stalls, in which girls frequently outnumber boys. In the same year (1967) out of 24,259 persons cautioned by the police for indictable offences, 18,230, or more than 75 per cent, were under 17 years of age. Of a total estimated in round figures at 40,500,000 persons over 10 years of age in England and Wales, more than 4,500,000 belong to the age-group 10 to 17, but their share of the offences committed is well over 10 per cent. If dark figures were established, this group would in all probability have more than any other age-group. If one out of every five boys aged 10 and under 17 has committed an offence, half of them against property, out of an estimated total of 2,360,000 in 1967, this would make 472,000 offenders. As for females, the ratio to males of those cautioned by the police is one to four and of those found guilty of indictable offences, one to six. Taking the ratio one to five as intermediate, and that the estimated total of females aged 10 and under 17 in 1967 was 2,247,000, this would make 449,400 female offenders within that age-group. Services could never be available for the treatment of all juvenile offenders. Fortunately, in most cases the offence is an incident which, without treatment of any sort, is not repeated. In other cases, the offences are tolerated and nothing is done, and the juvenile eventually becomes an habitual or persistent offender devoted to minor offences which actually do not harm society greatly, although certainly in many cases the victim may be seriously affected. This is frequently the case in offences against property when the victim belongs to the lower or poorer classes.

The above figures do not aim at any dramatic effect. They try to show that the problem of juvenile delinquency in the restricted sense of the term is complex, and too serious to be dealt with by a series of generalities, as was done in the White Paper here considered, which is certainly no better than its pre-decessor. Everybody has the right to express views and even to submit a project on any matter, but when the agency concerned is no less than the Home Office and the problem that of juvenile delinquency, it is not unreasonable to expect adequate presentation and analysis of facts instead of generalities in support of the project advocated.

In his letter to The Times of 1 October 1968, Hugh Klare, secretary of the Howard League for Penal Reform, stated that the value of the paper was to bring into a single machinery all children in trouble, without labelling as delinquent those who have been caught. My good friend Klare seems to have a broad and at the same time one-sided concept of 'trouble'. If this equivocal term has to be used, society is in no less trouble with juvenile delinquency than the delinquents themselves. One wonders whether it is not time that we stopped deluding ourselves and others by giving words a meaning which they do not possess. Juveniles in need of care and protection and juvenile criminal offenders are two different things and require separate machinery. The mistake has been that, whether it is called 'juvenile court', 'welfare board' or something else, a single machinery is dealing with two different problems. The fact that here and there they imperceptibly merge does not justify their amalgamation. Limits are seldom clear-cut enough to maintain an absolute separation, but this does not mean that everything has to be packed together. On the contrary, science and experience show that distinctions and classifications and different machineries are required. Otherwise a single machinery would be enough to tackle everything. As for the defence of the paper made by the presidents of a series of associations of children's officers, etc. (*The Times,* 12 October 1968), their main argument is the artificiality of the distinction between children in need and child criminal offenders, about which enough has already been said. Far more to the point and showing knowledge of reality and needs, the Chairmen of the Inner London Juvenile Court Panel point out the anti-democratic character of the proposals made, the dangers of political pressure, the lack of individual guarantees and the impossibility of implementing what is suggested. In sum, they hope that before it is considered by Parliament, the paper will be subject to more careful investigation.

The final result of this approach has been the *Children and Young Persons Act 1969* which, as pointed out in Parliament, is the grandchild and child of the White Papers of 1965 and 1968 respectively which have already been examined; the parentage is unfortunate. It is not my purpose to examine the Act in detail. As far as its application is concerned this has already been done by John Watson's *The Juvenile Court 1970 Onward,* 1970. Suffice it to say here that the Act persists in maintaining an image of home, child and young person which does not correspond to British reality, or in all probability, to that of the immediate future. This explains the traditional amalgamation of persons in need of care and actual criminal offenders, partly prompted by the broad meaning given to the term offence in England and elsewhere, and the individualistic approach of the Act centered around the child or the young person. The reference to public interest is a minor one and as Watson shows, it raises too many questions to be regarded as satisfactory. One of the main questions is, does the need for care and control justify the complicated machinery of the Act? There are others: What is to be understood by 'proper development' and 'moral danger'? Will only standard class or local levels prevail? Can the phrase 'beyond the control of his parent or guardian' still be used as one of the main foundations to justify the machinery and expenses involved? If applied within reasonable limits can it really be thought that all the ways and means required will be available in the immediate future or will the Act remain for many years to come a 'paper reality'? The difficulties of its application are aggravated by its length, casuistic content and obscurity. While the English language is clear and concise, legal language always manages to obscure the issue.

In Sweden the way in which cases are handled by the Welfare Board system does not permit a complete statistical picture of the extent of juvenile crime. Thorsten Sellin, in his interesting study, 'Into the Causes and Consequences of Juvenile Criminality', in *Industria* (1964), says that the progression of delinquency in Sweden is difficult to assess because of inadequate information. This is still the case. Available data show that in 1967 juveniles under 15 years of age committed 31,108 criminal code offences, out of a grand total of 437,042. In the case of serious criminal code offences, the age-group 15–20 accounts for 47 per cent of the total, so that the participation of this group in the total must be larger than that of any other group. Briefly, in Sweden as in any other country, the 'so-called children' commit as many serious offences as adults. I say 'so-called children' because the Swedish Welfare Act, 1961, applies to any person under 18 years of age in need of care or assistance or who has committed a criminal offence. In certain cases the Welfare Board jurisdiction applies to persons up to 21 years of age.

In France the 1958 Act abolished the principle of criminal responsibility and laid down the principle that the judge is supposed not to punish but to assist the minor. Before 1958 judicial intervention was only justified when the act had been previously defined by law as criminal. This legal approach was replaced by the notion of *état de danger* (dangerous condition) revealed by the commission of the criminal offence or by a series of personal, family and other environmental circumstances. This welfare approach, which allows the judge to intervene *ex officio*, implies the application of a series of measures, the ensemble of which constitutes what is called *éducation surveillée* (supervised education). Views on the increase or decrease of juvenile delinquency in France differ according to the figures considered and the meaning of 'juvenile delinquency' used. With respect to criminal offences in 1965, 43,767 juveniles aged 13 and under 18 were dealt with by the juvenile courts, i.e. by the *juges des enfants* or by the *tribunal pour enfants*, including the *Cour d'Assises des mineurs*. As a rule, nearly 70 per cent of the criminal offences committed were against property, about 10 per cent against the person, nearly 5 per cent sexual offences, and the rest were classified as miscellaneous. The number of minors under 13 years of age constituted nearly 9 per cent of the total, those aged 13 and under 16 about 34 per cent, and those aged 16 and under 18 nearly 57 per cent. Of the 43,767, 26 per cent were sentenced to a penal sanction, about 74 per cent subjected to special educational treatment and less than 1 per cent acquitted. As in many other countries, the 13–14 age group contributed heavily to theft and vandalism. The latest statistical data (March 1969) provided by the Prefecture of Police of Paris and *banlieu* show that 25 per cent of all criminal offences were committed by *minors* under 21 years of age.

In the Federal Republic of Germany, the 1953 Act defines a juvenile offender as any person aged 14 and under 18 who has committed an infraction which, in accordance with law, has been made punishable. As a category apart, juvenile persons in need of care or assistance but not criminal offenders are dealt with by tutelar judges whose functions are often performed by the ordinary juvenile court judges. Young adult offenders are those aged 18 and under 21. In 1967, a little over 11 per cent of all offences known to the police were committed by juveniles, the ratio between male and female being ten to one. In 1965, the last year for which judicial statistics are available, juvenile courts dealt with 41,846 offenders, of whom only 3,428 were females. In decreasing order, the five most important offences committed were larceny, serious larceny, sexual offences, bodily injury and embezzlement. There were 27 homicides and 60 attempted homicides.

In Japan the jurisdiction of the Family Court, 1949, applies to all juveniles between 14 and 20 years of age who have committed a criminal offence, as well as those whose tendencies indicate that they may commit one. The term 'criminal offence' is not only determined by the criminal code, but also by special laws and traffic laws. 'Pre-delinquents' are the juveniles who habitually disobey the proper control of the persons in charge, absent themselves from home without a proper reason, associate with persons who show a disposition to commit a criminal offence or are of immoral character or frequent undesirable places or habitually commit immoral acts, provided that, owing to their personal characteristics or environmental circumstances, there is a strong likelihood that they will become criminal offenders. In exceptional cases, minors over 16 years of age are dealt with by the ordinary criminal jurisdiction. Children under 14 years of age in need of care or assistance, whether or not they have committed a criminal offence, are dealt with by Child Guidance Centres. In certain cases they may be referred to the Family Court. Putting aside juvenile traffic offences, the number of which is rapidly increasing, criminal offences committed by juveniles are also increasing to such an extent that the reform of the Family Court by reducing the upper age-limit to 16 or 18 years of age is contemplated. The present law reflects in many respects an American influence, which, according to some distinguished authors, no longer corresponds to present Japanese reality. In 1967 the number of juveniles apprehended by the police for offences defined by the criminal code was well over 200,000 and that of adults well over 600,000. Nearly 69 per cent of the criminal offences were against property, about 24 per cent were violent crimes, i.e. bodily injury, physical assaults, intimidation and extortion, 4 per cent atrocious crimes (murder, robbery, arson and rape), 1·5 per cent immoral offences, and the remainder what are called 'intellectual crimes'.

In the socialist countries, the distinction between a juvenile offender and a juvenile in need of care and assistance is clearly made, but this does not deprive juvenile offenders of the care or assistance they need.[44] In the Democratic Republic of Germany the Juvenile Court Act of 1952, which in all probability will soon be replaced, considers as juvenile any person aged 14 and under 18. Children, who are all persons under 14, are not subject to criminal jurisdiction. The law provides a series of educational or rehabilitative measures as well as penalties which are carried out in special institutions for juveniles. The main purpose of the measures and sanctions is not the welfare of the minor, although this is not ignored, but to inculcate in him social consciousness, a sense of social responsibility, discipline and working habits. The administration of criminal justice, of which criminal juvenile justice is a part, requires the close co-operation of all agencies dealing with social guidance. This, according to Horst Luther, means that criminal procedure is of particular importance to achieve the above-mentioned aims. The impression is that what may be called a re-socialization process within the socialist framework begins as soon as the proceedings start, hence the importance assigned to the latter by Luther, Lekschas and others.

In the U.S.S.R. the provisions of the criminal and criminal procedure codes of the R.S.F.S.R. state that only minors who have attained the age of 16 years before the commission of a crime are subject to criminal responsibility. Persons from 14 to 16 years of age are subject to criminal responsibility if the crimes committed are homicide, intentional bodily injury causing an impairment of health, rape, assault with intent to rob, theft, robbery, malicious hooliganism, intentional destruction or damage to State or social property or the personal property of citizens with grave consequences, or the intentional commission of actions that can cause a train wreck. Persons under 18 years of age who have committed a crime not representing a great social danger, and who may be reformed without application of criminal punishment, may benefit from compulsory measures of an educational character which do not constitute a criminal punishment. The proceedings in cases of juvenile offenders are established by Chapter 32 of the criminal procedure code, and actually do not call for a special court, but for proceedings in which, at the discretion of the investigator or procurator or upon a petition of the defence counsel, a teacher may participate in the interrogation of the minor who has not attained 16 years of age. The participation is also possible in cases of minors over 16 who are considered to be mentally retarded. The teacher has the right to ask questions of the minor, to acquaint himself with the record of the interrogation and to make written remarks about its correctness and completeness. Parents and other legal representatives may be summoned to attend the proceedings, and they have the right to analyse the evidence, to submit evidence and raise questions. In order to strengthen the educational effect of the proceedings, the court must notify the school or other educational institution in which the minor has been studying, as well as social organizations at his place of study or work. If necessary, similar representatives of organizations at the place of work of the parents, guardian or tutor may also be summoned. The minor may be removed from the room when circumstances which may have a negative effect on him are examined. With some variations of no substantial character, this is the procedure followed in the other Soviet republics. The investigator, the procurator, as well as the court and the defence counsel, are supposed to obtain the necessary information about the personality of the offender and environmental circumstances in order to determine the responsibility as well as the measures, including penal sanctions, to be applied. In the essay previously mentioned Alexejew stresses the social-educational character assigned to the proceedings, actually mentioned by Article 400 of the R.S.F.S.R. criminal procedure code, as well as the necessity of creating a specific and comprehensive system of measures for offenders who are minors, inasmuch as he correctly states that the improvement of judicial proceedings only will never eliminate juvenile crime. As part of the policy for the prevention of juvenile delinquency, there exist in the U.S.S.R. Commissions for Minors' Affairs which, in co-operation with a series of agencies and organizations, try to help and improve minors and their surrounding conditions, also helping the parents if necessary. According to G. I. Kotscharow in *Jugend Kriminalität,* etc., already cited, their purpose is twofold; to prevent the causes of juvenile delinquency and to point out the responsibility of the persons who provoke these causes.

Unfortunately, reliable statistical data on juvenile deliquency and crime are not made available abroad, even at the gatherings of socialist countries. What is found is mostly fragmentary and more often than not propaganda references to progressive reduction percentages of juvenile delinquency, so regularly repeated that one wonders how there can be any left. The exception to this rule is Yugoslavia, where statistical data are published and made available to those interested in them.

As in other socialist countries, in Yugoslavia there is a clear distinction between juvenile offenders and juveniles who are non-offenders but who are in need of care or assistance because of personal or other conditions. This does not mean that juvenile offenders do not get the care they need. On the contrary, as I know, every effort is made to assist juvenile offenders, whether or not they are in institutions. A juvenile offender is a person aged 14 and under 18 who has committed a criminal offence. As far as treatment measures are concerned, some distinctions may be made between those aged 14 and under 16 and those aged 16 and under 18. The survey *Juvenile Delinquency in Yugoslavia* (SOA/SD/CS. 5–1967) commissioned by the United Nations, which covers the period 1947–62, shows that the number of minors sentenced for offences against property increased so rapidly that, while in 1947 they constituted 46 per cent of all offences committed by minors, in 1962 they constituted 80 per cent. As a compensation, the offences against the person showed a decline. As for male and female sentenced offenders, the ratio in 1962 was nine to one. The figures also show that the criminality of the 14- and 15-year-old groups was increasing, and that on the whole juvenile delinquency, if compared with the total number of persons sentenced, ranged between 2 and 3·8 per cent. According to the survey, it seems that juvenile delinquency is comparatively infrequent. Yet more recent figures show a considerable increase of juvenile delinquency in the last few years. While in 1962 the total number of juveniles sentenced was 2,898 (of whom 260 females), according to *Statistički Godišnjak SFRJ 1967, 1968 and 1969*, in 1965, 1966 and 1967 it was 4,682 (394); 5,572 (411) and 5,663 (383) respectively. Certainly the correlation between sentenced offenders and crime is not direct. Nevertheless, there is always a certain relationship which, unless contested by other findings, permits the tentative conclusion that the increase of juvenile delinquency is reflected in the increase of sentenced juvenile offenders. As a rule only a small number of minors were sentenced to imprisonment, the vast majority being submitted to educational, disciplinary and other measures. A measure frequently used is to return the offender to the parents with instructions to intensify their supervision.

In conclusion:

a Juvenile delinquency is a serious problem in most countries, particularly in well-developed countries, and is sometimes purposely minimized or resignedly accepted. On the other hand, the problem is considerably inflated by being treated as a child welfare problem, according to which there is no distinction so far as jurisdiction, prevention and treatment are concerned between juvenile criminal offenders and juveniles in need of care or assistance, inasmuch as both need one or the other. Political and sociological as well as scientific and welfare considerations are against such an amalgamation.

b The inflation is avoided in countries—particularly socialist countries—in which juvenile delinquency means only the commission of a criminal offence by a juvenile. Experience shows that by setting up different categories of behaviour instead of lumping them together, individuals receive better treatment and prevention is easier. With this in mind, the Secretariat of the United Nations raised the question of the convenience of the restricted definition in its study, *The Prevention of Juvenile Delinquency* (United Nations International Review of Criminal Policy, Nos. 7–8), submitted to the 1955 United Nations Congress. It was at the 1960 United Nations Congress that a recommendation was adopted according to which the problem of juvenile delinquency should not be unnecessarily inflated, and—without attempting to formulate a standard definition—the meaning of the term should be restricted as far as possible to violation of criminal law. Even for protection, specific offences which would penalize small irregularities or maladjusted behaviour of minors, but for which adults would not be prosecuted, should not be created. This concept already prevailed in socialist countries. On the other hand, the recommendation has not been followed by the United States and countries adopting the 'welfare' approach, among which the United Kingdom should be mentioned, in view of the attempts made to enlarge that approach.

c More often than not the welfare approach implies the infringement of human rights, not only of minors, but also of adults. Curiously enough, while the rights of the child are solemnly proclaimed in a well-known Declaration, these rights are ignored by welfare or informal proceedings dealing with juvenile offenders as persons in need of care. The question was raised at the Fifth International Congress on Social Defence (*Actes du Congrès*, 1958, published by the International Society of Social Defence) with particular reference to countries in which welfare boards were operating. That there was some foundation in the remarks made

162

was admitted years later by the reinforcement of the so-called legal element in the Swedish Child Welfare Act, 1961 (see particularly the Preface and Introduction to the official edition in English, published by the Ministry of Justice, 1965). As for juvenile courts, the case *in re* Gault decided by the Supreme Court of the United States on 15 May 1967 shows how unprotected human rights are when these courts are transformed into welfare agencies. Since then a series of decisions by state courts in the United States have tried to remedy a situation overlooked by social workers and medico-psychological professionals and judges as well.[45]

d The inflation caused by the welfare approach has led in some countries to the inflation of institutional and non-institutional services, which cost more than general services for the mentally and physically handicapped and the aged, and do not give as good results. Furthermore, in most of the developing countries this inflation has made it impossible to organize the services required. Since in many cases what is regarded as juvenile delinquency is a passing event which does not require treatment, one may ponder whether this lack of proportion between the inflated concept of juvenile delinquency and the scarcity of ways and means to deal with it is not a disguised blessing for the juvenile and society at large. What is certain is that the multiplication of services will never keep pace with an inflated concept of juvenile delinquency, however many millions are spent.

e Another serious shortcoming of the inflated conception of juvenile delinquency is that there is no way to determine its actual extent; the evaluation of the effectiveness of preventive and treatment programmes becomes an almost impossible task. The difficulties involved clearly emerged at the discussions on juvenile delinquency at the 1955 United Nations Congress. The inflation of the welfare conception of juvenile delinquency has brought into the field numerous governmental and non-governmental agencies and organizations dealing with the problem from every angle, making co-ordination and better use of the scarce financial resources extremely difficult, if not impossible. Yet, like many governmental agencies, each of them claims results the effectiveness of which cannot be evaluated because of the vague concept of delinquency. In the report by R. L. Morrison, *The Effectiveness of Current Programmes for the Prevention of Juvenile Delinquency in Certain European Countries, Council of Europe* (1963), eight of the thirteen countries approached stated that no evaluation had been or was being undertaken, and none of the remaining replies could be regarded as an evaluation of effectiveness. Close scrutiny of the answers confirms, as Morrison points out, that the remarks made by the Secretariat of the United Nations in 1961 in *Methods used for the Prevention of Juvenile Delinquency* (SOA 61/SD.4) and related notes and studies, remain unchallenged. They will so remain as long as juvenile delinquency, whether dealt with by juvenile courts or welfare boards, is understood so broadly and actual criminal offenders are regarded as 'children in trouble'. Both the above report and the United States President's Commission report on *Juvenile Delinquency and Youth Crime*, already cited, properly understood, are the most serious indictments of the prevailing juvenile delinquency policy in capitalist countries; this is also true of their followers, even if they claim to be socialist or anti-capitalist. There is no doubt either that this policy is partly the result of widespread professional deformation, as well as of vested professional interests which take advantage of a concept which offers them a boundless area for any kind of research project or grant.

f Neither the juvenile court nor the welfare board have prevented the term 'delinquency' from acquiring a social stigma which was deliberately avoided when the term was selected. What is a stigma? Should it be avoided? It means an imputation attaching to a person's reputation or a stain on one's good name. In a more definite sense, putting aside etymological or ancient meanings, the term was used by anthropological criminology to indicate physical or physiological criminal characteristics. At present it is often used with highly emotional-professional overtones by social workers and medico-psychological professionals to indicate something having irreversible effects on the personality of juveniles, which is fortunately not so in most cases. Experience and psychology show that in one way or another everybody at a certain moment in life carries a social stigma or has been for some reason stigmatized. Yet the effects are not, as a rule, deep or permanent. Of course, some juveniles are more sensitive than others, but quite a number of them are not affected at all, particularly those well known to be delinquents, but have not been brought to court. In fact, many of them boast of being offenders without impairment of any sort, when later by themselves they stop acting as such. In sum, the fact of being officially declared delinquent may or may not affect a condition of which the juvenile is fully aware, and which possibly does not bother him. Actually, many of them know that in contemporary society crime implies no social handicap to reaching a political or any other important position. All will depend on the type of crime, the surroundings in which one moves and the materialistic interpretation given to success. Therefore psychologists cannot pretend that stigmas produce a single general and irreversible effect. Delinquency has not only the meaning attached to it by them and by social workers, but also, more important, that assigned by individuals and society at large. Briefly, words acquire a meaning which sometimes has little to do with that originally assigned to them. It is unjust that the stigma attached to a particular kind of delinquent behaviour is extended to other types of juvenile behaviour or conditions which have nothing to do with criminal offences. The euphemism of calling all of them children in need of care or assistance does not deceive anyone—even the juveniles themselves, especially the offenders. Attitudes are very little changed by labels, because in many cases people know that the label is deceptive. Actually, stigmas cannot be avoided; what should be avoided is the emotional attitudes of many professionals to stigmas. In many respects, stigmas perform a social function of differentiation and classification that is more needed now than in the past, in view of the pseudo-scientific trend of putting together things which are essentially different. The most tangible result of this scientific and grammatical distortion is that to many people 'delinquent' means something worse than criminal. It has brought forward the image of a brutal, frightening and irresponsible person who is actually not met with as frequently as the stereotyped image suggests.

g It is often said that since juveniles constitute society's reserve capital, the welfare approach to juvenile delinquency is fully justified. This is, of course, true, but one of the liabilities involved in this particular reserve capital is juvenile crime. Following the same reasoning, it may be said that adults constitute the real working capital and deserve reasonable protection, particularly from the depredations of juvenile and young people. As for old people, who are increasingly preyed upon by criminal juvenile and young offenders, they also represent a capital deserving no less attention and protection than those given to juvenile offenders. Logically enough, the frequent use of the term 'capital' in connection with juvenile and young people in general and juvenile and young criminals in particular corresponds to the image of social problems in capitalistic societies. This image always implies a segmented approach to social problems, which is why juvenile crime, under the label of 'delinquency', has been construed and treated as a separate problem from that of crime. In this respect socialist countries seem to be more realistically *welfare*-minded, inasmuch as the term applies to society at large. Without advocating that socialism should be implanted in capitalist countries, one may ask whether the moment has not arrived to replace this segmented and unilateral approach to social problems by something more in accordance with contemporary socio-political needs.

3 The causes of juvenile delinquency

The variety of theories of the causes of juvenile delinquency correspond to the inflated concept of it. The most frequently mentioned are tension, frustration, rejection, deprivation of parental care, broken homes, lack of mental health or of educational and recreational facilities, slum living conditions, with the corollary of delinquency areas, maladjustment, immaturity, etc. Some of these directly or by implication are claimed to have irreversible effects, and as such to explain subsequent adult crime. Although many of them have a marked medico-psychological connotation, others are sociological in character, and some represent a mixture of both. By their combined action, they have built up the thesis that 'children' live in a world of their own, in which the fundamental distinction between right and wrong is regarded as irrelevant or in suspense until the minor reaches a particular age limit. The aim has been to consider all juveniles under a certain age as totally outside the fundamental system of values of a given legitimate order and therefore not responsible for what they do. Since it would not be possible to examine here all the causal theories, only a few are considered.

With respect to the broken home, the greatest difficulty is to define what it means and determine its effects, either by itself or combined with other causes. It may be defined as a home from which one or both parents are absent because of death, desertion, legal separation or divorce, employment as migrant workers elsewhere, sentenced to prison, or for any other reason unable to fulfil in continuous and due form what are generally regarded as parental duties and responsibilities. On the other hand, the physical presence of both parents does not ensure the appropriate fulfilment of these duties, particularly when both parents are at work. Against this it may be said that their daily absence does not deprive children of their attention or love; this is true in many cases but not in all. Furthermore, bad parents or parents estranged from each other may always be physically present and the home be as broken as if they were far away. Juvenile delinquency cases usually show a great percentage of broken homes among offenders. This may partly be explained by the fact that the structure and functioning of the home differs in each social class, and that as a rule the lower or underprivileged class is well represented in research projects. In my own inquiries I have seen homes which by generally accepted standards should be regarded as broken, and yet the family ties were working pretty well as far as the children were concerned, and also the parents—even if the husband kept his mistress at home, the mother was periodically running away, to come back more or less repentant, or both parents were drunkards. This agrees with other findings and is supported by D. J. West in his study, *The Young Offender* (1967), when he says that the closeness of the association between delinquency and broken homes is sometimes overestimated, and that the high figures found in the surveys he mentions, although quite striking, are difficult to interpret, first for lack of appropriate control groups and, secondly, because, among the inmates of institutions, there is an over-representation of boys from broken homes, which may occur as a consequence of the policy of the courts, who are more likely to commit a boy if he has no stable home. Gibbens, in *Psychiatric Studies of Borstal Lads* (1963), says that 'A home broken at birth or soon afterwards may be least traumatic, since adequate substitutes are more often to be found; the effects of parental discord or rejection can be more marked'.

The above and similar remarks by other authors raise the question of the present usefulness of the term 'home' and its conditions in contemporary criminology as a causal factor. Etymologically, 'home' has always had a meaning broader than that used by criminologists. On the other hand, as a restricted family structure it is more a Western creation than anything else. In fact, it has seldom existed as such in many developing countries and is fading in some developed countries. This is often ignored by the imitative criminology of developing countries, especially in Asian, African and Arab countries into which the image of the Western broken home has been transplanted. Actually, everywhere family and home are two different things, and in many developing countries, while the former still exists in robust form, the latter does not. In developed countries, under the impact of many factors home is becoming more and more an external structure which by itself cannot be used to explain a causal process, for the simple reason that the necessary elements to produce it do not exist or are less significant than they were in the past. This is partly due to socio-economic transformation, the increasing inability of parents to perform the traditional functions assigned to them and the no less increasing emancipation of juveniles from people in general and parents in particular. Divorce facilities, which I do not criticize, are breaking up more homes than before, but not necessarily family ties. To all this should be added the sometimes excessive interference of welfare policies in home matters, which, in different degrees, try to maintain a crumbling home structure. The question, then, is whether contemporary criminology should not look more into family ties—which do not necessarily mean a compact family—than into home structure and its functioning. I am fully aware that this raises many other questions, but in any case it seems that the causal role of home should be approached by criminologists in a different way, especially in developing countries in which family ties more than home fortunately play a paramount role.

The above leads to the question of the causal significance of the deprivation of maternal care in juvenile delinquency. The relationship has been much discussed, but it was Bowlby who brought it to the fore again when he found that of 44 thieves, 17 had suffered early or prolonged separation from their mothers during the first 5 years of their lives as against only 2 of the 44 controls.[46] Since then, the deprivation of maternal care as a causal factor of juvenile delinquency has been widely accepted. Fortunately, the World Health Organization decided to review the situation, and this was done in *Deprivation of Maternal Care: a Reassessment of its Effects* (1962). With respect to juvenile delinquency, the analyses of Lady Wootton and Andry are of particular significance. In her penetrating study, Lady Wootton concluded that in maintaining the hypothesis that the damaging effects of separation are irreversible, Bowlby has committed himself rather too far. She also refers to more conclusive evidence contrary to Bowlby's findings. In his study, Andry says that, according to his own findings, 'the hypothesis that there is a greater tendency for delinquents to have suffered from dual-parental separation than for non-delinquents proved negative'. In fact, his findings point to 'a greater degree of defective paternal leadership among delinquents than among non-delinquents'. Actually, the lack of parental care is only one aspect of the growing failure of the contemporary family to fulfil the role still assigned to it. We should be grateful that there are still some places where the family is not failing, but unfortunately as a primary institution it is losing ground. How are we going to remedy the increasing lack of parental care, family authority and sense of responsibility? Certainly not by opposing the democratic companionship family to the authoritarian family, as Ernest W. Burgess did in his essay, 'Mental Health in Modern Society', in *Mental Health and Mental Disorder* (1965). Like other images of the family, these were oversimplifications of one of the most complex institutions created by human nature. Suffice it to say here that, without rejecting companionship and participation, democracy requires authority, and sometimes more authority than is thought. In any case, as far as criminal delinquency is concerned, the success of the democratic companionship family in the United States is doubtful. In my opinion, the solution does not lie in the increase of family welfare services, but in organizing society on quite different socio-economic and political bases. As long as those existing at present are maintained, every speculation about the role of parental care is possible. One thing, however, is certain, that on these bases the 'rebuilding' of family care with welfare and medico-psychological programmes will be more theoretical than real.

Lack of maturity. Lack of maturity is still frequently advanced to explain the irresponsibility of minors for criminal acts. Since maturity is multiform and means 'having reached a stage of complete development', the term is ill-chosen, as no age is proof that the complete development has taken place in every respect. Yet under the impact of a series of assertions, mostly medico-psychological in character, the thesis has been accepted that before reaching a certain age minors are unable to distinguish right from wrong and even less to realize the meaning of some fundamental prohibitions of society. Therefore, owing to their incapacity, minors are supposed to live in a world of their own.

It was at the United Nations European Social Welfare Seminar in Paris in 1949 that this thesis received its professional consecration from social workers and others. After disposing of the existence of normal children and affirming that adjustment was the best way to prevent delinquency, it was decided that 'in European countries or at least in countries with Western civilization, it is desirable that full age for the purpose of penal law should not be fixed below the age of 18 years'. It was also stated that 'in general, adult ways of thought and behaviour cannot be considered with any certainty as being acquired before the age of 18'. Capping all this, it was said that the term 'juvenile delinquency' escapes purely legal definition, that, owing to maladjustment, there was no difference between delinquent and maladjusted children, and that the same treatment was suitable for all children (*European Welfare Seminar*, United Nations Publication, Sales No.1950.IV.9). This series of over-simplifications were regarded as 'progressive' and met with wide acceptance in many countries. Later, in order to become more 'progressive', the upper age limit of 21 was considered the most suitable, and was adopted by some countries in certain cases. Since this kind of progress is difficult to stop, later the limit of 25 was suggested, among others by the *Société Générale des Prisons et de Legislation Comparée* of France. A Belgian writer suggested 30 as the age of full maturity and hence of criminal responsibility.

The age-limit of 18 has been accepted by countries of such different backgrounds as Sweden, France, Colombia, Austria, Mexico, Jordan, Switzerland, Turkey and Thailand, in all of which I have discussed the reasons for adopting this limit. When some years ago I raised the question in Jordan, telling them that in Iraq, which has an almost identical background, the age was 15, the answer given was that 18 corresponded to the prevailing international trend. When, at the Fifth Social Defence Congress, Stockholm, in

169

1958, I criticized the fictional character of the age-maturity uniformity, the answer was that puberty ends everywhere at 18, that adulthood begins at 25, and that the reason for this is that the skeleton stops growing after this age (*Actes du Cinquième Congrès International de Défense Sociale* (1958). The incongruity of this uniform age-limit is maintained by the distinction of 16 and 18 upper age-limits in India for boys and girls respectively, if it is remembered that, whatever their age, females are far less prone to crime than males. During my mission in Iran some years ago, I pointed out the anomaly of 18 and 6 as the upper and lower age limits established by the Juvenile Court Act, 1959, for juvenile criminal offenders. The same applies to many of the Asian countries, such as Singapore, Malaysia, India and Pakistan, where the lower age limit is 7. This wide gap between limits barely disguises a compromise between the acceptance of 'progressive' trends and the maintenance of old criteria of discernment still deeply rooted, and not without reason, in these and other countries.

Certainly, general rules are convenient in some respects, but if anything was to be expected from a progressive criminology it was not uniform maturity criteria, which bio-psychologically are unfounded, but individualization. If this is proclaimed as fundamental in the treatment of offenders, the same should be done when determining individual responsibility. It is difficult to admit that the passing of the last minute makes a person all of a sudden responsible, especially considering that up to the last minute minors have been kept in a world of their own where fundamental social values are inapplicable. Individualization shows that many adults are less mature than many juveniles, and yet by virtue of the general rule they are regarded *prima facie* as responsible. Therefore, the assertion that minors must acquire first the 'ways of thought and behaviour' of adults makes little sense. What is required from them is to absorb the existence and meaning of certain fundamental prohibitions and behave accordingly.

Maladjustment. Ever since the 1920s, the stock-in-trade terms 'maladjustment' and 'juvenile delinquency' have been regarded as interchangeable, the implication being that minors are not responsible for crimes committed owing to their maladjusted condition. Sometimes the term 'unadjusted' is used; occasionally a distinction is made between them. Such was the case in India, where 'unadjusted' applied only to beggars, and 'maladjusted' to juvenile offenders in need of care (*Social Welfare in India,* New Delhi, 1955). More recently, I had the good fortune to see a paper in which the author maintained the thesis of 'pre-natal maladjusted children' to explain delinquency. At the present time, 'maladjustment' embraces the physically handicapped, the mentally subnormal, the retarded, the abandoned, the disturbed, the non-integrated, the deviated, the orphaned, the vagrant, the maladjusted, the nonconformist, the incorrigible or beyond control and the delinquent. Although stock-in-trade terms may be tolerated for brevity purposes, they are hardly justified as scientific concepts. The fact that the conditions enumerated may have something in common does not allow us to lump them together, inasmuch as they are markedly different. Certainly, to become orphaned is not the same as to be a juvenile criminal offender. The term 'non-integrated' is meaningless as long as a specific reference is not made to a particular integration requirement. The same applies to 'deviant' or 'nonconformist'. Leslie T. Wilkins, in *Social Deviance* (1964), has tried to evolve a general theory of deviance which, although theoretically attractive, has doubtful value for practical operation. Fortunately, Wilkins also says that social action should not be undertaken lightly on the basis of models. The tendency to express social phenomena in mathematical formulae—already attempted with crime in the nineteenth century—inevitably leads to high-level abstractions which have little to do with reality. Sociologically they are an oversimplification, and politically they are potentially dangerous, as they may be used to 'solve' social problems in a biased way under the cover of science.

The juvenile student who resists or attacks a policeman or damages a building because he wants a better kind of university or more respect for the autodetermination of peoples can hardly be regarded as deviated or maladjusted, and yet he is an offender. In fact the legitimate order, not to say society, maintains the distinction, inasmuch as it aims at the improvement of the educational system and proclaims the respect for autodetermination, but also defines what criminal offence is independently of the concepts of deviance, maladjustment, etc. The conclusion is that as a standard measure, deviance has little meaning. According to a standard measure of deviance, a juvenile opposing prevailing discriminatory attitudes and policies in his family and social group is deviant or non-integrated or maladjusted. The problem is to determine the criteria according to which the deviance or maladjustment must be established: family, group, state or federal standards.

Maladjustment has been defined as the failure to identify oneself with the aims and purposes of a particular group or society, or the inability to participate actively in conformity with these aims and purposes, or unsuccessful attempts to achieve individual goals or meet the expectations of a group or society.[47] Obviously, being a member of a group or society requires a certain amount of conformity, acceptance, participation and perhaps achievement, but between this limited adaptation and identification and expectations there is an enormous gap which cannot be regarded as maladjustment, especially when it is due to ideas or aims far superior to those of the group or even society at large.

The main questions involved are: What are the requirements that maladjustment implies and what is the extent within which one is adjusted and beyond which one is maladjusted? Does adjustment mean conformity, and if so what kind? Does it mean integration, and if so to what? What is the kind of acceptance that prevents maladjustment? These and many other questions show that maladjustment cannot explain delinquency, either in general or specific terms. Should the boy who gets money under false pretences be regarded as maladjusted when his father is involved in kick-backs and other shady dealings widely accepted by the group or society? In fact, the boy is well adjusted and yet, like his father, he is a criminal offender. The same applies to the promiscuous girl when promiscuity is accepted in her social *milieu*. Yet according to some statutes she is a delinquent and must be treated as such. Briefly, should we still maintain that because juveniles have been artificially relegated to a world of their own, they are automatically maladjusted when they follow patterns prevailing outside it? What is the purpose of declaring truancy, running away, wandering in the streets, etc., delinquent?

If an adjusted person is one who joins others in defining the objectives of his society and participates in the attempt to realize them, very few may be so regarded, because many are not interested in these objectives or may disagree with them. According to current definitions of maladjustment, those advocating stern discriminatory measures in a discriminatory society are well adjusted, while those opposing them are maladjusted. Here again the question is: Maladjusted to what? To the group or to mankind? Like deviance and nonconformity, maladjustment is too ambivalent a term to serve for general theories of delinquency and crime and behaviour in general. The mistake is to transform individual cases into general explanations.

Mental health and delinquency. Happy family conditions, adjustment, socialization, the ability to fulfil expectations, etc., are generally regarded as the greatest sources of mental health. Since juvenile delinquency is frequently related to broken homes, lack of parental care, maladjustment, etc., the inference is that mental disease or disturbances should be frequent among juvenile offenders. Here again the difficulties for discussion are partly due to what should be understood by mental health and partly to the vagueness of the term 'disturbance'. The World Health Organization has defined health as 'a state of complete physical, mental and social well-being and not merely the absence of disease or infirmity'. This definition seems to imply that, even if there is some lack of mental or physical health, there is still a healthy condition. If this is so, the term 'disturbance', so vaguely and generously used by psychiatrists, has no particular meaning unless the disturbance is specific and of some importance. To some extent the same applies to 'disorders', also widely used, although with a more serious connotation.

What is the relationship between the mental health of the family and that of its different members? In their interesting essay, 'The Child and the Family', in *Aspects of Family Mental Health in Europe* (W.H.O., 1965), D. Buckle and S. Lebovici point out that the mental health of the family is not at all the sum of the health of its individual members, although the mental ill-health of one of them will often affect the whole. On the other hand, the disturbing effects of the mental ill-health of one member may be compensated by the interaction of other family aspects. This, however, is not easily determined. As the authors say, the examination of the family requires the examination of each member, of each dyadic relationship and of each triad, and so on. Such an exhaustive procedure, although ideal, would rarely be feasible. In my opinion, these remarks show how superficial are some inquiries and conclusions about the relationship between the lack of mental health and delinquency. This seems to be the case with a survey currently being carried out in Puerto Rico, the tentative conclusions of which are that the lack of mental health is one of the most important contributing factors of juvenile delinquency and school absenteeism. The findings of Gibbens, West and others show that cases of mental diseases among juvenile offenders are seldom found, a conclusion which corresponds to the small ratio of mental illness among juvenile people in the general population. This lack of correspondence is significant, inasmuch as in many countries people under 21 years of age constitute between 40 and 50 per cent, sometimes more, of the total population, and their contribution to crime, which in some cases far exceeds their proportion, cannot be explained by lack of mental health in the family or in the minors themselves.

More controversial is the relationship between mental deficiency and delinquency and crime. Thirty years ago Cyril Burt (*The Young Delinquent* (1938)) found that among delinquents the proportion of mental deficiency was five times greater than in the school population at large. This and similar percentages should be appraised in the light of D. H. Stott's findings in his remarkable inquiry, *Delinquency and Human Nature* (1950), where he made the important distinction between impairment of mental effectiveness owing to emotional disturbance as an interfering element and the relative frequency among juveniles of simulated mental deficiency by 'playing daft'. Whether or not the latter may be related to other causes than mental dullness is another matter. More recently, referring to old inquiries, the report, *On the State of the Public Health for 1967* (Ministry of Health, H.M.S.O., 1968) shows the difficulties of ascertaining in the general population the proportion of mental subnormality, and how it may be more easily detected in rural than in urban areas, a circumstance which as far as I know has not received much attention in the studies on the prevalence of subnormality among juvenile offenders.

Are these and the other causes of juvenile crime different from the causes of adult crime? Although here and there the causes in the case of juveniles are labelled differently, there is no essential difference between both types of causation. The opinion here expressed contradicts that maintained by the majority of professionals to whom, since juvenile delinquency originates in a juvenile world, its causation must necessarily be different. West seems to support this view when he says:

> The offences committed by young people differ in kind and
> in motive from the typical crimes of adults. Infants
> may steal things not knowing that it is forbidden, older
> children may do so because they have not learned the
> self-restraint which normally develops with increasing years
> and adolescents may break the law to show their daring
> or to annoy their parents. Adults are more often credited
> with taking calculated risks for the sake of dishonest gains.

Statistical and non-statistical data do not support the generality of this. The truth is that a comparison of criminal offences committed by juveniles and adults shows only quantitative and not qualitative differences. In some cases juveniles commit comparatively more crimes against property than adults. With respect to bodily injury and other assaults, those committed by juveniles are proportionately more numerous than those committed by certain adult age-groups. The same occurs with rape and indecent assaults; examples of this have already been given. As for motives as identified in West's remarks with cause and factor, the artificial creation of a separate world has not made an essentially different type of motivation. Experience shows that the commission of offences for lack of restraint, if this may be regarded as a motive, is also present in a number of offences committed by adults. In fact, a number of assaults are due to lack of self-restraint. As for the

174

wish to annoy parents, may I say first that minors annoy other persons as well, and that adults also commit offences because they want to annoy somebody else. As for the calculated risk, which by itself is neither a motive, cause nor factor of crime, in many criminal cases juveniles or young people are more careful in the commission of criminal offences than adults.

4 The machinery

The thesis of delinquency as something apart from adult crime required machinery. This was promptly provided, although some-times only on paper, by the organization of a special jurisdiction in the form of juvenile courts, in some cases family courts and, in the Scandinavian countries, welfare boards. It is not the purpose of this section to discuss the comparative advantages of these systems; this has already been done in many international gatherings, with no tangible results. As long as juvenile delinquency is understood in the broad sense, neither system is adequate to deal with juvenile crime, as they reflect a welfare approach which does not satisfy the penal needs of contemporary society. Of course, machinery is not expected to solve by itself the problem of crime, but logically machinery should be replaced when it cannot achieve the purpose for which it was created.

If the United States, with all the ways and means at its disposal, has fallen short of the target, what is the situation in other countries? In Britain juvenile courts cannot cope with the problem of juvenile crime for the simple reason that they reflect a conception of juvenile delinquency which belongs to the past. In France common jurisdiction judges frequently act as juvenile judges, and the same occurs in Italy, Spain and other countries, where the necessary number of juvenile courts have not as yet been created.

In India up to 1967 only a few of the 17 states or union territories had promulgated laws on the pattern of the Central Children's Act, 1960. Some states, such as the Punjab and Madhya Pradesh, promulgated the laws, but up to now they have not been enforced. In others, such as Nagaland and Orissa, there is no special law at all. The Indian welfare conception of delinquency has been criticized in India by P. Varma (*Crime, Criminal and Convict*, 1963), who raises the question whether delinquency and crime are not aspects of the same phenomenon. He concludes that as two different concepts they are sociologically artificial. In Japan there are family courts everywhere, and yet their effective-ness against the growing flow of juvenile crime is now being questioned. In Laos and Indonesia there are no juvenile courts. In the Philippines there is only one since the law was passed in

1951. In Thailand the Juvenile Court Act, 1951, set up the system; up to now there are three, one in Bangkok, one in Sougkhila and the other in Nokara Rajsima; the Department concerned, however, had no information about the last two when I requested it. On the other hand, the Juvenile Court of Bangkok is doing a commendable job. Like many other countries in similar conditions, elsewhere juvenile offenders are dealt with by the ordinary courts, although occasionally some facilities for juveniles are made available. The situation is better in Ceylon and still better in Singapore, but far less satisfactory in Pakistan, where, according to A. A. G. Peters's *Comparative Survey of Juvenile Delinquency in Asia and the Far East* (Unafei Series, Fuchu, 1968), various Children's Acts have been enacted, but not enforced. The situation is satisfactory in Hong Kong, where there is a Juvenile Offenders Act, 1956, which is applied.

In Africa the situation is less encouraging. No juvenile courts exist in a number of countries, such as Mali, Mauritania, Nigeria and Chad. Perhaps the most informative study on the matter is W. Clifford's survey, *Juvenile delinquency in Zambia* (United Nations, SOA/SD/CS.3, 1967), because what he says applies to other African countries as well. It also confirms my opinion that in developing countries, which constitute the majority, the problem of juvenile delinquency cannot be dealt with in the Western way. The main specific characteristics of the problem are tribal concepts of juvenile delinquency, marked differences between urban and rural delinquency, and the role that customary courts play in civil as well as in criminal matters.

In the Middle East the United Arab Republic was the first to have juvenile courts, in 1905; in Syria juvenile courts—in most cases, common jurisdiction judges presiding over juvenile delinquency courts—apply the provisions of the penal code, but minors benefit from special institutions when available; those in Damascus, Hama and Aleppo were well operated in 1963. The situation was less satisfactory in the Lebanon, where there are no juvenile courts. According to the kind of offence committed, a judge of the court of the first instance or the civil section of the court of first instance may sit as judge of the juvenile court. In Jordan the role assigned to juvenile courts is performed by ordinary courts, which usually apply ordinary criminal procedure in a more flexible way when dealing with juveniles. In Morocco the Criminal Procedure Code of 1959 contains the procedure to be followed by the courts when dealing with criminal offenders and provides a series of educational measures.

In Latin America juvenile courts are provided by law in many countries, but as a rule they exist only in the capitals or other large cities. Elsewhere judges or courts of ordinary jurisdiction deal with juvenile offenders. Such is the case in Guatemala, Colombia, Chile, Mexico and Peru. Juvenile courts in the true sense of the term exist in Costa Rica and Uruguay. In Argentina the ordinary courts deal with juvenile offenders, and in some provinces special institutions for them are available. In Brazil some states have juvenile courts, and in others juvenile jurisdiction is exercised by ordinary courts or judges. In some of the states special institutions for juvenile offenders are available.

Thus it will be seen that the term 'juvenile court' is in practice nothing more than a special jurisdiction exercised by ordinary courts or judges when dealing with juvenile criminal offenders. This state of things may be regarded as unsatisfactory—which it is, but not for the reasons supposed. The juvenile court system has not necessarily failed because of the inability of governments to implement certain laws, but because these laws were pressed on them and presented as progressive when this was not so for the vast majority of developing countries. In other words, the experience of the historical process of some developed countries was regarded as suitable to all countries, under the pressure of a series of theories and assertions elaborated by distinguished professionals at international gatherings, where imitation and emulation are difficult to control. To the writer, the existing situation shows clearly enough the failure of imitative processes. The inability of developing countries to implement transplanted juvenile courts is partly due to their realization that juvenile offenders may be dealt with by ordinary courts, provided these have at their disposal the necessary social services; and also to the fact that although the extent and gravity of juvenile delinquency is often exaggerated, it has not reached the dimensions of well-developed countries. In sum, as I have stated in the past, by trying to imitate others the developing countries have evolved a two-track system, the results of which are questionable. The only possible solution is that imposed by reality in a number of cases, i.e the use in a human and social way of the ordinary criminal jurisdiction, coupled with the creation of adequate services and institutions. It is to this end that efforts should be intensified, and in assigning to professional judges two lay persons who should share with them the exercise of the special jurisdiction.[48]

As for the welfare board system as practised in the Scandinavian countries, I doubt if it has ever yielded the results claimed by its supporters, or if it could be transplanted into other countries. There are some significant differences between the way it is practised in Sweden and in the other Scandinavian countries, where the problem of juvenile delinquency is less serious. As a rule, the presence of what is called the 'legal element' as a guarantee is more significant in Finland, Norway and Denmark than in Sweden.

5 The need for a different approach

The thesis that juveniles and juvenile offenders should live and be kept in 'a world of their own' is not the outcome of a historical socio-political process, but the work of a scientific approach which is unrelated to social needs and the role of juvenile and young people. The historical movement in favour of children, in the right sense of the term, never aimed at keeping them apart from the adult world. In fact, the movement was one aspect of a two-pronged movement aiming at the improvement of children's as well as adults' conditions. The separation of the former from the latter, taking them apart from the socio-political maelstrom, was initiated and eventually achieved by a series of medico-psychological assertions and the intensification of welfare policies and programmes. Eventually, they succeeded in building up the fictional entity 'children' as representing any persons under 18, 20 or 21 years of age. The euphemism was completed by maintaining that if they did something wrong they were simply in trouble. The main slogans of this image were that 'children' were in constant need of 'love and protection', which nobody denies, provided other important aspects are not ignored; that 'the personality of the minor and not the act committed whatever its seriousness and atrocity is the only thing to be considered' which, under the nebulous concept of personality, dispensed with the sense of social responsibility; that 'children should be saved', which is quite correct, provided adults are saved from 'children's' atrocities; and that 'children constitute the capital of tomorrow's society', which is also true, although obviously other forms of working and used capital represented by adults and old people should also be considered.

The most tangible result of the theory of juvenile people as something apart was to make them beneficiaries of permissive policies, insulate them from reality, proclaim that all their needs should be satisfied, that no sense of responsibility was required for a number of years—in sum, juvenile people became sociologically parasitical. In fact, this approach reflected a larger one of human behaviour in general, provided by similar medico-psychological theories, according to which every aspect of human behaviour was exculpated by giving to drives, emotions, desires, etc., a prevalence over fundamental social values. Certainly some social values need urgent renewal, but this task is not facilitated by exculpatory theories, the constructive character of which is nil. The consequence was the rapid expanding of self-satisfying beliefs and the gradual weakening of the individual as well as collective responsibility in every respect. Permissiveness became the general rule instead of the exception in the juvenile as well as the adult world, especially in well-developed societies. Briefly, in the affluent society, which was put forward as a model, what matters is to maintain as high as possible the production-consumption equation and keep the individual essentially as a consumer-production being gradually taken over by automation—instead of raising his condition as protagonist. Consequently, life is governed by a few according to plans, the formulation and implementation of which for professional and other reasons are never made known.

Fortunately—and here again we see that often technological and scientific progress diverge from politico-social movements—in the last two decades youth has been rebelling against all this and has recently taken a definite stand against being regarded only as the recipients of love, care, etc., and above all of theories and policies. Actually, far more courageously than adults, they have reacted against the whole system. In the last few years youth has become more aware of the inadequacy of political and social structures and policies; of the deceptive character of the improvement of material living conditions with all the submissiveness it implies; that they are entitled to have their say on many things and intervene directly in others; and, finally, of their right to resist the system actively or passively.

If youth has to be limited by years, the present youth ranges from 14 to 21 years of age, i.e. it is constituted by the same age-groups which, with some upper age-limit variations, are regarded as 'children in trouble', 'immature people' or 'children in need of care and protection', and as such not responsible, especially as criminal offenders. Yet many of them are deliberately becoming offenders as one of the ways to provoke the change they are aiming at. Years ago I advanced the thesis that part of juvenile delinquency was an expression of protest against a number of things, among them the way juveniles were dealt with. Theoreticians and researchers assumed that they were unable to distinguish between right and wrong and therefore to pass judgment about what was going on around them. Actually, they are well acquainted with facts, policies and theories, and their judgment about many of them is already well known. Indeed, much of what they say is inarticulate and occasionally preposterous, but this should not create the belief that because sometimes they are utterly wrong their protest is a fading event. They have already made political history, and their protest is still in front of us. In sum, as far as the theory of juvenile delinquency is concerned, one may say that complacent psychology and sociology have failed because of a surfeit of theories. Frustration, lack of love, maladjustment, deviance, subculture and the like seem to be no more than empty names to explain this sudden maturity and self-reliance of juvenile people.

The above means that juveniles and young people play a definite role in contemporary society. It started by their adopting a particular way of dressing; at present they are asking for a different kind of life. The role has an irreversible character, and as such imposes among other things a revision of the present clumsy concept of juvenile delinquency. If the role of youth has changed, if they ask for greater participation and they seem to have a sense of social responsibility which was scientifically denied them, they have to be made more responsible in every respect, particularly in the commission of criminal offences. Participation without responsibility may perhaps be explained and justified by some medico-psychological theory and ancillary social thesis, but logically and politico-sociologically it does not make sense.

The steps to be taken are, first, to dispose of the theory of juvenile delinquency; secondly, to implement the recommendation of the 1960 United Nations Congress and consider as delinquency the commission of criminal offences, and hand over to social and medico-psychological services the cases of truancy, disobedience, running away, etc.; and thirdly, pending the organization of social criminal justice, assign to ordinary courts or judges a special jurisdiction to deal with juvenile criminal offenders. Their task should be helped by putting at their disposal as many treatment facilities as possible. Actually, this is already the pattern in some countries, owing to the unavoidable gap between legislation and practice. It is also the policy followed in socialist countries in which juvenile people were always considered as an integral part of the whole social framework. Putting aside monolithic interpretations of socialist systems, it is obvious that this integration is not only possible but necessary in non-socialist countries.

4   The expansion and distribution of crime

What follows is an attempt to examine the more relevant factors determining the expansion and distribution of crime. Although it is sometimes denied, crime is expanding everywhere, and more quickly in developed than in developing countries. This is contested by representatives of the former who maintain that, since developing countries lack reliable criminal statitstics, they appear in a better light than developed countries. But not all developed countries have reliable or complete criminal statistics, and the question is not only one of statistical data, but of the connection between development and crime. As a rule, the greater the development the greater the amount of crime, especially when development is understood as socio-economic development in terms of production-consumption and higher material standards of living. The main reasons for the expansion of crime are: (*a*) that the growing complexity of development usually demands greater penal protection, hence the increase of the number of criminal offences (*b*) increasing corruption and leisure time: and (*c*) greater individual as well as collective insecurity and protest against existing socio-economic and political systems, even in countries where everything is run according to a single political ideology, party and machinery. The common denominator of these factors is population growth and its age and sex distribution. It is not true that war, particularly World War II, is the main cause of the expansion of crime, although obviously it plays a part; however, like any other factor, the role of war is ambivalent, in the sense that it provokes but also reduces crime. Furthermore, as a factor the effects of war eventually fade and are replaced by others. Only metaphysically can it be said that by creating new conditions, which in turn provoke others, and so on *ad infinitum,* war effects are still in action. A close scrutiny of the facts shows that in most

181

cases war is not a sudden event but the culmination of a process, the causal effects of which start acting before the war begins. It is difficult to ascertain what are the criminogenic effects of war itself, those of the process preceding it and those provoked by contemporary but independent factors.

1 Population growth

The relation between crime and population is direct in the sense that the greater the population the greater is the total amount of crime. However, this relationship is affected by the action of a series of intervening factors, some of them inherent in the population itself, with the result that as a rule crime grows faster than population.[49]

Population projections are decisive in the formulation of many policies, but up to now their role in criminal policy has been modest. They have been more frequently used in the projections of prison population to determine the building programmes of penal institutions. Yet if criminological projections are to have a part in the criminology of the future, population projections must be used in other ways. The usefulness of criminological projections may be contested on two accounts: that those based on population projections are sometimes subject to substantial rectifications, and that, owing to the variables involved, they risk becoming high-level abstractions. Suffice it to say here that criminological projections will always be related in one way or another to population projections which cannot be regarded as abstractions even if rectified, and that as long as the researcher moves in close contact with reality and the manipulation of data is not transformed into an end by itself the risk of abstraction can be avoided. It is true that substantial rectifications are made to population projections, but the number and size are gradually decreasing with better statistics and the refinement of projection techniques. In any case, planning ahead is becoming a feature of every policy, and there is no reason why criminal policy should not make greater use of population projections. Certainly, projections and planning involve a series of variables some of which may act out of context, but in most cases this can be accounted for by allowing them some margins of action. For criminological projections, the medium variant of population projections seems to be the more convenient, not only because they represent the most plausible trend, but also because, if a variable is out of context, the compensation is easier to make. It is also important that criminological projections should limit themselves to relatively short periods of time; those of 5 or 10 years seem to be the most convenient. As the Secretariat of the United Nations has pointed out with respect to population projections, the longer the time-span of the future estimates, the greater the likelihood that unforeseen developments may cause the population to move outside the limits which appear plausible when the projections were made.

In 1938 in England and Wales the total indictable offences known to the police were 283,220 for a total population, excluding those under 8 years of age, of a little over 38 million, of which nearly 20 million were females. In 1967 there were 1,207,354 of the same kind of offences, and the population involved, excluding those under 10 years of age, was well over 40 million, of which nearly 21 million were females. The impressive increase of crime with respect to population may be minimized by saying that present police methods are better than those of thirty years ago, that the preparation and presentation of criminal statistics have improved since then and that the number of acts defined as criminal offences has also increased, etc. All this may be true, but it is also true that in 1938, with less technical police methods and a smaller police force, 50 per cent of all indictable offences were cleared up, while in 1967 the percentage was 41·2. This casts no reflection on the police. What it means is that most of the explanations advanced to belittle the rise of crime must be submitted to close scrutiny before being accepted. As for the presentation of statistics, it has remained very much the same, which is an advantage in some respects. It is interesting that a comparison of the percentages of certain offences gives the impression of relatively steady trends. Thus in 1938 larceny was up to 70 per cent of all indictable offences known to the police, while in 1967 it was 64 per cent. For breaking and entering the percentages were 17 and 21 respectively, and for offences against the person barely 1 and 2·3 respectively. On the other hand, sexual offences show a decline from 2·4 to 1·8 per cent. Needless to say, pending analysis of the intervening years, the above percentages are of limited value and cannot be regarded as indicators of well-established trends. However, they are significant in the sense that, in spite of all that has taken place between 1938 and 1967, partly reflected in criminal statistical fluctuations, their margins are not so far apart as to exclude the existence of relatively stable criminal trends.

With respect to the growth of the world population and the faster growth of crime, the following are significant enough: for 1970, 1980, 1990 and 2000, the world population estimates are 3,592, 4,330, 5,188 and 6,130 million respectively; the estimates for 1960 and 1965 were 2,998 and 3,297. This means that in the year 2000 the world population will have doubled. Assuming that crime will increase only five times as much—which is a conservative estimate —it will be staggering. This is confirmed by the regional decennial estimate. In Europe the increases for 1980, 1990 and 2000 are

6, 5 and 5 respectively, while those for Africa are 30, 31 and 31, and for Latin America 34, 32 and 38. Among the European countries the criminogenic effect of population growth will be less marked in Switzerland, Austria, Luxembourg and the Scandinavian countries; *mutatis mutandis*, the same applies to Czechoslovakia, Poland, Hungary and the Democratic Republic of Germany. The impact will be greater in Rumania, owing to her greater population growth. As for the U.S.S.R., the decennial increases 13, 14 and 12 are higher and in principle more vulnerable to the increase of crime. On the other hand, the severe losses of World War II are reflected in the sex ratio. At the time of the 1959 census, females outnumbered males by well over 20 million; although the gap will eventually be closed, barring other factors since crime is mostly a male event, for some time the accrued crime vulnerability to the increase of the total population will partly be offset by the prevalence of the female population. To a lesser extent the same applies to Germany.

The following selected countries are offered as an illustration of the different impact of population growth on the increase of crime:

Country	1965	1970	1980
		(in millions)	
Australia	11	12	14
Brazil	81	93	123
German Federal Republic	55	56	58
Ghana	7	9	12
India	483	543	682
Indonesia	105	118	152
Japan	97	101	111
Kenya	9	10	13
Mexico	41	49	70
U.S.S.R.	231	245	277
United Arab Republic	29	34	46
United Kingdom	54	56	57
United States	194	207	240

The increase in the Scandinavian countries is too low to be shown in round figures. In Sweden the estimates are 7·7, 7·9 and 8·3 million respectively.

As far as the population factor is concerned, developed countries are as a rule less vulnerable and more able to face the rise of crime. Yet in some of them the situation may prove to be extremely difficult; this would be the case in the United States if present criminal policies are maintained. According to *Uniform Crime Reports* (1967), between 1960 and 1967 the population has increased

10 per cent, but crime 89 per cent. Is the situation in the United Kingdom any better? It is not easy to say; for England and Wales, although the limited growth of the population is reassuring, existing data show that between 1950 and 1967 the crime-population rate of persons found guilty of indictable offences has almost doubled, while the corresponding population has increased by barely 3·5 per cent. Does this mean that by 1980 the above index will be doubled? With all the necessary reservations it does seem likely. This does not necessarily mean that the prison population will grow at the same pace, since other factors than population are involved, but certainly it will be greater than at present. As for non-institutional treatment, the number of offenders will no doubt increase noticeably, demanding more probation, parole and other facilities. Can all the difficulties involved in this increase be solved by multiplying the services, the number of judges and police, or by organizing a different but more effective system of criminal justice? In other words, is the present preventive-treatment policy with respect of crime justified? If it is remembered that the developing countries are beset by many other serious problems, including political unrest, the gap between them and developed countries in the control of crime, as in other aspects, will be widened instead of reduced. A factor to be considered in making projections is the age limit for criminal responsibility, which in some countries is as high as 18 or 20 years of age. In these countries, actual crime will be camouflaged under the term 'delinquency', which itself will rise considerably, owing to the expanding of the age-groups under 25 years. Needless to say, population growth may be affected by many factors and its impact on crime be less noticeable. Decreased fertility, birth-control policies, etc., may affect reproduction rates, yet the prospects are not encouraging. While developed countries have in general reached a population stability with a net reproduction rate of about one, many of the developing countries have a far higher rate of increase, which will affect the increase of crime.

2 Improvement of material living conditions

The improvement of living conditions is still regarded as one of the best methods of preventing crime; as a rule, the improvement refers almost exclusively to socio-economic conditions. These are basic, but there are others with a political, juridical and moral character. The question is not rhetorical, inasmuch as, in contrast with past policy, in the last few years the Economic and Social Council and the Secretariat of the United Nations maintain the view that preventive and treatment policies of crime should be regarded as part of socio-economic development. According to

Resolution 1086 B (XXXIX) of 1965 of the Economic and Social Council, 'the prevention of crime and control of juvenile delinquency and adult criminality should be undertaken as part of comprehensive economic and social development plans'. The Secretariat has stressed this policy by saying that 'social defence programmes should be necessarily attuned to national development policies', and, further, that 'social defence problems lay deep in the processes of economic and social development and had to be resolved within them'.[50] This narrow approach to the problem of crime is apparently based on three assumptions: (a) that crime is a socio-economic problem, therefore the improvement of these conditions will eradicate or reduce it; (b) that socio-economic reality constitutes a single entity; and (c) social defence success depends upon a balanced social and economic development.

With respect to (a), experience shows that the improvement of socio-economic conditions, even if carefully planned, has not reduced crime; the United States, United Kingdom, Sweden, Federal Republic of Germany, Switzerland and France are examples. The thesis criticized here overlooks the fact that socio-economic improvement may reduce or eradicate some old forms of crime, but new ones will inevitably appear, some of them as a consequence of granting penal protection to some aspects of the new socio-economic order. The definition of 'social' as 'everything that refers directly to the conditions in which people live', given in a recent United Nations report, *Social and Economic Development,* No. 3 (United Nations Research Institute for Social Development, 1966), does not help much to a better understanding of social problems or of social defence. Even if the term 'social' is used with quotation marks, the fact remains that there are many living conditions which by no stretch of the imagination can be regarded as social. Political conditions, juridical systems and moral patterns, to cite a few, are no less important factors with respect to crime. In this respect it should be added that under dictatorial régimes socio-economic conditions usually improve, sometimes rapidly, yet crime does not decrease, especially that committed under cover of official position or as the result of corruption and political resistance.

With respect to (b), the unity of socio-economic reality can be maintained only for the areas in which social and economic factors are dealt with together, but not in those in which each of them, according to its specific purposes, acts on its own. Only an ambitious concept of what 'social' and 'economic' are can identify co-ordination of policies with the unity of the social and economic and social defence problems. The mistake is to identify a particular situation in which factors of many sorts are involved with a conceptual appraisal of it. Criminology, sociology and economics have much in common, but also substantive areas in which each acts independently. As for the last two, the distinction has been made by the United Nations itself in its Covenant on Economic, Social and Cultural Rights of 1966. The social right to strike may run against economic development and only figuratively can be regarded as forming part of a single socio-economic reality. In fact, for economic and political reasons this right is denied in some countries The improvement of methods of production is a field in which social development has little or nothing to do. Briefly, the fact that in some respects social and economic development should go together does not mean unity of the aspects involved, and even less of the socio-economic reality. As for criminology, it is obvious that its subject-matter goes far beyond socio-economic development, the same applies to criminal policy, which certainly must be related to many others. Regarding the 'attuning' suggested, suffice it to say that the thirty desiderata of Resolution 1139 (XLI) 1966 of the Economic and Social Council which constitute the nucleus of socio-economic development make it illusory. The subordination of United Nations social defence activities to socio-economic policies explains why social-defence matters have been considered as affecting only 'special groups' or 'vulnerable groups' and crime the sequel of an 'imperfect society', which is not the case. A different approach was made in 1953 by the Secretariat itself, when it was stated that by its very nature the programme of social defence was directed towards the whole community and not to certain groups (*Programme of Concerted Practical Action in the Social Field of the United Nations and Specialized Agencies,* E/CN.5/291).

As for (c), putting aside the important question of the sense in which the term 'balanced' should be understood, the thesis of balanced development is valid only in the area in which the social and economic development are co-ordinated, but not beyond that, for the simple reason that outside those limits each development acts in accordance with its own specific aims. What is meant is adequate co-ordination of social and economic policies where they are supposed to act at the same time; the term 'balanced' therefore seems unnecessary. Certainly the report, *Planning for Balanced Social and Economic Development*: 1964 (*U.N.* Publication, Sales No. 64.IV.8), concerning India, the Netherlands, Poland, Puerto Rico, Senegal and Yugoslavia, shows not only the difficulties of such balanced development in limited areas of action, but also that the proclaimed unity of socio-economic reality is more a figure of speech than a correct conceptual expression.

The above questions are relevant to developing countries, inasmuch as the quotations made as well as the wishful thinking of some governments have already led them to regard criminal policy as having no substantive character of its own and crime as a problem which will almost automatically be solved by socio-economic development or planning. This was the mistake made in the past by most of the present developed countries, who are still paying for it. Even if the developing countries succeed in their socio-economic development, crime will not necessarily be reduced, as this development brings with it new factors of crime, to which should be added those having their origin in non-social and non-socio-economic conditions. In Sweden, a country with an excellent social record, crime has not decreased; in the United States, with an excellent economic record, it is increasing every year. According to a survey published by *Time* on 27 December 1968, since 1961 the gross national product in dollars increased 71 per cent, industrial production 51 per cent, and wages and productivity 48 and 30 per cent respectively. Between 1960 and 1967 crimes of violence increased 73 per cent, and against property 91 per cent; even granting that in the United States there is in many respects a lack of co-ordination between social and economic development, this will not explain the increase of crime. As for the success of developing countries in their socio-economic development, the *1967 Report on the World Social Situation* of the United Nations (E/CN.5/417 and Add. 1 and 2) as well as the Secretary-General's *Report on the World Situation,* 1967 (A/7248), show not only that the gap between developed and developing countries is widening, but that in many developing countries social and economic development is not what it should be, in others it is stationary and in some actually deteriorating. The difficulties faced by these countries are serious, but they are aggravated by internecine struggles, dictatorial régimes, privileges of the *élite* and nationalistic pursuits. Moreover, there is the crucial question of what is meant by socio-economic development; certainly it is not socio-economic equality, even in socialist countries, where socio-economic categories are different in some respects, but still as prominent as in capitalist countries. What seems to be meant is the achievement of certain standards and levels of living. The choice of the indicators was made by the United Nations in an excellent report on *International Definition and Measurement of Standards and Levels of Living,* 1954 (U.N. Publication, Sales No. 54.IV.V). Since then other reports have been published; health, food, working conditions, education and human freedoms were taken as indicators, and all these levels have improved in many developing countries. The most marked exception is human freedoms, in which developing countries are far behind, a matter of crucial importance, as the violation of these freedoms is one of the most important sources of contemporary crime. Should the index of crime be regarded as one of the indicators of a desirable standard of living? At the time of the preparation of the report I was asked for my opinion, and after some hesitation I decided against; today I would not hesitate, as I regard a 'reasonable' index of crime as an indicator of a good standard of living.

Another significant aspect of socio-economic development and accompanying technological and scientific progress is the gradual increase of leisure time and its obvious impact on crime. Experience shows that free time, boredom, mischief and crime often go together, particularly among the young. In his provocative book, *Les 40,000 Heures* (1965), Jean Fourastié advances the thesis that in the twenty-first century the number of working hours per year will not exceed 1,200. Assuming an average life of 85 years, this makes 700,000 hours, of which only 40,000 will be devoted to work. Even if a substantial part of the balance is needed for transportation, education and family duties, leisure time will be too plentiful to be ignored as an important factor with repercussions on crime. Fourastié's assertions are a mixture of factual data, projections and high-level abstractions; yet leisure time is already playing a part in crime which has been largely ignored. The situation is probably different in developing countries, where free time is mostly unoccupied, but not leisure. In the developed countries leisure time is frequent and often accompanied by the increasing boredom provoked by mass communication, mass education, mass entertainment and every conceivable mass technique to increase the capacity of man as a consumer. Leisure and youth were discussed at the International Conference on Youth, 1964 (Final Report, UNESCO/ED/211). The recommendations were for greater development of cultural activities connected with intellectual and general training, more particularly for sport and physical education, and that governments and organizations should promote youth tours and international exchange of youth groups and the development of holiday camps and youth hostels. All very nice, peripheral and remote from the role already played by youth in contemporary society. In fact, the Conference stressed the image of a parasitic youth always engaged in intellectual and physical pursuits which should be continued in their already excessive free time. There is no doubt that primary and secondary education must be general, compulsory and free. The situation is different with higher education, in which, irrespective of class, individual qualifications are paramount. The policy of the open door has unfortunately identified equality of rights with equality of qualifications, with the result that the student mass of our time is to a great extent inarticulate, frustrated and negatively-minded. Yet as a mass, the product of a mass education policy, they get more benefits, grants and privileges than other social groups, some of which have already proved their usefulness, such as old and retired people. As a social status, 'student' is in need of redefinition. Undoubtedly, as a group as well as an individual the student is fully entitled to protest and participate, but on the other hand he should justify the benefits he gets from society and more particularly from taxpayers. There is little doubt that the present protest and participation would have been more intelligible and constructive if more selective policies had governed access to college and university education and the condition of the student. This should no longer be conceived as a parasitic and in many cases parading condition, but as one in which study and work, including manual work, are combined; grants and other benefits have to be made good by studying and working. Otherwise, as a group students will become the masters of everything and the students of nothing. It is obvious that the present status of students has increased crime by the way students behave as reformers. I repeat that individually as well as in groups students are fully entitled to protest and participate, and that in many respects their attitude is justified—but not the senseless violence they use. Like other groups, students think violence pays; unfortunately, the permissive society of our time authorizes the conclusion. Certainly by their violence, which may be justified in certain cases, students have abundantly demonstrated that higher education—for many, only contact with it—does not reduce crime. On the contrary, since many of the offences committed benefit from impunity, the chances are that they will increase.

To the writer there is a relationship between expanded welfare policies, boredom, excessive permissive attitudes, less sense of individual and social responsibility and juvenile crime. Since as a rule youth stands monotony and boredom less patiently than adults, this explains to some extent the greater proportion of crime in the 14–25-year age-group. Boredom and monotony are later replaced by worries and responsibilities, and these contribute to the decline of crime from 40 years of age onwards. The contrast between Nordic and Mediterranean juvenile delinquency cannot be explained by the better quality of the statistics of the Scandinavian countries—in Sweden the statistical extent of juvenile crime cannot be ascertained, nor, since 1964, can the age and sex of adult offenders—but by the role of boredom and monotony in general and among juvenile people in particular. It is true that the Welfare State has brought many advantages, but it has also brought boredom and monotony to the already excessive number of factors contributing to crime.

3 Growing insecurity

Individual and collective insecurity is becoming one of the most marked characteristics of our time.[51] In the era of social security, individual security, as the ability to perform significant tasks by oneself, to believe in the justification of fundamental values or in the authenticity of one's own or another's sentiments or attitudes, is getting less, partly because of the greater importance given to State or other forms of political security and partly because of the growing intromission of science, technology and welfare in daily life. As for minority groups which exist almost everywhere, their feeling of insecurity is greater than ever. By reducing initiative and freedom through a series of protective, assistance and control policies, society, without making effective its promises, has made man more insecure. In some respects the situation is worse in developed than in developing countries, although the latter, owing to their lack of imagination, are learning fast how to introduce greater security policies which would be unnecessary if they were democratically organized. The situation is no better in socialist countries where the individual is subject to constant supervision, which itself breeds insecurity and dissatisfaction.

More specifically, the reasons for this growing insecurity are: the expanding complexity of contemporary life, of which bureaucracy and meritocracy are two of the most outstanding features; frequency and intensity of national and international conflicts; greater economic and financial vulnerability, in spite of planning and rising taxation, production and consumption; growing dogmatism in the political as well as other fields, including recent youth movements which ignore or exclude everything which is not in conformity with what they advocate, even if they do not always know how to express it; expanding bio-psychological knowledge which reduces our confidence in our own feelings or makes individuals more subservient to every kind of propaganda; greater reliance on specialization and interference by experts and services in the form of advice or assistance in every aspect of individual and collective life; growing dependency on mass communication, mass education, mass production, etc., and more frequent and bolder deprivation of human rights. The temptation to add the loss of religious faith, which should not be identified with assistance at religious services, is great. Suffice it to say that, in order to become a greater source of security, religion has to adapt itself more rapidly than it is doing to contemporary social needs and problems and politically disassociate itself from anti-democratic régimes.

Some of the above factors are ambivalent and therefore bring in benefits, but taken as a whole they have reduced the individual to the condition of a cog in an enormous and complicated machine governed by systems, ideologies or plans. It may be argued that it has always been the same. Even so, progress was supposed not only to improve material conditions, but also to increase the individual feeling of security. Instead, man is more subordinated than ever, and the net around him, although piously intended for his benefit, remains a net and certainly does not reinforce his sense of independence and hence of security. Needless to say, the picture is not the same everywhere, but as a rule the greater the complexity of society and State intervention the greater the feeling of dependence and insecurity. The reasoning that the lack of individual security has been compensated for by better material living conditions is the kind of argument usually put forward by dictatorial régimes.

Certainly security and insecurity have always existed; the old thesis of man as the *animal insecurum* as opposed to beast as *animal securum* is too metaphysical to be discussed here. Man has gained in many material respects, but is rapidly losing his feeling of individual and collective security. In many countries even social security offers only a modicum of it. Undoubtedly incertitude and risk are inherent in every human undertaking, but nowadays both are intensified. Science, technology and welfare have brought many good things but also a constant shrinking of individual and collective security, making man more dependent. It is not that all three should be banished, but that they are not used to make the human condition secure. According to Peter Wust, the capacity of man to face the insecurity inherent in security and, conversely, the security inherent in insecurity is rapidly vanishing, as far more things are done for him than by him. In sum, whatever his affluence, technological skill and scientific knowledge, or perhaps because of them, man is becoming more subordinated than in the past. The most tangible result is that insecurity is gaining a new significance at both national and international levels. In a subtle way it is permeating many aspects of life, such as individual and collective attitudes *vis-à-vis* the fundamental system of values, the national and international legitimate order and the purpose of life. While society is getting better organized and controlled except in crime, mankind is getting ever more insecure. The distinction is important, since some crimes should be regarded as more serious when they are against mankind than against society. A revision of the list of crimes against society will show that some of them could be abolished without danger either for society or mankind. Such is the case with some offences having a political or ideological character and quite a number of petty offences against property.

Instead of creating security as a powerful unit embracing the fundamental aspects of life, contemporary society provides only a piecemeal security, the assemblage of which is often purposely prevented—especially by anti-democratic régimes. Indeed, associations, unions and the like aim at greater security, mostly material in purpose, yet for political, financial and other reasons man and society are becoming more vulnerable. One may ask whether this is not part of the price to be paid for the greater role of economics, technology and science in life. This growing feeling of dependence, insecurity and risk has led to more sceptical attitudes with respect to the fundamental system of values, which indeed need to be changed, but are still fundamental enough to have a primordial governing character. What is the connection between these growing sceptical attitudes and crime? If by 'connection' is understood absolute causal relationship, the answer is 'None', but if it is understood as it should be in dealing with social problems, such as crime, as the highly probable effect of a markedly negative factor, then there is a connection. Therefore, excessive individual and collective insecurity is a contributing factor to the extent of crime.

4 Corruption

Corruption has always been a close companion of crime. This explains the multiple forms it takes and the varied terminology used to describe it: bribery, graft, gift-taking, kick-backs, sharp business practices, etc.[52]

As with crime, society is supposed to stand a certain amount of corruption without being seriously disturbed. The question is whether corruption has not become so widespread in many countries that is constitutes an important contributing factor to crime. In the last ten years the following countries have passed Acts or conducted official inquiries, sometimes more than once, on corruption: Algeria, Argentina, Brazil, Canada, Ceylon, Ghana, Greece, India, Indonesia, Italy, Nigeria, Morocco, South Vietnam, Syria, Uganda and the United Arab Republic. In the United States official inquiries, reports and court cases show that corruption is frequent among politicians as well as in administrative services, police and business. In the U.S.S.R. some of the economic crimes, often severely punished, are the result of corrupt practices in State production. Although varying in form and sometimes in motivation, corruption in both capitalist and socialist countries is often a pattern of life.

The main contributing factors of corruption are the concentration of power, wealth and status, anti-democratic régimes, excessive bureaucracy, monopolies, trusts, big corporations and the like, patronage, governmental concessions for economic and industrial development, a poorly organized and paid civil service, and, as a general ingredient, a materialistic conception of success in which money and ostentation play a primary role. In the developing countries tribal and family loyalties and the accepted use of 'legitimate gifts' should be added. Tribal and family ties are strong enough to demand and get protection and posts from anyone holding an official position of importance, the dispensing of which often implies corrupt practices as well as the commission of criminal offences. More often than in Latin America, in African and Asian countries the concept of public service and the distinction between public administrative function and private interest is lacking. This explains why even among cultivated persons the claims of relatives are often considered 'justified'. As for 'legitimate' gifts to public officials and civil servants, while some have a remote origin and are difficult to eradicate, others are of recent creation. The most significant difference is that, while in the past most of these presents were in specie, nowadays money is used, and apparently with better results.

Occasionally corruption has been explained as a feature of national character, poverty or lack of education. Some years ago the writer advanced the thesis that the only difference between developed and developing countries is that in the former bribery involves higher sums, and that in developing countries corruption is sometimes aggravated by corrupt practices introduced by businessmen from developed countries; the Philippines is a good example. As for the lack of education, I share the view of Wraith and Simpkins that it may reduce corruption with the qualification that in developing countries I have found well-educated and highly-placed persons who used corruption to get what they wanted, and that in developed countries, such as the United States, corruption as a criminal offence is more serious among advisers, administrators and politicians than among less educated groups. Among the police, cases of corruption are frequent, and in some states some of them have reached notoriety. The fact that senators guilty of corruption which, if committed by anybody else, would have led to criminal prosecution, are still acting in state as well as in the U.S. Senate seems to indicate that corruption has something like a recognized political status. As a remedy, the 1967 Ethics Code adopted by the U.S. Senate will accomplish very little. In Italy the Marotta case shows that educated people are cleverer than the non-educated in corruption. The majority of the military régimes trying to justify themselves as cleansing operations become more corrupt than their predecessors. The most marked difference is that the man on horseback favours the monopoly of his own group. Publicity has sometimes been suggested as the best remedy. While I favour its use, the snag is that under undemocratic régimes the Press is not free. The growth of professional classes as well as workers' organizations has also been considered a remedy; here again over-optimism should be avoided. Among lawyers, corruption is more frequent than the cases reported to bar associations show. The boast that there are few cases of disbarment does not mean that corruption is non-existent, but, on the contrary, that it is tolerated. The situation is worse where no association of any kind exists or where membership is not compulsory. Some trade unions are known more for their corrupt practices than for anything else.

Corruption is also closely related to treason, espionage and disclosure of State secrets. Nowadays almost every country has special laws and sometimes special courts to deal with these matters. Divided loyalties, ideological affiliation or sympathy and other factors may play a role in the commission of these criminal offences, but, besides not being incompatible with them, corruption is often the determining factor. I should add that the immoderate idea of State security in some countries is a contributory factor.

Organized crime cannot exist without official corruption. The Kefauver Report stated: 'The most shocking revelations of the testimonies before the Committee is the extent of official corruption and connivance in facilitating and promoting organized crime.' More than twelve years later the connection between corruption and crime is mentioned by many others: Robert K. Woetzel in 'Overview of Organized Crime: Mores versus Morality', Henry S. Ruth Jr., 'Why Organized Crime Thrives', and John A. Gardiner, 'Public Attitudes towards Gambling and Corruption', in *The Annals of the American Academy of Political and Social Science* (May 1963 and November 1967), stress the role of corruption in the increase of organized crime, which is also stressed by the President's Commission report on *Organized Crime* already cited.

Finally, the connection of corruption with unethical professional practices and from these to criminal offences is well known in insurance, advertising, merchandising, sport, television contests, etc.

Although corruption and criminal corruption are legally different, both are expressions of the same attitude to morals, ethical principles and public function. That a certain amount of corruption is unavoidable cannot be denied; the difficulty lies in knowing what are the bearable limits for corruption in general and criminal corruption in particular. The latter may take many forms, according to the nature of the act and the persons who commit it. It may be against justice or public administration, security regulations, public health or other interests, illegal professional activities, etc.

As such, it constitutes one of the most significant segments of unknown crime and of known but unreported crime, and this is why criminal statistics seldom reflect this type of offence. The main reasons for it are widespread tolerance of corrupt practices, especially in societies where success is measured in money or ostentation, and the various and often subtle ways in which corruption is carried on. In some countries a public official or even a judge will never be corrupted by money, but will become 'supple' enough to do what is requested if a promotion or a decoration is promised. Criminal corruption is a two-way affair in which one of the partners, if not both, are often highly-placed or influential persons, which makes criminal prosecution difficult. Finally, even if the act constitutes a criminal offence, the matter is often handled first by administrative authorities or bodies which recommend dismissal, demotion or transfer instead of criminal prosecution. Owing to the connivance of those directly involved, as well as a generally tolerant attitude, corruption frequently benefits from impunity, and therefore it pays. The offenders do not belong to any particular criminological type, and since in their social groups corruption is tolerated or accepted, their rehabilitation is doubtful. Recent inquiries in the United States show that as long as the taxpayer is not directly affected, corruption among minor- and medium-grade officials is tolerated. The reaction was different with respect to high-grade and police officials, but even here a distinction was frequently made according to which the corrupter is regarded as less responsible than the corrupted. The explanation of this seems to be that in business matters outright corrupt practices are regarded as permissible for competitive reasons. What are the remedies for corruption? Some have already been examined; others, like better organized and paid public administration, watch-dog committees, etc., have also been suggested and may yield good results, but it is doubtful if they will sensibly reduce it. People seem to have a high margin of tolerance to it, and often professionals come to the rescue by saying that no criminal corruption has taken place. That is what happened with white-collar crime, so close to corruption—its criminal character is still denied by distinguished professionals. The result is that corruption in developed as well as in developing countries, whether capitalist or socialist, is one of the important sources of crime. As for the offenders, they not only enjoy impunity, but often public recognition as well.

5 Sex and crime

Demographic data show that in the vast majority of countries the population is almost equally divided between male and female; the most significant exception is the U.S.S.R., where women still outnumber men by several millions. But the participation of men in crime far exceeds that of women. The excess varies according to the different stage at which crime is dealt with; as a rule, it rises from police to court and from court to prison statistics. Unfortunately, police data are not always available, hence the more frequent use of judicial and prison data. For brevity, as far as male-female ratios are concerned round figures are used.[53]

In England and Wales in 1957 and 1967 the male-female ratio of persons cautioned by the police for indictable offences was 6 and 4 to 1 respectively. The average per 100,000 of the corresponding population was 81 and 124 male to 13 and 32 female respectively. In 1957 females over 8 years of age outnumbered males of the same age by 1,700,000, and in 1967 females over 10 years of age outnumbered the males by 1,200,000. In the same years the male-female ratio of persons found guilty in all courts was 8 and 6 to 1 respectively. However, the ratio varies when specific indictable offences are considered. In offences against the person, the male-female ratio in 1957 and 1967 was 19 and 17 to 1; in sexual offences, 103 and 132 to 1; receiving, frauds and false pretences, 6 and 7 to 1; breaking and entering, 43 and 40 to 1; and 5 to 1 in both years in the case of larceny. On the other hand, there are some specific offences in which females found guilty usually outnumber males. Such is the case with infanticide, cruelty to children, abandoning children under 2 years of age, procuring abortion, concealment of birth, larceny from shops and stalls and brothel-keeping. As a curious contrast, men far exceed women in cruelty to animals and, what is more significant, in malicious wounding, causing death by dangerous driving, as well as in reckless or dangerous driving. As for prisoners under sentence, Borstals and detention centres included, the male-female ratio, with some reservations owing to the different presentation of data, was in both years virtually the same, 25 to 1.

In the Federal Republic of Germany in the period 1963-67 the average male-female ratio in adult crime dealt with by the police was 7 to 1. The male-female ratio in 1965 for persons convicted by courts was 8 to 1. In the prison population at the end of 1966 and 1967 the male-female ratio was virtually the same, 23 to 1. In France in 1965 the ratio among persons found guilty by the courts was 10 to 1. The ratio for the prison population in 1966 and 1967 was 23 and 25 to 1 respectively. In Belgium the average male-female ratio of persons found guilty in the period 1956-65 was 5 to 1. In the prison population the male-female ratio in August 1967 and August 1968 was 17 and 20 to 1 respectively.

197

In Spain the ratio among those brought to trial before the courts in 1965 was 10 to 1; with some fluctuations, it has been the same since 1954. If anything, there is a slight downward trend in the last few years. For sentenced persons, the male-female ratio in 1965 was 16 to 1. In 1966 and 1967 the male-female ratio of sentenced prisoners in the prison population was 20 and 22 to 1, and of prisoners awaiting trial 22 and 28 to 1 respectively. In Italy in 1965 the male-female ratio of sentenced persons was 5 to 1, and in the prison population 18 to 1. In Switzerland the male-female ratio of persons found guilty of criminal offences in 1966 was 6 to 1. In Norway in 1966 among persons charged by the police it was 10 to 1, for persons found guilty by the courts in the period 1963–65 it was 11 to 1. In Yugoslavia in 1964 among sentenced adults and juvenile offenders it was 3 and 10 to 1 respectively.

In the United States in 1967 male arrests outnumbered female arrests by 7 to 1, but the latter rose by 7 per cent while male arrests rose only 4 per cent. Females were arrested in 14 per cent of murder, robbery, aggravated assault, burglary, larceny and automobile theft. Their involvement was primarily for larceny, which accounted for more than 1 of every 6 female arrests; they accounted for 21 per cent of the forgery, 23 per cent of the fraud and 19 per cent of the embezzlement arrests. Long-term trends between 1960 and 1967 reveal that arrests for females under 18 years of age rose 71 per cent for automobile theft and 76 per cent for burglary. While the arrests of young males greatly outnumbered those of females during this same period, nevertheless the percentage increases in both these offences were not so pronounced: 53 per cent for automobile theft and 40 per cent for burglary. In the case of aggravated assault, arrests of males outnumbered those of females by almost 7 to 1. Nationwide the ratio of arrests for murder was more than 5 males to 1 female. Owing to the large number of illegal police arrests in the United States, statistical data on arrests are subject to caution, but they are significant enough to conclude that there is an obvious gap between male and female crime. In Canada in 1966 the male-female ratio of persons charged by the police was 10 to 1 in the case of adults and 7 to 1 among juveniles. If only criminal code offences are considered, the ratio is 9 and 8 to 1 respectively. For persons found guilty by the courts, the ratio was nearly 8 to 1 in 1965. In Japan female crime has fluctuated considerably since 1964; the increase in the last few years is mainly due to negligent homicide and bodily injury in traffic accidents. The rate of criminal code offenders per 1,000 female population in 1966 was 1·4, while that of males in the last 20 years has fluctuated between 15 and 21. Admittedly, females are in general more leniently treated than males. In 1965, 70 per cent of females sentenced to imprisonment were given suspended sentences, against 50 per cent of males; those sent to prison in 1966 constituted only 3 per cent of the whole prison population. In Argentina in 1965 the male-female ratio of sentenced offenders was 15 to 1.

In most developing countries the male-female ratio is difficult to establish, either because statistics are not available or are unreliable, or, if available, they are quite often not classified by sex, partly because of the relatively small number of female offenders. This is the case with India, where only scattered information about female crime among juvenile offenders is available. Police data on female crime are not available in the United Arab Republic, and judicial statistics, although very useful, make no reference to female offenders. In this and other countries the most reliable—although not the most significant—data are prison statistics. The information gathered by the writer from official sources is good enough to give an idea of the extent of female crime. In the United Arab Republic in 1965 the ratio among sentenced prisoners was 9 to 1, and for those awaiting trial 12 to 1. In Jordan in the same year the prison male-female ratio was 45 to 1, and in Iran in 1966 among sentenced prisoners it was 40 to 1. No information was available on those awaiting trial.

The small proportion of female crime has often been denied. For years there has been a criminological fashion well represented by Otto Pollak's *The Criminality of Women* (1950), according to which female crime is masked as a result of a combination of factors, such as tolerance, lenience and women's ability to avoid detection. The expression *cherchez la femme* is still used to convey the idea that, if not as material authors, women are the hidden principals in the vast majority of crimes committed by men. It is said that, since women are participating more than ever in activities originally the preserve of men, eventually female crime will equal male crime. Undoubtedly there is some truth in all this; but the fact remains that even in well-developed countries where women participate in almost every aspect of life, their participation in crime is still small.

In order to be understood, the study of female crime requires the consideration of the following aspects: the real status of women in each country; the role of sex; the analysis of female crime and the bio-psychological characteristics of women and men. Here I shall content myself with some remarks which, owing to the interdependent character of the questions involved, may overlap in some respects:

a Status of women. There is no doubt that partly due to the activities of the United Nations in the field of human rights and the status of women, as well as those of governments, non-governmental organizations and leaders, most of them women, their equality in some countries and the improvement of their condition in others has been accomplished. Yet, as Jessie Bernard says in her remarkable essay, 'The Status of Women in Modern Patterns of Culture', in *The Annals* cited (January 1968), a distinction should be made between enacted rules, such as legislation and administrative regulations, and crescive rules, i.e. mores, custom, traditions and convention. In many countries the political and legal rights of women are constitutionally proclaimed, but not always recognized. The right to equal employment, which is seldom accompanied by equal remuneration, is an example. To the writer the matter is important for two reasons: one because of the growing number of unmarried women with children in developed as well as in developing countries, and the other because of the greater frequency of divorce. A third might be added: the shorter average span of life of males compared with females. All three make women more socio-economically vulnerable than men, and thus more prone to some types of crime. As for tradition, experience shows that in many countries the political and legal equality declared by law is prevented by the still powerful crescive rules. The recent inquiry conducted by Nicole Bernheim shows that in Morocco and Algeria girls, either as students or as employees, although dressed in the Western way, are often forced by the family to wear the veil and avoid contact with males. Even professionals are often handicapped by a series of traditional restrictions. In Algeria, with all her revolutionary impetus, the Family Code is still little more than a project and polygamy and repudiation have not as yet been officially abolished, in spite of the proclaimed equality of men and women. The situation is far better in Tunisia, where women are rapidly moving towards effective equality. In Syria I remember the case of a woman chief of social services in an important town who had to wear the veil every time she had to perform her duties outdoors. I have found similar situations in some Asian and Latin American countries where women are prevented from performing professional activities as soon as tradition and custom are involved. Jessie Bernard raises the important question of the woman's right to privacy and contraception. Both are frequently denied by men, even if they accept political and legal equality. To the writer both are particularly important because their denial contributes to the commission of criminal offences, such as procuring abortion, still regarded by many as a traditional female offence. Promiscuity is taken for granted by many young people in developed countries, but when pregnancy occurs because the male refuses to submit to some precautions he may turn his back, and the alternatives left to the women, usually young and unmarried, are to have an illegitimate child, abortion, infanticide, to abandon the infant or give him in adoption. Even if the latter is made easier or abortion in some cases legalized, the problem is badly solved. Abortion is relatively easy for those with financial means, but they constitute a minority. As for contraception methods, some of them are not easy to get and others not cheap enough, and male co-operation is often refused. Statistical data show that abortion and infanticide prevail among women of the less-privileged classes. The same applies to illegitimacy, and it is in this class that men act more frequently as genuine representatives of crescive rules.

b The role of sex. By itself sex has nothing to do with the legal equality or inequality of men and women; these are conventional creations. What determined the extent and type of participation of women in the socialization process was pregnancy and all that it implies in rearing children, passiveness and limitation of activities and interests. Indeed, female sex and pregnancy are closely related, but contraceptive methods have demonstrated that sexual relations and procreation are two different functions, the total separation of which cannot be excluded if the generation of human beings can be achieved by other methods than copulation. As long as female sex, pregnancy and child-rearing, and to a lesser extent home care, in which men are already participating in developed countries, go together, political and legal equality will be effective only for a minority. This is because the effectiveness of their equality is only relatively compatible with the role performed by the female sex. The results of this relative equality are not very encouraging— not only for women, who often have to give up professional careers, but more significantly for children, who are caught between the two different roles which are seldom performed as they should be. To the objection that the maternal instinct is innate in women, it may be said that not all women possess it and that its lack does not make them abnormal; and, secondly, that, even if phylogenetically rooted as a response, it may disappear or be sublimated by replacing the stimulus. This already occurs when for various reasons women do not have children. In the long run, if sexual relations and generation are separated, the maternal as well as the paternal instinct will fade.

With respect to the sex role, two alternatives seem possible: one to maintain the traditional female role and functions with a more effective political and legal equality, including the rights to privacy and contraception as well as socio-economic equality; and the other to dissociate as much as possible sexual relations, pregnancy and the rearing of children. The first runs contrary to contemporary thinking, but it would be a mistake to discard it on the grounds that it represents the return to old ideas. Actually, if properly developed, it offers many possibilities and deserves consideration by the developing countries, which may become as developed as they wish in this and every other respect. Development does not mean imitation. For the dissociation of sexual relations, pregnancy and the rearing of children the process is more complex. To begin with, it implies total recognition of the right to privacy, which many males in developed countries will resist. The rearing of children is already taking place, especially among women, through a series of services and facilities. As an intermediate solution, the results are not satisfactory. The step to be taken is to hand over the rearing of children from the beginning to special services or agencies, with no intervention from the mother. This will no doubt be resisted by many. Actually, although for different reasons, it was suggested by Plato centuries ago. Pending the suppression of pregnancy by the fertilization of the human ovum outside the body, it is the step which, if supplemented with an effective right to privacy and equal socio-economic opportunity, will bring nearer male and female equality. This means a type of family different from the present one, where the equality of the sexes is more rhetorical than real in most cases as long as women are trying to perform two different tasks at the same time. Pending the 'a-human' suppression of pregnancy, the only thing to do is to relieve them from the rearing of children. The questions raised here need more detailed consideration, but one thing seems certain: in spite of welfare policies and the claimed equality of women, which is mostly in the upper classes, the present structure and functioning of the family, which contribute greatly to the increase of crime, are bound to change radically, whatever well-intentioned attempts are made to maintain them.

c *Female crime*. In dealing with female crime, a distinction should be made between its extent and its forms. It is obvious that the growing participation of women in activities previously monopolized by men and in social life in general has increased the volume of female crime, although it has never equalled male crime—first, because male crime also increases and, secondly, because the traditional female role prevents it. The data already produced for England and Wales demonstrates this. More specifically, the remarkable survey, *Studies of Female Offenders* (Home Office Research Unit, 1967), shows that, although there are some fluctuations, female crime is increasing steadily. In some cases, the analysis of data tends to support the thesis that this increase is due more to the socio-economic vulnerability of women than to anything else. This is particularly noticeable in the groups over 40 years of age. Of course, other factors must be taken into account, but in all probability that vulnerability is the most significant. In France a study conducted years ago and made available to the writer by Interpol shows that during the years 1955 and 1965 crime, including police and gendarmerie data, has steadily increased, but the increase among males is greater than among females. As for female juvenile offenders, a remarkable study conducted by the Centre of Research of Vaucresson shows that between 1953 and 1966 the volume of juvenile delinquency remained in the region of 4,000 every year.

It is true that police and courts are sometimes more lenient to women than to men, but the margins are too wide to be explained away so simply. It is probably true that it is more difficult to detect women in minor offences, such as small thefts and larceny from shops and stalls and some forms of fraud, but not in the case of serious offences, which, after all, are more important. What prevents detection in many cases is the smallness of the illegal appropriation, which is not reported because it is covered by insurance. The same happens with men in cases of larceny from houses and factories and from automatic machines and meters, as well as in frauds by agents, in which they far exceed women. Leniency by the police is only exercised in minor offences, and the same applies to men, although perhaps to a lesser extent. The leniency of the courts does not affect the number of offences known, but the greater use they make of suspended sentences, probation, fines and short-term imprisonment in favour of women.

The forms of crime traditionally assigned to women are abortion, infanticide, abandonment of infants, prostitution, theft and frauds. In developing countries, insults and defamation are also frequent. In the same way as the expression *cherchez la femme* is used to explain some male criminal offences, *cherchez l'homme* may explain many cases of abortion, infanticide and abandonment. Actually, in some cases the abortion has been envisaged in advance by both man and woman, and if not the male partner often provides the address or the money or both to procure the abortion. The fact that abortion has to be performed on women, and often by themselves or by another woman in the less-privileged groups, does not make it a typical female offence. Moreover, in some countries doctors, seldom women, specialize in abortion, whether in the country of residence of the women or in another where legislation is more tolerant or progressive. It is not true that abortion is difficult to detect; more often than not a number of persons know about it, but are reluctant to say anything, even in countries where religious beliefs are very much against it. Unless socio-economic reasons are admitted as a ground for abortion, the present legalization will reduce but not eradicate illegal abortion; it continues in both Sweden and Japan.[54]

Only countries, such as the United States, which are still not parties to the United Nations Convention of 1950 regard prostitutes as criminal offenders. Since prostitution is a crime *à deux*, it is difficult to understand why only the woman is punished. The practice introduced in New York City some years ago of prosecuting men as well as women and the small number of men prosecuted shows how strong the crescive rules are. In brothel-keeping women usually outnumber men, but are in turn outnumbered in the traffic in persons and the exploitation of prostitution. In this respect, financing prostitution, one of the main activities of organized crime, is almost exclusively a male undertaking. In 1967, according to the *Uniform Crime Reports,* the percentage of women in commercialized vice and prostitution was 77. The amalgamation of both offences so clearly separated by the above-mentioned Convention gives a distorted picture of reality. In fact, in the United States commercialized vice is mostly a male preserve. In Britain the Street Offences Act, 1959, makes a 'common prostitute' of any woman who loiters in a street after a warning by a policeman. As has been said, the Act has merely 'swept under the carpet' something that should have been faced up to. By creating this curious type of offence, the crescive rules, which in most cases favour males, won a victory on behalf of what is commonly known as public morality. In 1967, 2,422 women were found guilty as 'common prostitutes' at the magistrates courts, but only 10 men for aiding, etc., offences by prostitutes. Needless to say, the less-privileged, fortunate or intelligent prostitutes constitute the majority of the short-termers sent to prison. This I was able to ascertain during my visit to Holloway in 1968. The frauds committed by women are increasing, but as a rule are far less serious than those committed by men.

Although not a typical female offence, cruelty to children is more frequent among women than among men, and this in spite of the more tender character assigned to maternal instincts. Whether the greater number of women offenders is due to personal characteristics of the mother involved, socio-economic conditions, that the child was unwanted or is difficult, or that there are too many cannot be discussed here. In all probability, each case involves a series of factors the action of which cannot easily be prevented without long assistance, supervision, etc. What is obvious is that generally the cases are more frequent among the less-privileged classes. Statistically their number is small, but in all probability the dark figure runs into the thousands even in developed countries. This touches the question whether, if known, criminal sanctions should be applied to those who ill-treat children. The answer is not easy, since the term 'battered children' is sometimes loosely interpreted. If by 'battering' is understood more than bruises, it is obvious that a criminal offence has been committed. The reasoning put forward that family life is highly emotional, that criminal law can destroy instead of rebuilding a child's family relationship— already destroyed in many cases—that guilt is difficult to prove, etc., cannot be entertained, first, because in one way or another many criminal offences imply the same if not greater emotional involvement, secondly, because criminal law is supposed to protect anyone, particularly the defenceless person brutally attacked, thirdly, because the hypothetical rebuilding will be difficult to achieve or merely temporary, and, finally, because the effectiveness of criminal law may not protect a child as it should while protecting many others who are victims of brutal parents. In this respect, whatever is said to the contrary, criminal law, like any other sort of regulation, has a preventive effect which, although not absolute, acts in many cases. Moreover, the condition of parent carries no privilege. The solution would be that as soon as battered children are detected, they should be taken away by the social services and criminal proceedings instituted later. I do not see any benefit for the child to keep him terrorized with the parents while these are convinced that they should be nice to him and the conditions generating the battering, some of them not easy to solve or requiring a long time, are remedied. The thesis that family environment is better than any other or that certain homes may be rebuilt should be revised, not for the benefit of criminal law or of the family, but of the individual, particularly when it is a child.

d Bio-psychological characteristics. Although some of the characteristics of the opposite sex remain in men and women, each of them presents bio-psychological differences and contrasts which partly explain their diverse participation in crime. According to Anthony Barnett (*The Human Species* 3rd Ed., 1968), women do not reach their high level of sexual activity until much later than men, commonly in the thirties, and later in life they are potentially more active than men. On the other hand, he adds, some women, but few men, seem able to live contentedly with little or no sexual outlet. Physically, men are heavier in size and shape than women, usually taller, with greater muscular strength and on the average have a higher metabolic rate. Intellectually, women seem less able than men in activities requiring analytical, enterprising or aggressive attitudes, such as mathematics, engineering, banking, big business, and trade and legal and related activities. In political matters they are as good or bad as men. On the other hand, in social and some economic matters they are more realistically-minded, have a greater sense of security and responsibility and are better equipped to face problems or situations. Women are more prone than men to mental illness, a condition which some think would increase their quota of crime if they were not institutionalized or taken care of: this is true. In Britain the *Annual Report* of the National Association for Mental Health for 1967–8 states that 'One in every nine women and one in every fourteen men in this country can expect to spend part of her or his life in a mental hospital'. But this does not mean that the crime gap is explained by the fact that more women than men are kept in institutions, since the connection between mental illness and crime is minor. Moreover, there is no correlation between the peak of female crime and the prevailing ages of women institutionalized for mental reasons. That any mental condition affects every aspect of behaviour is an assertion that some schools of thought maintain, but others deny. As for the expression 'taken care of' by mental care, the fact is that many of the women are released without actually being taken care of in the proper way, owing to lack of personnel and other facilities. Yet when released there is no proof that these women are more prone to crime than others.

Whether the different male and female characteristics can be explained genetically or by environmental factors or both is irrelevant here. What they show is neither superiority nor inferiority, but diversity, and that this diversity explains more than anything else the different extent as well as the less violent forms of female crime. Briefly, women are far less aggressive than men; all statistical data show that the number of violent offences committed by females is far less than that of men, and that this is not affected by lenient attitudes or detection difficulties. The following table shows this:

United States: arrests for violent crimes,
'Uniform Crime Reports', 1967

Offence	Total	Male	Female	Percentage (round figures)
Murder and non-negligent murder	9,145	7,650	1,495	16
Robbery	59,789	56,689	3,100	5
Aggravated assault	107,192	93,343	13,849	13
Vandalism	109,299	102,540	6,759	6

In Mexico, another country where violence is a normal feature of life and not a subcultural characteristic, according to Artemio

Niño Galván's *Epidemiologia del homicidio en México* (1965), which is probably one of the best inquiries on the matter so far made in that country, between 1928 and 1963 230,432 persons were apprehended for homicide, of whom only 7,392, or 3 per cent, were women. Of those sentenced for murder in the same period, only 2 per cent were women. As far as leniency is concerned, it should be noted that while nearly 50 per cent of those arrested for homicide were not convicted, only about 30 per cent of women were acquitted. In India, where violence and murder are also widespread, although proportionally less than in the United States and Mexico, the interesting study by S. Venugopal Rao, *Murder* (Ministry of Home Affairs, 1968), shows that out of 12,310 murders reported in 1965 only between 6 and 7 per cent were committed by women. Briefly, even if violence is a typical characteristic of daily life, women are far less affected than men. In England and Wales in 1967 out of 63 persons found guilty of murder only 1 was female. In the same year the male-female ratio of persons found guilty of crimes of violence against the person was, in round figures, 18 to 1, and in breaking and entering 40 to 1.

The final query is whether the dissociation of the female sex, pregnancy, rearing of children and related subordinated tasks, if achieved, will bring female crime to the same level as male crime? With respect to crime in general, in all probability the gap will become small enough to be regarded as virtually closed. For violent forms of crime the answer is that, whatever her competition with men within a real socio-economic and legal and political equality, woman's bio-genetic formula will prevent criminal parity. The answers do not imply that crime may be explained by bio-psychological factors only, but that some crimes may be explained more readily by them than by others.

6 Age-groups and crime

The age-group distribution of crime has been deprecated by some authors, owing to the many variables involved in the age-crime ratio. That the variables are numerous and complex cannot be denied. On the other hand, in spite of its limitations, the age distribution of crime is reliable enough to draw some valid conclusions, establish useful projections and formulate within reasonable limits effective criminal policies and programmes. Some hazard is involved, but no more than in similar techniques used by other policies. After all, not even in the natural sciences is it possible to operate with complete certitude when a particular factor is seriated in order to establish some relationships between the series and a particular phenomenon. Certainly population statistics are not always as good as they should be, but pending further improvement, they have to be used. The same may be said of criminal statistics. Leslie T. Wilkins is right when he says in *Social Deviance* (1964): 'It is often claimed that statistics are misleading or that figures can be found to support any argument. It is true that figures can be misleading, but more often the figures are correct enough; it is their use which is misleading.' In other words, the age distribution of crime makes possible a better understanding of crime as a social phenomenon and permits projections which undoubtedly have a policy-making value. Certain comparisons between countries should be avoided. As for the countries themselves, the age-crime distribution should always be accompanied by some explanation about the socio-economic and other roles played by the groups under consideration. Significant in this respect is the different meaning of age when applied to a population in general and to different groups in particular.[55]

Individually, age means not only a length of time, but also a socio-economic and political status and activity, different ways of living, personal characteristics, conflicts and aims of a changeable nature and a certain amount of contentment, success or failure. In sum, it means a diversity of attitudes and reactions to the daily challenge of life. All this is present in age groups at large, but the ageing process of the population as a whole differs from that of individuals and groups as separate units. To begin with, the age of a population is determined by that of the different groups. This means that in each population there is a constant process of rejuvenation which does not occur in age-groups and even less in individuals. Age-groups and individuals are replaced, but not rejuvenated. On the other hand, a population becomes younger even if the number of aged persons increases, provided that at the same time the number of young persons increases more rapidly. This is what is happening at present in many developing countries in which children and young persons under 19 years of age constitute about 50 per cent of the population. *Prima facie*, in view of the growing rejuvenation of crime, this would mean that juvenile crime is greater in developing than in developed countries. As will be seen later, the answer does not lie only in the numerical amount of young people, but in other factors also. In sum, age structure and crime are closely related, but in order to be understood their relationship has to be studied in the light of the corresponding socio-economic and political system. The system is to some extent determined by the composition of the different age-groups and their respective roles, but as a structure the system prevails over the attitudes of age-groups in capitalist as well as in socialist countries. This strength, however, is at present challenged by young groups in some of these countries, who claim a greater participation in the shaping and functioning of the system. In this respect, the theses of capitalist and socialist thinking of which an excellent exposé may be found in *The Determinants and Consequences of Population Trends,* cited in note No. 55, have been badly shattered by contemporary events. As far as crime is concerned, there is little doubt that the welfare concept of delinquency cannot be maintained, and unless the system is radically changed in both types of countries juvenile crime will become more serious.

With regard to England and Wales, the data below give an idea of the importance of the age groups in crime:

1959–67: Males

Age-group	Estimated number in each group during the whole period	Average number per 100,000 found guilty of indictable offences
Under 14	16,016,000	1,462
14 and under 17	9,753,000	2,786
17 and under 21	12,178,000	2,518
21 and under 30	24,333,000	1,514
30 and over	112,513,000	339

1959–67: Females

Under 14	15,176,000	47
14 and under 17	10,110,000	378
17 and under 21	11,923,000	276
21 and under 30	23,898,000	176
30 and over	128,550,000	23

Since in 1964 the age of criminal responsibility was raised from 8 to 10, the data from 1950–63 and 1964 onwards are not strictly comparable. Yet they are illustrative enough to draw some tentative conclusions for policy-making purposes. By raising the age of criminal responsibility, the group under 14 has been considerably reduced, a fact which should be kept in mind in evaluating its contribution to crime.

For specific indictable offences the following table is significant:

Violence against the person

Under 17		17–21		21–30		30 and over	
M.	*F.*	*M.*	*F.*	*M.*	*F.*	*M.*	*F.*
14,179	650	31,753	782	38,048	1,860	27,300	2,623

Sexual offences

9,418	25	9,138	39	11,809	107	22,297	167

Receiving, frauds and false pretences

25,592	3,144	16,434	2,403	32,939	3,619	49,774	7,149

Breaking and entering

164,100	5,184	78,145	1,840	80,047	1,186	40,801	761

Larceny

271,881	48,516	161,911	27,333	200,714	33,010	223,566	91,824

During the period 1959–67 1,813,141 persons were found guilty of indictable offences. The percentages of the different age groups are as follows:

	Percentage
Under 14	14
14–17	17
17–21	19
21–30	23
Over 30	27
	——
	100
	——

In 1967 the percentages were:

Under 14	10
14–17	15
17–21	22
21–30	25
Over 30	28
	——
	100
	——

In 1967 the estimate of the population aged 10 and under 30 years was about 22 per cent of the total, but their share in the number of persons found guilty of indictable offences was about 72 per cent.

For the period 1964–67, in which the age of criminal responsibility was fixed at 10 years, the prevailing decreasing order of the contribution to crime of the different groups of persons found guilty of indictable offences in magistrates courts and assizes and quarter sessions courts was as follows:

1964–67

Magistrates courts		Assizes and quarter sessions courts	
M.	*F.*	*M.*	*F.*
21–30	21–30	21–30	21–30
17–21	14–17	17–21	17–21
14–17	30–40	30–40	30–40
Under 14	17–21	40–50	40–50
30–40	40–50	50–60	50–60
40–50	50–60	14–17	14–17
50–60	Under 14	Under 14	Over 60
Over 60	Over 60	Over 60	Under 14

I say prevailing because, apart from possible error, there are some fluctuations. Thus in 1964, when the age of criminal responsibility was raised to 10, the male 14–17 age-group was the second and the group under 14 was fourth. In 1967, the male 30–40 group was fourth and the group under 14 fifth; for females, the fluctuations do not substantially alter the order given.

The data refer to persons found guilty, and not to police statistics. This means that the actual number of offenders was larger, and that the participation of the different groups might be different if police data were considered. In all probability, the greatest beneficiaries of the system of judicial statistics are the juveniles, and especially the females. Yet the judicial data are good enough to draw some tentative conclusions:

a Crime is mostly a male problem to a great extent confined to the 14–40 age-range, the greatest concentration taking place in the 21–30 age-group, followed by the 17–21 group. In the magistrates courts, which deal with the vast majority of indicted persons—in 1967 about 90 per cent of all persons found guilty of indictable offences were sentenced by them—the 14–17 and under-14 groups are the fourth and fifth. Their place, however, is taken at the assizes and quarter sessions courts by the 30–40 and 40–50 groups respectively, partly due to procedural and jurisdictional reasons because of the gravity of the offences involved. Occasionally, the type of offence may alter the order given by bringing forward a particular group. This happens with vandalism, in which the under-14 group surpasses all others. Other offences are concentrated in a wide age-range. This is the case with murder, the bulk of which is in the 17–40 range, but more particularly in the 21–25 age-group. This finding does not essentially differ from those of Terence Morris and Louis Blom-Cooper in their remarkable study, *A Calendar of Murder* (1964).

b The downward trend begins in the 30–40 age-group and is already very marked in the 40–50 age-group.

c For males, the lowest group is the over-60s. Among females, the over-60s rank higher than the under-14-years in the case of serious offences. Recent figures point to a steady increase of the contribution to crime in the oldest group. The same is happening in other countries. This is to be expected, owing to the expanding span of life and all it implies, particularly among women, whose average span is longer than that of men. On the other hand. for the time being their criminality will not be more serious than it is at present. What is certain is that in the long run the growing span of life will change some of the patterns of the present age-group scale and with it some aspects of criminal policy.

d For females, like males, the greatest contribution to crime is made by the 21–30 age-group, followed by the 14–17 in the magistrates courts and the 17–21 in the assizes and quarter sessions courts. In both the 30–40 age-group is the third. The reversal of the groups under 14 and over 60 in magistrates courts and assizes and quarter sessions courts confirms the typical characteristics of female crime, which are also visible when the order of female groups is compared with male groups, characteristics about which enough has been said when sex and crime were discussed.

What are the roles of these age-groups which explain their different contribution to crime as a social phenomenon? The following explanations are submitted:

a As a group, the 21–30 is the most crucial, since it constitutes the passage from young to definite adulthood with all the finality which that implies, whatever changes may take place later. To men as well as women it means the period in which, for better or worse, assertiveness and aggressiveness play a role in laying the foundations of the future. Any change in these foundations, even if eventually successful, implies new difficulties, disappointments and conflicts. It is the period in which family, professional, economic and social aims and purposes appear, if not yet well defined, more pressing and demanding of more prompt solutions than at a later stage of life, in which problems and difficulties are taken more calmly. Needs, antagonism, security and effort may be regarded as the main elements of this period of life. Even if the new generations understand them in a different way, they will still play their determinant role, whatever degree of rebelliousness and dissatisfaction are displayed. Eventually life imposes itself, and some sort of adaptation begins to take place, but not without serious resistance and negative attitudes against the prohibitions of a legitimate order which has to be reckoned with. Yet before this is done criminal law has frequently been broken. It is in this period that youth fades away and the need for a stable future asserts itself, hence the importance of chance and risk to ensure it and the greater number of criminal offences committed.

b As the second most important age-group, 17–21 is a mixture of resentment, illusion and rebelliousness because, more often than not, the young person feels cheated and unprepared for the task looming in front of him. The rebelliousness is marked because the permissiveness he has until then enjoyed brings him into frequent conflict with a world for which no appropriate image was offered him. The search for a job or the pursuance of further study constitute a new source of conflict and negative attitudes. Often the job is not what is wanted. As for higher study, the open-door policy of our time is indeed promising, but in a number of cases young people feel they are not equipped to go ahead. Whether this policy is democratic or not will not be discussed here. Suffice it to say that it is based on a principle of equal aptitude which does not exist. Furthermore, socio-economically as well as politically it is disrupting and a waste of time and effort. Everybody has the right to protest and to participate. On the other hand, the open-door policy of access to college or university has not only debased the quality of both, but inflated the student body, at present made up of a large number of young persons well aware that they will never succeed as real students. The result is a type of student who wants to reform everything and is not equipped to do so. To the writer there is no doubt that present educational policies in many countries have contributed to the increase of individual failure at a young age. The process has been going on for years, but it is only now that the cumulative effect is seen. This is not an argument against higher education or its accessibility to those able to benefit from it, but mostly against the system, of which present college and university organizations are a part. In sum, whether as worker or student, the role forced upon the juvenile group is the greatest source of juvenile crime. It is in this period that the person officially regarded as a 'child' or a 'child in trouble' faces things of which he has no idea, for the simple reason that he has been kept in a world of his own, completely invented by distinguished professionals and public officials and accepted by no less distinguished policy-makers. Bio-psychologically, young people in many cases represent the maximum that the individual will ever reach. Yet between them and the system there is an enormous gap, because the latter persists in regarding them as something apart. The claim that physical and psychological maturity are at present more separate than ever before, and that this is the reason why juveniles are less responsible and more criminal, misses the point that what is involved is a political and socio-economic process. Physically and psychologically, juveniles are sufficiently well equipped to understand the fundamentals of individual and social life and act accordingly. Juveniles as a group are playing a greater role than ever, but it is doubtful whether they are fully prepared for it. It is in this general unpreparedness that the high index of crime of this particular age-group has its roots. Fun still plays a part in it, because they were brought up to permissiveness and the lack of discipline, a sense of social solidarity or responsibility. Socio-economically, the 17–21 age-group is to a great extent parasitical. Its most tangible contribution to society is that it is the second most important group from the point of view of crime. The fact that the female 14–17 age-group is the second in the case of less serious offences does not significantly alter the conclusion.

c For the 14–17 age-group, the criminal category of which varies according to sex and type of crime, but which occupies a prominent rank, its members are the typical inhabitants of the artificial juvenile world. The expansion of vandalism and other violent offences against persons and property are better explained by the widespread permissiveness of that world created by a series of medico-psychological assertions. As a group this is the most parasitical of all—even more than the under-14s, from whom far less should be expected. They are the beneficiaries of a series of policies and programmes in which the consideration of the fundamental values of society are seldom if ever considered and yet, like the 17–21 age-group, their most marked contribution to society is crime. It is not suggested that this group or any other should be socio-economically and politically regimented, but that sociologically they should be taught to adhere to fundamental social values and standards. This should not be asking too much, but it can only be achieved if the present educational system is radically changed. The main question involved in the criminality of this group is not the unsettling effect of pre-puberty and puberty changes, which are exaggerated and could be reduced to a minimum with an educational system with greater social content and purpose. This will not be achieved by raising the school-leaving age to 16: the only effect of this will be to increase the already serious frustration of the juvenile generations. I share H. Mannheim's misgivings about the beneficial effects of a rise in the school-leaving age; furthermore in England and Wales it is very doubtful that by 1973–74 the necessary number of teachers—already seriously deficient—will be available. The latest prediction is that by that time the deficit will be no less than 20,000. As long as the last years of school as well as those of college and university are not combined with some kind of work, whatever is done will be delusory. My own experience is that the enlarging of educational programmes will merely postpone problems which should be solved at an earlier stage, and that the maturing process will not be improved.

d The decline of crime, which begins in the last years of the 30–40 age-period, is mostly due to the fact that it is then that family and professional or occupational roles are to a great extent settled, although not always satisfactorily from an individual point of view. By then work or professional activity constitute a daily pattern of life, and more responsibility must be faced. Whatever has been said to the contrary, there is a close connection between sense of responsibility and the decrease of crime.

One of the problems that will affect all age-groups, but more especially those in the 10–40 range, is the use of leisure time, which for many reasons is increasing and will increase still more. Leisure time and crime, particularly among juvenile and young people, are closely related. If leisure is used for entertainment which is in the hands of private initiative, it will accelerate the present process of depersonalization already promoted by technology. Not that these should be rejected, but an improvement should be made in the way in which they are used to reduce contact among human beings. Too much leisure time coupled with a welfare sense of security leads to boredom. In this respect the comments of Georges Guéron, quoted by Fourastié (*op. cit.*, p. 174), are significant.

215

According to him '*le phénomène suédois*', even if exaggerated, shows that complete stability entails the risk of provoking beyond boredom the pure psychopathic act as well as the gratuitous delinquency for the sole purpose of damaging or destroying.

In the United States crime committed by persons under 25 years of age has been steadily increasing for years past. The *Uniform Crime Reports* for 1966 and 1967 show that the greater proportion of arrests is of persons under 25 years. In both years in decreasing order the greatest contributors were the 16-, 17-, 18-, 15-, 19- and 20-year-olds, followed by the 21-year-olds. On the other hand, the criminality of the 13-14 age-group has been rapidly increasing. The second most important concentration takes place in the 24–44 age-range, with the greatest percentage in the 25–29, followed by the 40–44 age group. From 45 years onwards the percentages decline rapidly. It is significant, however, that the arrests of persons over 50 have also been increasing during the last few years.

In France the decreasing order of the different age groups is as follows:

1959–1963: Persons Sentenced

Delits		Crimes	
M.	F.	M.	F.
20 & under 30	40 & under 60	20 & under 30	20 & under 30
30 & under 40	30 & under 40	30 & under 40	30 & under 40
40 & under 60	20 & under 30	40 & under 60	40 & under 60
Under 20	60 and over	Under 20	Under 20
60 and over	Under 20	60 and over	60 and over

In his interesting study, *Pour une Politique du Crime* (1966), Georges Picca points out the rejuvenation of crime in France, that the number of juvenile offenders indicted before the courts doubled between 1954 and 1964, and that of every two sentenced prisoners one is under 30 years of age. The same rejuvenation and the increase of crime among those under 25 years of age is stressed by G. Stefani, G. Levasseur and R. Jambu-Merlin in their *Criminologie et Science Pénitentiaire*, (1968), with the important remarks that crime is concentrated in the 18–35 range, that from the latter limit onwards crime decreases—although less rapidly among females—and that the criminal-age pyramid is more flattened out than that of the general population.

216

In the Federal Republic of Germany, according to police statistics, the criminality of those under 21 years of age, with some fluctuations, has been steadily increasing for the last fifteen years. In 1967 persons under 21 years of age identified by the police as authors of criminal offences were 27 per cent of the total, while the estimate for 1954 was 18 per cent. Yet to the writer the analysis of data conveys the impression that in terms of population percentages the situation is not as serious as in other developed countries.

In Yugoslavia in 1964 the decreasing age-group order of persons sentenced by all courts was as follows:

M.	F.
30–39	30–39
25–29	40–49
40–49	25–29
50–59	50–59
21–24	21–24
18–20	60 and over
60 and over	18–20

Other countries show similar although not identical trends. It is to be regretted that Swedish *Kriminalstatistk* (*Polis-statistik*) contain no reference to age-groups other than that concerning the offences committed by juveniles under 15 years of age, which, although significant, do not allow comparisons with any other group. The mention is made for no other reason than that Sweden being a highly developed country with a well-developed welfare system, it would have been extremely convenient to have included her in the exposé made here.

The data presented are taken from statistics of different sorts, all affected by the shortcomings inherent in any statistical presentation. Certainly police and judicial statistics offer two different views of the extent of crime and the age-groups involved, yet between them there is always a correlation. They are reliable enough to compare trends and draw some general conclusions quite adequate for policy purposes aimed primarily at the prevention and control of crime as a social phenomenon. The general conclusions are the following:

a   As a predominantly male social phenomenon crime is mostly concentrated in the 10–40-years range;
b   Juvenile and young person crime, including females, is steadily increasing in the 14–25 years range; and
c   the rejuvenation of crime is partly due to the rejuvenation of

217

the population in many countries and to the growing role of juvenile and young persons in every aspect of life, not only as far as they themselves are concerned, but also in connection with other groups and society at large.

Although in a different way, the rejuvenation of crime raises a serious challenge to developed as well as developing countries. In the developed countries the growing role of juvenile people will be far more significant than their numerical growth. In the developing countries the factors are reversed, in the sense that the impact of the number of juvenile people is generally greater than the impact of their role.

According to projections, in the developed countries the proportion of persons under 14 years of age would actually be reduced from 29 to 26 per cent of the population in the period 1960–2000. More specifically, in the European countries the percentages of persons aged 15–24 in the 15–64 range would be 24 and 23 in 1980 and 2000 respectively. In northern European countries the percentages would be 23 and 22 respectively. With respect to the United Kingdom, these averages do not differ greatly from 1967, according to the population estimates of that year. Yet the increasing role of youth as well as the trends of crime allow the tentative conclusion that by 1980 the amount of crime will in all probability be doubled, and by 2000 trebled. Certainly many things may happen to prevent this, but there might be others which would make the increase still bigger. One of the methods of reducing crime is to abolish the criminal character of a series of acts. Undoubtedly some revision has to be made, inasmuch as some portions of criminal law in Britain and elsewhere are obsolete. In a timid way this was done in England and Wales by the Criminal Law Act, 1967, ch. 58, which abolished champerty but not embracery, being a barrator and the like. More drastic would be the adoption of the 'children in trouble' policy, advocated by the White Papers, which, without abolishing offences, would abolish the sense of social responsibility in a substantial part of the population. To what has already been said against this failure to protect society at large I would add that the State has no right to offer society as a propitiatory victim for any groups, whatever the desire to protect the latter. Such a policy may be defended and adopted, but if this is done the State should commit itself to indemnify the victims of the so-called 'children in trouble'. In other words, the protection and care of one group cannot be undertaken at the expense of other groups. The protection of 'children in trouble' involves far more than their supporters have in mind.

The rejuvenation of crime in developing countries will create a more critical situation: first, because of the rapid rejuvenation of their population; and, secondly, because, apart from other reasons, through an imitative process already evident, juvenile people will try to play a greater role than that played up to now. In the less-developed regions the percentage of persons under 15 years of age will decrease from 40 to 35 in the period 1960–2000, which represents a certain advantage. On the other hand, the proportion of persons aged 15–24 per 100 persons aged 15–64 in some African and Latin American countries will be almost 38 per cent by 1980, and in others 37 per cent by 2000. The following data for a few selected countries may give an idea of the magnitude of the problem unless present policies are radically changed:

1980: Medium Assumption (in thousands round figures: males only)

Country	15–29 age-groups	30–44 age-groups
Mexico	10,343	6,422
Brazil	14,904	9,025
Peru	2,841	1,637
Venezuela	1,606	943
Argentina	3,211	2,529
Chile	1,300	853
Ceylon	2,356	1,429
Indonesia	19,090	11,041
Philippines	6,748	3,878
Thailand	5,639	3,299

The quality of the censuses on which these assumptions are based varies, but although the figures cannot be uncritically accepted, they still constitute a good point of reference which governments should not ignore. This fast rejuvenation of the population will be accompanied by an economic growth, greater urbanization and internal migration, an expanding educational system with accompanying intensified intellectual and political protest, political instability and a general improvement of material living conditions, but a growing gap between rich and poor. In the meantime, developing countries will benefit from the less parasitical character of the juvenile groups, especially in the rural areas. Some years ago in countries like Turkey, India, Thailand, Peru and the United Arab Republic, children and juvenile people constituted a substantial part of the economic force. In some of them it was considered that at least a fifth of the juveniles between 10 and 14 years of age were part of this force, while in the United States, New Zealand and Sweden the corresponding proportion was less than 4 per cent. But the expansion of juvenile crime in these three countries and the fact that it is less serious in those mentioned above cannot be explained only in terms of economic occupation. On the other hand, liberation from this occupation with nothing to take its place helps to explain the juvenile crime in countries in which the juvenile and young adult population is mostly parasitical. Here again we see that, however high the level of material conditions of living in developed countries, this has not been accompanied by a decrease in juvenile crime.

Is there any way of establishing the percentage of persons who will become offenders? Not yet with reasonable certitude, but the question is one that criminology should try to answer as accurately as possible. It is a question I have frequently been asked, and to which a definite answer was often expected, especially in developing countries. Putting aside professional, organized and habitual crime, as well as crime committed under cover of official position, which are separate problems, according to my research on the matter I should say that almost everyone sooner or later commits a criminal offence. Whether sooner or later depends to a great extent on the type of offence. For trivial offences, the most usual age is in the 40s in most countries, or perhaps in the early 50s in the developed countries. Many offences as well as many offenders are of a kind that society can withstand without serious disturbance; many of them remain undetected or, if detected, unreported. In all probability from 10 to 15 per cent of the population come in contact with the machinery of criminal justice, although not all require its full application. On the other hand, this criminal population is not evenly distributed as far as age is concerned. This means that in all probability between 5 and 8 per cent of the persons included in the age-range 15–40 will come into contact with this machinery. In the way it is now organized, it cannot handle the present offenders and therefore will be even less able to handle them in 1980 or 2000.

The last point to be examined here is the thesis of 'delinquent generations' raised somewhat dramatically in Britain, New Zealand and other countries. Leslie T. Wilkins, in his excellent piece of statistical research, *Delinquent Generations* (Home Office Research Unit, 1960), implied their existence. Obviously there is a relationship between generations born in certain periods of time and circumstances and their eventual participation in crime. The relationship with 'proneness to crime' is far more difficult to establish because of the ambiguity of the term 'proneness'; many people prone to crime are no more prone to it than to any other form of asocial or antisocial behaviour. Yet the relationship between generations and delinquency has not as yet been demonstrated: first, because the term 'generation' embraces far more than a cluster of cases, and the term 'delinquency' is vague enough to include what is not actually criminal. A close analysis of Wilkins' work shows that his conclusion does not go beyond the assertion that some birth years are associated with excessive criminality, which is correct, but does not demonstrate the existence of delinquent generations. In fact, as he says, his study 'raises more problems than it solves'. Even in countries like the United States and Sweden where juvenile delinquency is greater than in Britain, it would be difficult to maintain the existence of delinquent generations. The question has been brought up because in criminology, as in any other branch of knowledge, certain phrases become very popular without an adequate foundation and are used to undertake further research or to formulate policies which are not justified.

7 Migration and crime

The term 'migration' is somewhat vague; to the writer it means the change of residence for a substantial time or on a permanent basis in order to find work or to start a new life. The definition differs from those currently accepted, because in the last twenty years migration has acquired characteristics which make it difficult to accept the distinction between coerced and non-coerced migration and to explain the latter for economic and social reasons; these play a role, but political reasons are also involved. In the past political reasons were frequently overshadowed by the poor economic and social condition of migrants; this is the case of displaced persons and political refugees. More recently, the relationship between migrant workers and crime has been studied in Britain, Switzerland, the Federal Republic of Germany and by the Council of Europe.[56]

An analysis of some relevant inquiries shows that certain conclusions are dictated more by emotional attitudes than by an objective appraisal of facts. This is the case with the assertion that the high criminality of foreign labour migrants is a xenophobic myth. A dispassionate appraisal of facts shows that their higher criminality in certain offences is as real as that of the nationals in others. To cite an example: in 1967 in the Federal Republic of Germany police statistics show that the percentages of foreigners, many of them migrant workers, in the case of murder, attempted murder and bodily injury, is out of proportion with their number,

221

but the same applies to Germans when the figures for some sexual offences, certain types of bodily injury and offences against property are considered. The crime migration problem is an inflated problem, actually of modest dimensions when compared with the benefits that workers' migration brings into the country concerned. This may be regarded as outside the criminological field, but in fact it is part of it, since the incorporation of a substantial number of aliens into a country, even if on a temporary basis, necessarily implies an increase of certain crimes. The German statistics show that as a rule the higher percentages belong to Turks, Italians, Yugoslavs and Greeks, all, in principle, representatives of different cultures. I say in principle, because in many cases they do not represent culture of any sort, but only extremely poor living conditions. In fact, cultural or subcultural elements play a modest role when it is remembered that the same statistical data show that Americans occasionally exceed Italians in the commission of certain offences, and that most of them are visitors or members of the American Forces.

Should a theory of crime migration be evolved or further research pursued? With respect to a theory of crime migration, the basic element, a general theory of migration, is lacking. Among others, E. S. Lee, in 'Theory of Migration', in *Demography,* iii (1966), tried to produce one by saying that the characteristics of migrants tend to be intermediate between the characteristics of the population at origin and the population at destination. The thesis cannot be entertained, since it is difficult to envisage when and how that curious intermediate condition is acquired. Experience shows that migrants maintain some of their original characteristics, lose others and acquire some, but in most cases no amalgamation takes place. Old and new characteristics co-exist, and this co-existence may sometimes lead to as well as prevent crime. Certainly it would be difficult to apply this thesis to migrant workers, because in most countries they are allowed to remain for only short periods, usually not more than ten months or a year, and to come back. Many of them go to other countries and later still to others, returning after two or three years to the first one. Sometimes they go back home and return to the same country or go to another. In these conditions the acquisition of an intermediate set of characteristics is not possible. In fact, this restrictive policy, instead of reducing what might be called criminogenic effects of migration, will, in all probability increase them, since the difficulties of adaptation are repeated even if the migrant is an old hand, because he may be sent to a different area and take another job in less favourable surroundings and conditions. Economic competition between migrants and native workers, even if the former are confined to unskilled or semi-skilled jobs, is unavoidable. Unemployed, sick or disabled migrants create problems aggravated by language difficulties, racial discrimination, political propaganda, etc. Crime and anti-social behaviour on the part of migrants who either do not feel a strong attachment to the new country, especially when they know they have to leave after a certain period of time, or who break down mentally under the strain of making their way in a strange environment the most frequent feature of which is discrimination, raise further problems for the receiving country. All this was pointed out by the United Nations study on *The Determinants and Consequences of Population Trends* already mentioned. On the other hand, migrants are often propitiatory victims of many criminal offences, particularly violation of human rights and bodily injury, the latter often perpetrated by young offenders partly misled by political assertions. Such is the case with the 'skin-heads' in England.

The answer to the higher or lower criminality of migrant workers cannot be found in the study of all the hypotheses and mechanisms dealing with criminogenetic processes and differential personality patterns involved, since the results yielded by this operational criminology benefit only those in charge of it by promoting further peripheral research. The explanation has to be sought in the greater role that chance and risk play in the behaviour of migrant workers. Certainly, both elements may be affected by some personal factors, but generally they operate independently, owing to a series of unfavourable circumstances by which these workers are surrounded. The thesis may be formulated as follows: the probability of the happening of an event—here crime—is the ratio of the number and magnitude of circumstances favourable to that event to the total number of possible circumstances. Without going into causes, the number of circumstances favourable to crime surrounding migrant workers is greater than the number of those surrounding nationals. This means that in some cases the crime of migrant workers may be regarded as an 'accident', and the only way to reduce their contribution to certain forms of crime is to reduce the number and magnitude of surrounding circumstances favourable to crime.

The migrant may or may not be the spearhead of something desirable. As a rule, he is neither better nor worse than the national of the country of destination and should be accepted as equal, particularly when his work is needed. It is unjust to discriminate against them by exploiting them, keeping them apart or depriving them of benefits or assistance to which workers are entitled. It should not be forgotten that migrants are subject to close scrutiny by everybody and even closer supervision by the police. Proneness to certain offences does not make the members of a particular ethnic group more criminal than others, and if the receiving countries want to reduce crime by migrant workers, the best thing to do is to treat them as far as possible as nationals. Unfortunately all the signs are that migrant workers, although needed, will continue to be considered as second-class labourers in some countries. In this respect, some of the new African countries are already excelling and becoming as discriminatory for racial, political and economic reasons as South Africa and Rhodesia. It would not be surprising if, like their models, these new countries maintain the thesis of the higher criminality of the non-nationals.

8 Urban and rural crime

Traditionally, urban crime has been regarded as more serious in extent and gravity than rural crime. This is still valid, but like all general assertions, it must be qualified.[57]

To begin with, it does not mean that crime is exclusively an urban phenomenon. It means that, after fundamental concepts have been clarified and relevant data compared, proportionally urban crime is more serious and hence more important for prevention and control than rural crime.

The second qualification is that the distinction between urban and rural is not always easy to make. 'Urban' means a particular form of dwelling environment, the old *continentia aedificia,* as well as of living, in both of which the number and concentration of persons plays a predominant role. 'Rural' implies a different kind of dwelling in closer contact with Nature and a more simplified way of living, in which number and concentration are less important. More specifically, 'urban' is a setting in which occupation, communication and transport are determined by three main factors: mass, quicker tempo of life and multiplicity of services. The larger the city the greater the mass, the acceleration of tempo and the complexity of services. Man is more independent and isolated in some respects in an urban setting, but also extremely dependent on others. In the rural habitat, the conglomeration of people is minimal and the 'lonely crowd man' does not exist, transport is limited and frequently organized on a personal basis, services have a less impersonal character than in the city, and the amount of time available is greater. These differences have a marked impact on individual and family as well as professional and social life. Modern mass communication media, such as television and radio, have established a powerful common link between urban and rural ways of life, but their impact is less than is claimed.

All the above factors and more are behind the classification of urban and rural areas according to a fixed limit of the number of inhabitants. The criterion is useful provided it is not interpreted in purely numerical terms, but as an expression of what has been said above. In the United States the figure of 2,500 inhabitants is currently used as the dividing line between urban and rural areas. By some the limit is considered too low; on the other hand, it reflects fairly the prevailing uniformity of the urban habitat in the United States, broken only by small and somewhat isolated communities. In the United Nations Secretariat's *World Urbanization Trends, 1920–1960*, urban population is defined as 'that of localities with 20,000 or more inhabitants', and rural and small town population 'that of smaller localities or the open country'. It is stated that the definition, which has come into wide use in international research, must be used with caution, since it may exclude some places that are actually urban in character, while including others that may be merely densely settled rural villages. The remark is important because the definition itself excludes from urban the small-town population, which, however small it is, may not be rural at all. The explanation of the assimilation of rural and small town may be found in the fact that the latter, although somewhat different in character, is also near enough to Nature to be regarded as rural. According to the report, the figures 20,000 and 100,000 suggested the use of a multiplier of five to arrive at a more detailed size classification, viz:

20,000 and over	Urban population
100,000 and over	City population
500,000 and over	Big-city population
2,500,000 and over	Multi-million cities
12,500,000 and over	Metropolitan regions (i.e. those of New York and Tokyo)

The classification is particularly useful to criminology, because it refers to different types of concentration, each of which, although having something in common with the others, acts differently upon life in general and crime in particular. Although they may exist in smaller urban areas, the increase of professional and organized crime, narcotic offences, criminal corruption and white-collar crime is in direct relationship to the big and multi-million cities and metropolitan regions. In this concentration scale the growing number of people plays a primary role, but what is eventually determinant is the way in which the concentration is organized, where socioeconomic as well as political factors play significant roles. Even if they are numerically identical and the features and structure are similar, each city behaves in a different way—behaves because cities, especially from the category of big cities onwards, constitute by themselves a system with their own forces which imposes itself on individuals and groups as well as on policies and services. This explains why comparisons on numerical considerations are necessarily superficial, and also why the megalopolis makes the functioning of public services difficult, particularly those of police and the administration of justice. It is also why cities in the same country have different indexes of crime.

Another qualification is that required by the extent of the urban area. The terms 'city' and 'town' are frequently used when crime is discussed, but they are not precise enough to give a clear idea of what should be understood by 'urban area'. The old concept, *urbs*, as the city surrounded by walls was insufficient as soon as the city expanded beyond them. The case of Rome discussed by Jerome Carcopino in his *Daily Life in Ancient Rome* (1941) is illustrative; in the second century, when the growth of Rome was probably completed, the city had at a conservative estimate, 1,200,000 inhabitants, a great part of whom lived outside the walls. For that time it was as much if not more than present-day New York or Tokyo. For crime, the inner city and the trans-Tiber area constituted a varied but single unity. Nowadays, the expressions 'residential', urbanized' and 'suburban area', as well as 'conurbation', are frequently used. Whether a clear distinction can be made between them will not be discussed here. What is of interest is that with respect to the urban-rural dichotomy, all of them are part of the urban concept and as such considered as urban areas, even if in some crime presents specific characteristics. 'Suburban' means an adjacent area which may or may not possess some of the main characteristics of the nearby city, but which nevertheless is neither rural nor a small town. 'Conurbation' means the aggregation or amalgamation of different urban districts; more specifically in Britain they are defined by the Registrar-General as 'areas of urban development where a number of separate towns have grown into each other or become linked by such factors as a common industrial or business interest or a common centre for shopping or education'. The common characteristic is that, whatever their form and purpose, they are urban in character and way of life. So they should be seen as urban in the evaluation of urban crime when this is compared with rural crime.

A further qualification is that the distinction between urban and rural area has sometimes to be supplemented by a third category, partly urban and partly rural, which is neither a conurbation nor a suburban area. Some of them act as commercial, financial and educational centres and have some kind of industry, and as a rule serve at the same time a surrounding agricultural region. Their size varies, rarely exceeding the 30,000 mark, and yet they cannot be regarded as rural towns. They exist in countries like the United Kingdom, France and Germany, and in many respects constitute an important part of the socio-economic and political structure of the country. As such they may also deserve special criminological attention; if this is not possible, they should be considered as urban rather than rural.

No less significant as a qualification is the distinction between 'urban' and 'urbanization'; it is not easy to make, and even in highly technical papers the terms are sometimes used interchangeably. 'Urbanization' is an expanding process, usually of an already existing urban area or by creating a new town or city. Although both are aspects of growth, urbanization as a rapidly expanding urban process and the normal development of a city are not the same thing. It may be said that while urban development is mostly a condition, urbanization is an accelerated growing process with greater disruptive effects. Criminologically, urbanization may be more interesting than urban areas. The fact that urban areas, conurbations and urbanization are coincidental in many respects makes it difficult to consider them separately; as a rule, 'urban area' is used to express all three, and yet for criminological purposes the distinction is desirable.

Two other questions closely related to urban crime should be mentioned, both provoked by the increasing transport facilities: one is the offences committed by groups of vandals coming from the cities into rural and semi-rural areas, and the other is the growing number of robberies and breaking and entering by professional and organized crime coming in from urban areas, frequently big cities. Administratively these offences are often classified as rural, while actually they are urban. To the writer it would be difficult to regard the 1963 train robbery as a rural affair; the same applies to the robberies committed in the country by urban professional offenders and criminal gangs.

The above shows that, although essentially different, urban and rural areas have borderline zones in which the distinction is not easy, and that the content of the term 'urban' makes general urban crime indexes meaningless unless they are accompanied by some specifications as to the size and character of the urban areas concerned. On the other hand, the indexes of rural crime will probably decrease in some countries because agriculture as an occupation is decreasing. This means that rural areas will be less populated and more mechanized. Countries like Denmark, the Netherlands and to a great extent Switzerland, Puerto Rico and Uruguay tend to become what I would call 'urban countries'. Will the fading of rural-agricultural areas increase crime? There are enough contrasts in the countries mentioned to make a general conclusion difficult. And yet, with respect to Puerto Rico, parallel to the spreading urbanization is the rapid increase of crime. This is not an argument against urbanization, but against the anarchic way in which it is carried out, even if, as in Puerto Rico, planning commissions are at work. This is typical of other Caribbean islands in which the expansion of urbanization is facilitated by activities and interests in which gambling, entertainment and commercialized vice play a role.

With respect to Britain, the annual reports of Her Majesty's Chief Inspector of Constabulary and of the Commissioner of Police of the Metropolis as well as other sources offer enough data to maintain the thesis of the prevalence of urban over rural crime. The fact that in 1967, out of 1,207,354 indictable offences known to the police, 932,202 were recorded by provincial police forces should not be interpreted as an argument against the prevalence of urban crime, because provincial forces also operate in urban areas, including conurbations, as is shown by the location and functioning of the different regional criminal records offices. To the writer the findings of F. H. McClintock and N. Howard Avison in their excellent survey, *Crime in England and Wales* (1968), confirm this thesis. They reject the outdated thesis that criminal behaviour is almost exclusively a phenomenon of the large urban area, or that the incidence of crime in the Metropolis is very much higher than elsewhere. According to them, in

> . . . London and the seventeen largest cities and towns . . .
> that is areas with populations of at least 200,000
> inhabitants and which together account for approximately
> one-third of the population of England and Wales,
> it is found that in 1955 such urban areas accounted for
> more than 43 per cent of indictable crimes recorded
> by the police. By 1965, after the substantial increase in
> total volume of crime, those urban areas still accounted
> for only 45 per cent of the total volume of crime.

Although the authors seem to minimize the amount of crime in urban areas, the fact is that it is significant enough to justify the thesis of the prevalence of urban crime. This is confirmed by the percentages of the other 29 towns with populations between 100,000 and 200,000, plus 28 towns with less than 100,000. To this should be added to the huge crime percentages that the authors have found in the six conurbations studied by them. In spite of some variations, the findings are that in 1955 and 1962 the six conurbations accounted for almost half the crimes recorded by the police in England and Wales. Even if there is some overlapping between London as the Metropolitan Police District and the City and London as a conurbation or Greater London and related statistical data, it is obvious that the contribution of urban areas to crime in England and Wales is far higher than that of rural areas.

The complexity of urban crime was demonstrated in France and Belgium some years ago by Denis Szabo in his remarkable survey, *Crimes et Villes* (1960). Quite often his findings have been interpreted as a rejection of the thesis of the predominant role of urban crime; actually Szabo's main conclusions do not imply this. What he said was that the opinions about the criminogenic effect of urban environment *based on ancient observations* should be corrected, and that it is to be expected that with the fading of the urban-rural antinomy the specific characteristics of the two types of societies will also fade, and consequently the two types of crime will be brought together. Both conclusions are correct, but neither denies the fact that urban crime is more significant than rural crime. His first conclusion means that the old explanatory thesis should be abandoned, and the second that the difference between urban and rural crime will continue for the time being. These differences are in extent and gravity and do not necessarily mean, as Szabo points out in his analysis, that they refer to all forms of crime. The old explanations were largely based on the conditions of the cities in the nineteenth century, which were highly 'criminogenic', particularly for the lower classes. According to Jacques Droz's *Europe between Revolutions 1814-1948* (1967), Berlin, with about 400,000 inhabitants, had about 10,000 prostitutes, 4,000 beggars and 10,000 prisoners. For Britain, Henry Mayhew's four volumes on *London Labour and the London Poor* (1851 and 1862) contain a great deal of information about the socio-economic and political condition of the lower-class citizens, crime, prostitution, begging, etc. At that time, for many not belonging to it, the working class was regarded as dangerous and plagued with physical illness, moral corruption and crime. Since then the situation has changed, and crime has shifted or become more selective in the sense that, although the less privileged are still the main source of offenders the more privileged also have their share, which in all probability would be greater if their privileged treatment was reduced to more equitable limits.

The complexity of urban crime and its relationship with less-privileged groups, whose conditions are usually worse in the big cities than in rural areas, has again been demonstrated by V. V. Stanciu in his remarkable survey, *La Criminalité à Paris* (1968), published by the Centre National de la Recherche Scientifique. He speaks of the multiplicity of urban aspects and their greater corroding effect in this urban geography of crime, from which emerges the author's conclusion that the criminal man is no different from the non-criminal.

In the United States the prevalence of urban over rural crime is obvious, partly because of the urban character of the country even in small communities, and partly because of the uniform cultural patterns prevailing all over the country. The *Uniform Crime Reports* show that the number of arrests in metropolitan city areas and cities far exceeds that of the rural areas; even if the coverage of reported crime in the latter is less, the gap is still too big to be explained by this.

In the Federal Republic of Germany the populated areas are classified into big, medium and small cities, and rural areas. Big cities are those with more than 100,000 inhabitants, medium with 20,000 to 100,000, small with 5,000 to 20,000 and rural or country areas with up to 5,000. The following table is illustrative:

Criminal Offences known by the Police (percentages)

Year	Big city	Medium city	Small city	Country area	Unknown
1965	51·9	19·1	12·1	16·4	0·5
1966	51·5	19·3	12·2	16·5	0·5
1967	50·4	19·5	12·7	17·1	0·3

These and other data allow the conclusion that crime is more serious in extent and gravity in urban areas. This does not mean that the prevalence is absolute in every respect; it may safely be said that female, juvenile, young adult, migrant, habitual, professional and organized crime are greater in urban than in rural areas. As for offences, the most prevalent are murder, violence against persons, robbery, breaking and entering, petty larceny in stalls and shops, serious breaches of public order, vandalism, white-collar crime, criminal corruption, crimes committed under cover of official position and narcotic drugs offences.

The above conclusions may be doubted and criticized, but they are supported by data. Even if statistics are not what they should be, their shortcomings benefit urban as well as rural areas. In the latter, there is usually greater cohesion among the population, their needs are less, and there is more direct social control. Even gossip, as Marshall B. Clinard said years ago, plays a preventive role. This does not exclude that in certain countries crimes of violence against the person may be more frequent in rural areas than in urban areas. The Latin European countries offer examples of this. The same applies in general terms to Arab, Asian and African countries, but these and other exceptions do not conflict with the conclusions made here. It should be added, however, that these crimes of violence are no worse than those against persons and property committed in the cities of every size in many countries. Here again the old explanation of primary relationships, isolation and fierce individual independence put forward to explain the violence against the person in rural areas seems to be contradicted by contemporary events and crime in urban areas. The primary reactions and independent feelings prevail also in the modern cities more than in the past for socio-economic and political reasons. As for isolation, the country is far less isolated than in the past. An objective appraisal of contemporary protest attitudes against socio-economic, political and educational conditions and policies shows that, unless radical transformations take place, for years to come the cities will increase their contribution to crime. The fact that the motivation is different does not alter the criminal condition as long as the law remains unchanged.

The last question to be examined in connection with urban crime is the validity of the thesis of 'delinquent areas' advocated by Shaw and others in the United States, which is rather discredited. Although still favoured by some, it cannot be explained by ecological theories. The distinctions made between areas of 'criminal production' and 'areas of crime commission' or 'areas of crime commission' and 'areas of delinquent residence', 'social and psychological delinquency' and many others are inconclusive generalizations. Unfortunately, some developing countries have tried to explain their growing delinquency in the big cities according to the 'delinquent area' theory. Among other attempts I remember the one made in the United Arab Republic with respect to Cairo. The truth was that the so-called 'delinquent areas' were underprivileged in every respect, and delinquent and non-delinquent juveniles coexisted as usual. Moreover, with some exceptions, the type of offences committed were of a minor character, particularly when compared with those committed by civil servants, professionals, white-collar workers, etc., in other areas of the city. The distinction made by T. Morris in *The Criminal Area: a Study in Social Ecology* (1967) between areas of crime-commission and areas of delinquent residence may be valid if 'delinquent' is replaced by 'criminal offender', and factors motivating the commission of crime in other areas are disconnected from the theory of 'delinquent area', of which he was critical. Recently in some papers general references have been made to the fact that according to Japanese data, rural crime is increasing and urban crime decreasing. Even if numerically attested, it will not invalidate what has been said here.

With respect to the process of urbanization and crime as coincidental but differing from urban crime as far as preventive policies are concerned, the analysis of relevant literature and data, especially on African countries, shows that the most significant factors leading to the increase of crime are the following:

a That in spite of widespread planification, urbanization is proceeding more rapidly than the improvement of social and economic conditions, with the possible exception in some countries of health services and in others of social services. This rapid expansion of urbanization is sometimes due to 'prestige policies' and sometimes to the way in which international bilateral assistance, as distinct from United Nations assistance, is given. In many cases the combination of traditional and metropolitan cannot be avoided and in some respects should be preserved. On the other hand, interests sometimes make it difficult to apply the formula found to solve some obvious shortcomings without undesirable criminogenic effects. As for the few new towns, some of them are badly planned or imitate developed countries by creating low-income housing areas which are actually the new slum areas, as happened in New York, Cairo and Bombay and other big cities. Moreover, by concentrating efforts on the urban area of the capital, some African countries become over-urbanized, with all the usual harmful effects.

b The number of employed urban wage-earners in most African countries has not increased much over the past decade, chiefly owing to the falling-off of export prices, political uncertainty, lack of productive methods, etc. This has had different effects in the urbanization areas as far as the structure of the population is concerned. Some cities are predominantly male, with the majority between 15 and 45 years of age, which, as a group, may be regarded as the most crimeprone. In others, however, females prevail, doing a series of legal as well as illegal tasks. Eventually, the sex-gap will be filled, but in all probability it will take some years. In the meantime the possibility exists that some patterns of crime may become so rooted that they will persist for a long time afterwards.

c In spite of what is often said, the family and socio-economic link between the dweller in African towns and the countryside, with all the benefit this brings, is still strong. In fact, in some of them it has been reported that the major features of traditional life, such as tribe, clan and kinship, continue to regulate areas of social life, although some governments do not seem particularly interested in reinforcing and adapting these features to a more modern setting. On the other hand, changes of many kinds which particularly affect the young are taking place, particularly as a result of the failure of the educational system, which no doubt is seriously affected by the socio-economic situation. The large number of drop-outs in the rural areas is increasing the mass of unemployed, underemployed and unskilled in the big cities. Job opportunities for the educated and semi-educated are very limited. Civil services are comparatively well remunerated, but political uncertainty, patronage and an incipient administration do not make the posts secure enough. To what extent this situation may lead to criminal corruption is difficult to ascertain, but the factor is there. The question of an increase of juvenile crime is acute, in view of what has been said by some of the reports of the United Nations already mentioned. One of them states: 'the educational expansion that has taken place has resulted in the dreams of African youths for further educational attainment and occupational success, neither of which, in most cases, they have much hope of attaining'. Perhaps a partial remedy for this situation may be seen in the recent discriminatory policies of some African governments against foreign employees and traders, many of them of Asian origin. In any case, the result has been for many rural youths to flock to the towns, often to face disappointment. More specifically, it has been said, 'The indications are that the incidence of juvenile crimes and offences is on the increase in African cities' (*International Review of Criminal Policy*, No. 22, 1964, p. 66).

d In many developing countries, police, courts and institutional and non-institutional treatment services are scarce, badly organized or disrupted by political events in the cities, and non-existing or barely functioning in rural areas. In some, obvious improvements have been introduced, but often not enough, owing to more pressing priorities, some of them of a purely political character.

The above reflects a criminological point of view which may differ from that of politicians and economists. Progress has been made, especially in some aspects of social services, but these are already overtaxed with their own work and can hardly undertake the preventive action which they are supposed to perform in a more direct way. Urbanization, like economic and industrial growth, should be encouraged and planned, not only by economists and industrial experts, but the participation of the criminologist. Unfortunately, his participation, even in developed countries, has not as yet received due recognition. This does not mean that with this participation socio-economic policies will solve the crime problem, but that in some respects they may substantially reduce it.

5 Final considerations

The appraisal made here allows for some final considerations and the following are submitted:

a Contemporary criminology regards crime as a socio-economic or a psycho-psychiatric entity or a combination of both. Actually it is primarily a socio-political concept and only secondarily a causal event. The fact that crime is a conventional concept stresses rather than reduces its importance in individual and collective life. As such it is necessary for the survival and progress of a given society. It may be argued that many of the crimes committed under cover of official position, against international law or as the sequel to patriotic, political or revolutionary ideology or action are not crimes in the usual sense of the term or that if they are, they are outside criminal law and criminology. Without denying that exceptionally this may happen, the truth is that the crimes enumerated are as criminal as those committed by the 'man in the street', that they are clearly defined as such by the respective national codes, and that the legal penal system very seldom specifically authorizes the perpetration of these crimes. Thus the injury caused by police torture is nothing other than the bodily injury described by national criminal law. The same applies to the cases of 'liquidation' and brutal violations of human rights, the latter solemnly proclaimed by the corresponding national Constitution. Even if the provisions of the latter are suspended in case of emergency the suspension does not authorize the perpetration of crimes. The same applies to political persecution. In Indonesia nearly 300,000 persons were murdered in a few months less than three years ago. As for atrocities against prisoners or civil population, they cannot by justified by saying that the country committing them is not party to the international conventions protecting both. That would be tantamount to admitting that because some groups are not parties to a penal code or disagree with its contents, they are free to commit any kind of crime. As for being outside criminal law, this is true in quite a number of cases but it is mostly due to the way in which the penal system operates. The vast majority of crime escapes criminological research. This, however, has not deterred criminologists from formulating theories about crime in general or certain crimes in particular. Whatever is done I doubt that criminology will ever be able to deal with a substantial part of crime and if this is so, theories and sub-theories of crime, including delinquency, seem to be unnecessary.

The thesis already suggested, that a 'collective conception' of human rights will prevail, will open the door, as it did in the past, to greater criminality for the benefit of a particular minority or ideology. The truth is that at present, human rights are inherent in the human condition, a fact that proves how a conventional concept may become more important to individual and collective life than causal explanations.

b The purpose of a penal system is not retribution, social defence, rehabilitation, etc., but social justice. The latter is seldom referred to by contemporary criminology, still too much devoted to prevention and rehabilitation, which can only be achieved in a very limited way as long as society is organized as it is. Experience shows that the contemporary penal system, still rooted in the nineteenth century, is unable to cope with crime as a socio-political phenomenon and the same happens to criminology. What is needed is a new penal system; suffice it to say here that it requires a different kind of society and the reduction of criminal law to a minimum. The thesis is not new and has been advocated on several occasions; Nigel Walker in *Sentencing in a Rational Society,* 1969, calls it reductivism. This new penal system requires a different kind of judge and lawyer who cannot be produced by the present Faculties of Law. This means that the current interchangeability of judges still obstinately maintained in the Report of the *Royal Commission on Assizes and Quarter Sessions,* 1966–69, must disappear. The problem is not the re-organization of the system of 'administration of justice', but of creating through gradual planification a system of social criminal justice. Speedier justice, although badly needed, is not the same thing as social justice. Here again, the socio-political approach, not to be identified with political ideology or a particular 'establishment', is decisive. The thesis that the new criminal law should be drawn from criminology, besides being a rehash of what has been said in the past, ignores first, that the formulation of the criminal law of the immediate future demands far more than criminology, and secondly, that contemporary criminology has completed its historical cycle and is no longer up to the task.

c Is punishment necessary? Some are against it. Karl Menninger's

The Crime of Punishment, 1968, represents an extreme view the reasoning of which may equally be used to maintain that of the crime of psychiatric treatment. Pauline Morris's *Put Away, A Sociological Study of Institutions for the Mentally Retarded,* 1969, and many data concerning the United States, France and other countries, offer enough support to show that in many cases psychiatric treatment is as badly organized as penal treatment. Neither of them can be properly organized as long as the prevailing socio-political structure persists and yet both are necessary within certain limits. The thesis occasionally advanced that imprisonment has no future in a free society ignores the fact that this kind of society requires it, although certainly not as it is now conceived. In most cases imprisonment has no purpose beyond keeping people inside. As such, it facilitates the increase of crime and constitutes one of the most obvious forms of criminal injustice. With all the reservations that this kind of measurement implies, I should say that according to my own research, the average daily world prison population, political prisoners excluded, is between 1,500,000 and 2,000,000 of which approximately no less than 1,300,000 are sent to prison for less than six months, and in most cases to less than three. Obviously, this prison population, which is only a small part of the total world annual turnover, cannot be rehabilitated. As for the remainder, only a minimal part is kept for periods long enough to attempt what is still regarded as rehabilitation; even if it is understood in accordance with the United Nations Standard Minimum Rules for the Treatment of Prisoners, very few countries are equipped to apply them.

d Is criminology necessary as a discipline? It would be unfair to say that what is known as criminology has not contributed to the prevention of crime and the treatment of offenders but one may still ask if, as a branch of knowledge, criminology has justified its existence or whether it would not be better to replace it by a planned criminal policy. The present all-embracing content which includes penology and criminalistic and its condition of a *meta-science* claimed by some does not make much sense. Hence the efforts made to integrate a content that actually defies integration. Yet this boundless content has its supporters, perhaps because it allows a proliferation and repetition of research that would otherwise be difficult to justify. The third listing of Criminological Institutes in the United States and Canada, recently circulated by the National Council of Crime and Delinquency and the lists of projects undertaken in developed countries, show that in a substantial number of cases the purpose and the splitting of projects is unjustified. To some extent the same criticism applies to international agencies and non-governmental organizations. To most of them crime is only a portion of what may be called conventional crime and not the rapidly expanding socio-political phenomenon of our time and of the immediate future. There are exceptions, such as the Institute of Criminology of Cambridge, which is mentioned not because I am related to it but because of its pragmatic approach which gives preference to applied and not to purely theoretical criminology. The main tasks of the new criminology or perhaps a better planned criminal policy are: to contribute effectively to the planification of a social system of criminal justice; to determine as nearly as possible the amount of crime according to a restricted meaning of it that a given country may stand without being seriously disrupted; to assist in the formulation of a concept of social responsibility which may be used by the new criminal law, which cannot confine itself to the present concept of culpability and responsibility; and finally, to formulate a series of methodological concepts and principles of criminological research which may be applied anywhere, leaving to each country the task of evolving her own criminology which does not exclude a reasonable transplantation of what is done elsewhere. This criminology or planned criminal policy presupposes a different kind of criminologist, sociology, psychology and psychiatry than those at present prevailing in the criminological field, also a good training in political science and history as well as in methodology. The latter cannot be identified with the borrowing of methods and concepts from the natural sciences or manipulation of data and the use of impressive but inadequate terminology. Crime, including delinquency, is not an expression of 'deviant' behaviour. Even less should it be regarded as a 'behavioural problem' according to a 'behavioural' sociology, psychology or psychiatry. Biological progress has opened new avenues in the control of crime or more specifically of certain types of offenders. In this respect the pioneer work of Dr José M. R. Delgado and others in the United States on remote physical control of the brain should be mentioned.[58] Yet the door should be opened with great caution inasmuch as this kind of control raises questions of particular importance with respect to human rights. Two remarks must be made; one that technological and scientific progress enlarges rather than reduces the field and hence the protection of human rights, and secondly that the growing acceptance of reasonable forms of control makes unnecessary the search for the causes of crime for theory building. What Leon Radzinowicz said almost ten years ago in *In Search of Criminology*, 1961, is still valid: 'In the present state of knowledge the very attempt to elucidate the causes of crime would be better put aside. The most that can be done is to throw light upon the combination of factors or circumstances associated with crime'. At its best, criminological theories are an ensemble of conjectures. Even accepting what Karl R. Popper says in his remarkable book, *Conjectures and Refutations: The Growth of Scientific Knowledge*, 1963, that 'The way in which knowledge progresses, and specially scientific knowledge, is by unjustified (and justifiable) anticipations, by guesses, by tentative solutions to our problems, by conjectures', this cannot justify the formulations and implementation of criminal policy on the assumptions put forward by criminological theories, first because all can reasonably be refuted; secondly, because as Popper says, scientifically, nothing can be established as true nor even as probable, and finally because criminal justice must be based on something more than criminological research—in fact it must be based on the necessity of protecting the legitimate order democratically established. Science and technology influence our way of living and the structure of society, but in turn these two influence science and technology.

e The new approach to crime, criminal law and criminology demands a new activity at the international level in what incongruously is still called social defence. In 1950 the United Nations assumed leadership in the prevention of crime and the treatment of offenders with the cooperation of other international and non-governmental organizations mostly following the prevailing conventional conception of crime. The situation, with numerous historical antecedents, has radically changed in the vast majority of countries. Crime is no longer the scientific entity elaborated by distinguished criminologists but a rapidly expanding socio-political phenomenon closely related to the total structure of society which cannot be identified with the image of a particular 'establishment', whether capitalist or socialist. Will the United Nations policy-making bodies accept the new approach to crime and undertake the tasks that it involves? The greatest difficulties will come not from the Secretariat but from a number of Member States some of which maintain that according to paragraph 7 of article 2 of the United Nations Charter, crime as well as criminal justice is a domestic matter. This was the thesis of some socialist countries. If it is remembered that the vast majority of the 126 Member States are enduring anti-democratic regimes it will not be surprising if this thesis is reinforced. My experience is that democracy is essential for the planification of a social system of criminal justice and objective and independent criminological research. This may be attested by the reader by comparing a political map with a criminological or penal one. Indeed, under antidemocratic regimes, penal reforms are made, criminological research conducted and institutes or centres organized, but close scrutiny will show that what is done is seldom the penal reform or criminological research required. It cannot be denied that in some developing countries serious efforts are made to

238

improve the prevention of crime and the treatment of offenders but here again the problem of ways and means arises. Probably no less than 80 Member States are developing countries with average annual incomes that range from US $40 in Chad to well over US $1,000 in Venezuela. In the latter the penal system is by no means satisfactory. In all these countries the socio-political character of crime is undeniable. The lack of ways and means is often put forward to explain a system of priorities in which criminal justice is not included. In any case, it seems that dictatorial or personal regimes are not particularly interested in the problem of crime. For what it is worth, I should say that while in 1952 with 60 Member States the United Nations granted 43 fellowships in social defence, in 1969 with 126 Member States, only 3 were granted.

I am fully aware that my analysis of crime and the compressed character of these final considerations are vulnerable to criticism and controversy, yet the risk had to be taken in view of the expanding socio-political character of crime. Ortega y Gasset in *El Tema de nuestro tiempo*, 1921, said that any given situation may provoke two different attitudes, one markedly oriented to the past and present which favours a pacific continuity of what existed and exists, not excluding some innovation and progress; and another of a militant character which, without trying to destroy the past and the present, tries to understand its own age, not that which has just come to an end but that which is just begining.[59] To me there is little doubt that the second attitude must be taken with respect to crime, criminal justice and criminology. This does not throw the offender overboard but certainly pays more attention to crime itself as a socio-political concept which is far better supported by facts, conjectures and refutations than any theory of crime.

Notes

1 See *Second United Nations Congress on the Prevention of Crime and the Treatment of Offenders*, London, 1960, United Nations Publication, Sales No. 61. 3.

2 With the equally excellent study, 'Social Background and Criminality', by Risto Jaakola, both in *Kriminologinen Tutkimuslaitos*, Helsinki, 1966.

3 Oba, a Japanese public prosecutor, raised the question of 'Dunkelziffer' in his doctoral thesis, *Unverbesserliche Verbrecher und ihre Behandlung* (1906), frequently mentioned by German authors. Some parts were quoted by Dr Bernd Wehner in his excellent monograph, *Die Latenz der Straftaten* (1957), published in the *Schriftenreihe* of the Bundeskriminalamt, Wiesbaden.

4 See Sauer, Wilhelm, *Kriminalsoziologie*, (Berlin and Leipzig, 1933). To him *Latente* means *Geheime*, which is equivalent to secret or hidden crime. It comprises the cases in which the accused is freed for lack of evidence: when, for various reasons, the reported fact is not followed up by the police, or when the offence is not reported because it would be a waste of time, for fear of revenge, making family matters public, etc. In his *Kriminologie* (Berlin, 1950), Sauer also used the term *'Latenz Kriminalität'* with equivalent content.

5 See *A Study of Self-reported Crime*, by Nils Christie, Johs. Andenaes and Sigurd Skirbekk, in *Scandinavian Studies in Criminology* (Oslo, 1965), i.

6 See 'Surveys of Population Samples for Estimating Crime Incidence' by Albert D. Biderman, in *The Annals of the American Academy of Political and Social Science* (November 1967), devoted to 'Combating Crime'.

7 See 'Undetected Delinquent Behavior', by Martin Gold, in *The Journal of Research in Crime and Delinquency* (January 1966), iii, No.1.

8 In Mexico in December 1967 a Presidential Bill was introduced to reduce the illegal possession of arms, especially guns, and curb the tradition of settling disputes or redressing grievances with them. The law is badly needed, as the resort to arms has steadily increased since 1910, when the long Mexican Revolution started. In some rural areas the carrying of guns is encouraged by officials and

police in order to maintain a sort of *cacicazgo,* or local tyranny, over the community. Whether or not the law will be passed and, if so, whether the use of arms will be reduced is still open to question, as, according to the President's message, the bearing of arms is justified when the authorities of the country are unable to afford the people immediate and effective protection. It is in the inability of the local authorities to provide security or impartial decisions on the questions submitted to them, not in the abuse of the term 'subculture of violence', that the origin of the widespread use of arms may be found. This concept of individual justice was also widespread for similar reasons in the American Far West. During the recent discussions in the United States to introduce stiffer controls on the possession of firearms, it was revealed that no less than 200 million guns existed in the United States, i.e. more than one for every inhabitant. This 'armed' country contrasts with Britain, where citizens and police are unarmed and where gun control has never been resisted, as it is in the United States. The *Uniform Crime Reports* for 1966 show that 44 per cent of murders were committed with guns, 7 per cent with rifles and 9 per cent with shotguns (i.e. 60 per cent of all murders). It is obvious that without expecting to eradicate murder, the possession and use of firearms should be as restricted as possible.

9   The literature on organized crime in the United States is abundant, although sometimes repetitive, and any book on criminology provides bibliographical references. Of particular interest are *Crime, Incorporated* (1935), by Martin Mooney, which contains a good list of organized crime activities; *Organized Crime and Law Enforcement*, prepared for the American Association Commission on Organized Crime (1952, two vols. edited by Morris Ploscowe), which not only contains a long series of facts, but also interesting data about legislation and a series of recommendations for legislative action; and also in a general but more limited geographical area, the annual reports published by the Chicago Crime Commission and prepared by its able Executive Director, Virgil W. Peterson, also author of *Barbarians in Our Midst* (1952), in which the connection between politics, corruption and organized crime is amply and objectively established. The 1965 and 1966 Chicago Crime Commission *Report* contains detailed data about still-unsolved gang murders. As for the connection between organized crime and organized labour, which is one of the most important sources of unknown and known-but-unreported crime, see *Crime on the Labour Front* (1950), by Malcolm Johnson, *Interim Report of the Select Committee on Improper Activities in the Labor or Management Field,* No. 1417, U.S. Senate (1959), where, among others, the case of Hoffa shows the close connection between organized crime and labour, and how the latter, under unscrupulous leaders, becomes an almost unpunished source of unknown and known-but-unreported crime; and *The Enemy Within* (1960), by the late Robert F. Kennedy, particularly chs. 4, 7, 8, 12 and 15. The reading of this and other literature on the matter shows how right was the *Kefauver Committee Report* (1951), in saying that the Federal Government cannot reach the roots of organized crime, since they lie deep in the everyday administration and functioning of the criminal law in the self-governing units of the United States: cities, towns, counties and states.

10 On the extent, ramifications and sources of the manufacture of and traffic in narcotic drugs, and the way governments fulfil their national and international obligations, see the reports regularly prepared and submitted by the Division of Narcotic Drugs of the Secretariat of the United Nations Commission on Narcotic Drugs, the 22nd Session of which was held in Geneva in January 1968. The report of this session (Doc. E/4455) is particularly illustrative, and contains information on the most significant areas of the Americas, Europe and the Near, Middle and Far East in which illicit production, manufacture and traffic take place. The world-wide control of narcotic drugs, which started in 1912 and rested upon ten multilateral conventions, was replaced in 1961 by a single convention to which, in January 1968, 62 countries were already parties. The suppression of the traffic in persons and of the exploitation of the prostitution of others is carried on at the technical level by the Section of Social Defence, which also deals with crime-prevention and the treatment of offenders. The policy decisions are made by the Commission for Social Development, which, like the Commission on Narcotic Drugs, submits its reports and decisions to the Economic and Social Council. The Convention was adopted in 1959. On prostitution see *Study on Traffic in Persons and Prostitution,* by the Secretariat, United Nations Publication, Sales No. 59.IV.5.

11 See Cressey, Donald R., *Methodological Problems in the Study of Organized Crime as a Social Problem,* and Ruth, Henry S., Jr., 'Why Organized Crime Thrives', in *The Annals,* cited in note 6.

12 From an inquiry conducted in Florida in 1959–60. The quotation is from an authoritative source.

13 Resistance movements against enemy occupation should be praised and encouraged, but it would be naïve to conclude that under the label 'resistance' no common crimes are committed, many of which remain unknown or, if known, unreported. Among others, Greece and Yugoslavia may be cited without detracting from the patriotic effort of partisans in both countries. The case of France is better known, as some studies have been published about crimes committed during the occupation, not only by the Germans, but by them in connivance with the French, particularly officials of the Vichy Government, and by the French alone. The most recent and probably one of the best studies is *Traffics et Crimes sous l'Occupation* (1968), by Jacques Delarue, formerly a member of the French Resistance, historian and police inspector. The second part of his book is devoted to what has been called in France *un travail de démystification,* demonstrating objectively and with all the necessary evidence that of 13,400 candidates for the L.V.F. 3,000 were rejected owing to their heavy criminal records, 5,800 were admitted although their records were only slightly better, and later some of them were shot by the Germans as common criminals. Although obviously many of them did not commit common offences, some of them did. As for the complicity of the French in the Black Market activities openly carried on by the Germans, Parts I and II of the book are very informative; both French and Germans included high officials.

14 See *Report on the Feasibility of a National Computer System for Police Records* (H.M.S.O., 1966). For English criminal statistics,

the pages devoted to them by Mannheim in the first volume of his *Comparative Criminology* (1965) are extremely useful.

15 The working papers of the experts mentioned are part of the documents of the 1950 meeting of the International Group of Experts on the Prevention of Crime and the Treatment of Offenders. Professor Verkko's papers dealt with such matters as definition and object of criminal statistics, the problem of the number of crimes, comparison questions, methodological matters, police statistics, different aspects of judicial statistics, prison statistics, etc. The Secretariat's report on international statistics (Doc. E/CN.5/337, 1959) was mainly the responsibility of Dr Albert G. Hess, at that time member of the Section of Social Defence and currently Director of International and Project Services at the National Council on Crime and Delinquency, New York. The report (167 pp.) examines the technical aspects of the problem, the classification of offences, the preparation of schedules of inclusion and exclusion and the questions arising from the analysis of the three offences chosen. Another 56 pp. are devoted to the comments of United Nations correspondents in Social Defence and other experts.

16 All statistical data in this and other sections are taken from official publications, gathered by the writer or provided by officials or services on his request.

17 See López-Rey, M., 'Analytical Penology', in *Studies in Penology* (1964), edited by him and Charles Germain, and 'Administrative Penology—England and Wales', in *The British Journal of Criminology* (January 1965).

18 See *Actes du Congrès Pénitentiaire International de Saint Petersbourg* (1890), iii, 741–89. M. Beltrani-Scalia's report contains altogether 21 tables.

19 Max Weber's theses have been much criticized on account of his sociological, analytical or formal approach, because he was contradictory, too oriented to economics, and above all by his German colleagues because he never succeeded in building up a 'well-rounded sociological theory'. Probably all this is true. Personally, I never thought that Max Weber tried to produce a complete theory of the social system. What attracted me in his thought was his objectively restrained, theoretical assertions so clearly manifest in the following: that it is impossible to reach a total perception and even less conception of the universe; that concepts do not reproduce reality, but are only instruments for better knowledge; that value and meaning are determined by the attitudes prevailing at historical junctures; and that social science is a science of reality, but this reality cannot be conceived and treated as the reality dealt with by natural science: this means that the empirical-inductive study of reality is not all that has to be considered; history and attitudinal processes also play a definite role; in dealing with social problems, individual social behaviour, social structure and social development. and their respective interrelationships are no less important. As far as criminology is concerned, this means that, although individual ideas, emotions or conditions play a role, what is eventually determinant is the significance of individual behaviour in the light of its purpose and intrinsic value within a particular socio-economic and political framework. Weber's most significant publications are *Gesammelte Autsätze*

zur Soziologie und Sozialpolitik (1924), *Zur Wissenshaftslehre* (1922) and *Wirtschaft und Gesellschaft, Grundriss der Sozialökonomik* (1922).

20 See Sutherland, Edwin H., *Principles of Criminology* (3rd Ed., 1939); also *The Sutherland Papers* (1956), edited by Cohen, A., Lindesmith, A., and Schuessler, K. After his death, the *Principles* appeared under the joint authorship of E. H. Sutherland and Donald R. Cressey. References to social disorganization and crime may be found in most of the American books on criminology. In his distinction between deviant behaviour and social disorganization, Marshall B. Clinard, *Sociology of Deviant Behaviour* (1964), pp. 22–3, makes one of the most apt criticisms of the latter term. Taft, Donald R., *Criminology* (1942). The 4th Ed. is by Taft and Ralph W. England, Jr.

21 The most representative book on social pathology and crime is Barbara Wootton's *Social Science and Social Pathology* (1959), in which the reader may find one of the most outstanding contributions to analytical criminology. Her analysis of a series of criminological theories is masterly. However, her 'Conclusions—Methodological and Practical' may be challenged. For practical purposes, Lady Wootton regards the common denominator of social pathology as all those actions on the prevention of which public money is spent. To me this is *a posteriori*, and has little if anything to do with the intrinsic character of crime, delinquency, divorce, illegitimacy, marital separation, etc. In other words, public policy and the moneys spent are merely the recognition of the existence of a problem and add nothing to its condition.

22 The problem of norm and criminal law is of equal interest to jurists and criminologists. From a juridical point of view, the problem was studied by K. Binding in his monumental work, *Die Normen und ihrer Übertretung*, the first volume of which appeared in 1872. The distinctions between norm, prohibition, conduct and the like provided for many years an ample field for discussion to German professors. According to Binding, the norm is a juridical mandate prior to criminal law. By infringing the norm the offender adapts his behaviour to criminal law, i.e. he actually acts in conformity with criminal law. In Mayer the norm acquires a wide sociological content and embraces a series of mandates and prohibitions through which society demands a specific form of behaviour in accordance with its interests. Mayer's ample concept of norm raised serious criticism because it was extremely difficult to ascertain what had been taken by criminal law from the so-called cultural norm and what was in sum the kind of conduct required from the individual. *Kultur* as a criminological element was examined by W. Sauer in his *Kriminalsoziologie* (1933). To him crime is related to cultural values and culture in general, but this relationship does not mean that crime may be explained as a cultural conflict. On the contrary, it often reflects cultural adaptation. Furthermore, culture is closely related to morality, law, education, etc. A similar position is maintained in his *Kriminologie* (1950), in which he adds that less crime does not correspond to greater culture, but usually the opposite. He also states that crime does not produce culture. In his curious scale of factors leading to crime, the place assigned to culture is rather modest. In sum, in German criminology the

C.—R*

expression *Kulturkonflikt* has never had the meaning and extent
assigned to it by American sociologists dealing with criminological
questions. Neither Mezger, Exner, Seelig nor H. Mayer ever
thought of using 'culture' as the equivalent of an ensemble of
capacities, ideas or artifacts. In the United States T. Sellin, in
his essay *Culture Conflict and Crime* (1938), raises the question in
a wide socio-juridical context, which is maintained years later in
'Les grandes conceptions de la sociologie criminelle', in *Bulletin
de la Société internationale de Criminologie* (1955) and more
recently in the extracts, with editorial alterations, of his 1938 essay
included by Wolfgang, Saviz and Johnston in *The Sociology of
Crime and Delinquency* (1962). In Sutherland-Cressey's *Principles
of Criminology* (7th Ed., 1966) the expression 'culture areas' is used
in such a broad sense that it has no meaning at all. A more
restrained concept may be found in Taft-England, Jr.'s *Criminology*
(4th Ed., 1964), and this explains why the remarks on American
culture make far more sense than those made by other
criminologists.

23 See Reckless, Walter C., *The Crime Problem* (3rd Ed., New York,
    1961), p. 323.

24 Tappan, Paul W., *Crime, Justice and Correction* (1960), is the
    only American criminologist who categorically stated: 'there is
    not a criminal subculture'. Incidentally, it should be noted that
    his professional background was as much legal as sociological.
    Probably the main source of the concepts of culture and sub-
    culture prevailing among American sociologists may be found in
    Talcott Parsons *The Social System* (1951), which, as he repeatedly
    states, is a purely theoretical enterprise. To him culture consists
    in 'patterned or ordered systems of symbols which are objects of
    individual actors and institutionalized patterns of the social system'.
    Although partly patterned, culture does not constitute an ordered
    system of symbols; in fact, substantial aspects of culture are not
    ordered at all; and, secondly, although institutionalized patterns
    of a social system play a role, many important cultural aspects are
    not only outside but also against these patterns. With due respect,
    the fact is that in Talcott Parsons there is no clear distinction of
    fundamental concepts. This explains why society and social system
    are often used interchangeably. As for subculture, he identifies it
    with deviant behaviour; as examples he mentions 'hoboism' and
    'bohemianism', and as a 'legitimate possibility' schizophrenic
    behaviour, which as such does not seem to be well equipped to
    transform internalized personality processes into patterned systems
    of symbols. Other forms of subculture are constituted by criminal
    and delinquent gang patterns. This 'grand theory approach', which
    was criticized by C. Wright Mills in his excellent study, *The
    Sociological Imagination* (1959), is attractive, but without real
    sociological and philosophical foundations.

25 See Gasset, José Ortega y., *Misión de la Universidad* (1930). The
    subject is dealt with by Ortega in many of his philosophical
    publications. To him the individual is only one aspect of the social
    ensemble; the same applies to culture. What social and culture
    mean is not always *querido* (wanted) or *entendido* (understood)
    by the individual. In other words social and cultural are human
    in the sense that they refer to man but to a great extent originate
    outside him.

26 To some the questions raised here may seem outside criminology, and for that matter sociology, which monopolizes it. Yet as part of a philosophical and epistemological foundation they are essential if we want to remedy the prevailing conceptual confusion, lack of systematic presentation and methodological carelessness of both disciplines submerged in a flood of manipulated data, models, mathematical programming and formulae. Does all this imply that, as a science, sociology is going through a crisis of disintegration or is only the sociology operating in criminology affected?

27 Social change as an all-embracing sociological concept is dealt with by the majority of American books on criminology. This wide concept is gaining ground in some European countries. Occasionally the expression 'changing society' is used, which, by itself, does not clarify anything, since all societies are changing in one way or another.

28 See United Nations reports already mentioned. With respect to the 1965 Congress, the Discussion Guide as well as the experts' report summarizing the discussion on the topic 'Social Forces and the Prevention of Crime', enumerate as such public opinion, religion, the family, education, urbanization, migration, industrialization and occupational opportunities, many of which were discussed as part of the topic 'Social Change and Criminality' at another section of the Congress. The need to define what was meant by social force before continuing the confusing discussion was raised by the writer, but without result.

29 See De Greeff, Etienne, *Introduction à la Criminologie* (1937), *Ames criminelles* (Collection Lovanium, 1950) and *L'homme criminel* (1956). *L'Homme devant l'Humain* (1956) contains a series of valuable essays about De Greeff's work and ideas. It has been maintained that he was oriented towards a psychoanalytical and phenomenological interpretation of the criminal act. On the other hand, according to the writer's view, some of his psychological assertions do not seem to confirm it. Because of his own point of view and his analysis of De Greeff's views, Hesnard, A. *Psychologie du Crime* (1963), deserves special mention. His conclusion is that only through a combination of De Greeff's clinical conception of psychoanalytical thesis and phenomenology would it be possible, if not to elaborate a synthesis, at least to use their respective contributions to a better understanding of criminal behaviour. Like others psychoanalytically oriented, Hesnard thinks that in order to deal with social or human problems it is sufficient to unveil the symbolic character of social phenomena; Tullio, B. di, *Manuel d'Anthropologie Criminelle* (1951) and *Principi di Criminologia Clinica e Psichiatria Forense* (1960); Eysenck, H. J., *The Scientific Study of Personality* (1952), *Crime and Personality* (1964) and *Fact and Fiction in Psychology* (1965); Guttmacher, Manfred S., 'Medical Aspects of the Causes and Prevention of Crime and the Treatment of Offenders', a study prepared for the World Health Organization for submission to the United Nations Social Commission, published in *Bulletin* of the W.H.O., 1949, 2; Penrose, L. S., 'Mental Disease and Crime: Outline of a Comparative Study of European Statistics, in *British Journal of Medical Psychology* (1939), xviii; and *The Roots of Crime* (1954), edited by the late Sir Norwood East, which contains excellent essays on different psychiatric, legal and criminological matters. Particularly relevant

are those by Sir Norwood and D. D. D. Curran and Peter Scott; Gibbens, T. C. N., 'Psychiatry and the Abnormal Offender', a study prepared for discussion by the United Nations European Consultative Group on the Prevention of Crime, 1956 and later published in the *Medico-Legal Journal* (1956), xxiv; *Abnormal Offenders and Criminal Responsibility*, by the Secretariat of the United Nations; *The Treatment of Abnormal Offenders* by Professor P. Cornil, as well as the corresponding parts of the Summary Records and of the Report of the Group; López-Rey, Manuel, *Introducción al estudio de la Criminología* (1945), ch. 4 section 3; *On the State of the Public Health*, Annual Report of the Chief Medical Officer of the Ministry of Health for 1966 (H.M.S.O., 1967), *Health and Welfare Services in Britain in 1975*, by D. Paige and K. Jones, National Institute of Economic and Social Research (1966), and the corresponding criminal statistics and reports already used; and 'The Unitary Concept of Mental Illness' by Karl Menninger and others in the *Bulletin of the Menninger Clinic*, xxii, 1 (Topeka, January 1958).

30 According to the Press, the 1967 Report of the National Association for Mental Health states that well over 500,000 people are receiving treatment for mental disorders in Britain. Since mental disorders, like crime, have their own dark figures, it is difficult to establish any correlation between them. The usual practice of referring to statistical data is the most reliable, in spite of its obvious shortcomings, as long as nothing better is produced. For what it is worth, the case of Japan may be mentioned. In 1963 the survey conducted by the Ministry of Health and Welfare showed that there were approximately 1,240,000 mentally disturbed persons throughout Japan. The rate was 12·9 per 1,000 of the total population. Since 1950 mentally disordered persons have been subject to compulsory treatment, and certain officials—in this case the police, public prosecutors and prison authorities, as well as any individual—may initiate the necessary procedure. In 1965 the number of persons reported by criminal justice authorities was 7,267, of which 5,895 were declared mentally disordered. In the same year the number of persons apprehended by the police was 706,827.

31 See *The Basic Writings of Sigmund Freud* (1938) translated and edited by Dr A. A. Brill; *The Evolution of Modern Psychology* (1935), by Richard Muller-Freienfels, particularly pt. 5; *Contemporary Theories and Systems in Psychology* (1960), by Benjamin B. Wolman, a well-written, clear and systematic exposé and useful in every respect; *Schools of Psychoanalytic Thought* (1957) by Dr Ruth L. Munroe, also excellent, with analytical considerations, and the conclusion that none of the psychoanalytical systems reviewed may be regarded as 'true'; *Freud and the Post-Freudians* (1961), by J. A. C. Brown, constitutes a compact and clear exposé, with special consideration of the British schools; with a final chapter on 'Assessments and Applications', at the end of which the remark is made that the very real danger today is that neuroses may be treated pharmacologically or medically instead of psychologically; see also Mannheim, Walker, Wootton and Sutherland-Cressey. Mannheim's exposé and bibliographical references are the most complete. 'The Offender's Attitude towards Punishment', by Dr. Melitta Schmideberg, in the *Journal of Criminal Law and*

Police Science (1960) li, No. 3, with very pertinent remarks on the problem and lack of evidence about the unconscious wish for punishment; *Uses and Abuses of Psychology* (1953), by H. J. Eysenck, and 'The Psychoanalytic Theories of Crime Causation', by Gerhard Falk, in *Criminologica* (1966), iv, No. 1. More specifically about psychoanalysis and crime or delinquency, Alexander, F., and Staub, H., *Der Verbrecher und seine Richter* (1929), Aichorn, A., *Wayward Youth* (1925), and, constituting a series by themselves, three books with the same title *The Roots of Crime* (1935, 1954, 1960), by Alexander and Healy, by E. Glover and by Sir Norwood East, cited above; Abrahamsen, D., *Crime and the Human Mind* (1954); Reik, T., *Geständniszwangund und Strafbedürfnis—Probleme der Psychoanalyse und der Kriminologie* (1925), a collection of lectures, in two of which, the fifth and sixth, he makes a series of rash assertions about the talion and revenge content of criminal law, which only psychoanalytical faith can explain. The position was not substantially altered years later in *The Unknown Murder* (1936). The faith in psychoanalysis is the same, if not stronger, in Paul Reiwald's *Society and Its Criminals* (1950).

32 The reader will be interested to know that Juan Huarte de San Juan, in his remarkable treatise, *Examen de Ingenios para las Ciencias* (1575), referred quite clearly to inherited experiences of the remote past to explain, with no anti-Semitism, some of the characteristics of the Jews and how these past experiences still manifest themselves in some of the abilities assigned to them. The term *ingenio* means here aptitude or natural ability for a particular science. Huarte's purpose was to offer a treatise by which, according to anatomical, physiological and psychological characteristics, individual aptitudes to the study of the different sciences could be ascertained in order to avoid failure. Huarte de San Juan was a medical doctor. Several editions of the book were made both inside and outside Spain, in spite of the fact that it was included by the Inquisition in the *Index* of 1581.

33 From the detailed information given by P. Montes—no less than a full chapter—Dr. Esteban Pujasol's treatise *El sol sólo y para todos sol de la filosofía sagaz y anatomía de ingenious* (1637). Roughly translated: 'The only and for everybody sun of sagacious philosophy and anatomy of aptitudes'), a more justifiable work than that of his predecessor, Bautista dalla Porta, may be regarded as one of the most prominent pioneers of Lombroso's anthropology, especially concerning the lack of sentiment, atavism and physical characteristics of certain offenders. As usual in this kind of treatise, there is a mixture of medical knowledge, astrology and creative fantasy which some may scorn; in all probability, the same will happen in 300 years with everything at present written about anthropology and for that matter criminology. Pujasol's treatise was divided into four books, and probably for the first time plates were introduced into the text to show the physiognomic anomalies described by the author.

34 German terminology differs considerably from the English and requires some explanations. The biological complex is called *Anlage* and that constituted by outside factors *Umwelt*, or sometimes, as in Mezger and others, *Milieu*. Conceptually they are separable, but in each individual case they constitute an inseparable acting

whole. This means that by themselves neither *Anlage* nor *Umwelt* has causal significance, they have to act together. Often *Anlage* is translated as *disposition* which, although not really incorrect, is somewhat misleading. Actually, it means a potentiality or series of potentialities or something like a directional development which is not specifically determined, but subject to its own variables and those brought in by the *Umwelt*. The latter has been translated here as 'surrounding world' and not as 'environment', which, in the writer's opinion, has a broader context. The term *Ursachen* (causes) is usually used to refer in a general way to the etiology of crime. Such is the case with Seelig and Mergen, who nevertheless use *Anlage* and *Umwelt* in the sense mentioned.

35 As far as I remember, Mezger never referred to political matters in the lectures and seminars I attended for two winter semesters as a post-graduate student of the Faculty of Law, the Bavarian Criminal Biological Centre and the German Institute for Psychiatric Research in Munich. Exner's teaching and writings were never tainted by references to Nazi ideology.

36 The 3rd Ed. was published as *Kriminologie* (1949) after his death in 1947. In the Preface he explained that because the Criminal Biological Service had been abolished the old title was unnecessary. Under either title, the components were the same. However, the 3rd Ed. contains important innovations, especially on methodological research matters, recidivism, juvenile delinquency types and the complex *Anlage–Umwelt*-crime.

37 There is already a great deal of literature on the XYY chromosome and crime, although it is frequently reduced to short communications published in medical journals. Only a few are here cited: Court Brown, W. M., 'Genetics and Crime', in *Journal of the Royal College of Physicians of London* (1967), 1 (3); Price, W. H., and Whatmore, P. B., 'Criminal Behaviour and the XYY Male', in *Nature* (1967), 213; Court Brown, W. M., and others, 'Further Information on the Identity of 47 XYY Males' in the *British Medical Journal* (1968), 2; Telfer, Mary, and others, 'Incidence of Gross Chromosomal Errors among Tall Criminal American Males', in *Science* (1968), 159; Wiener, Saul, and others, 'XYY Males in a Melbourne Prison', in *The Lancet* (January, 1968); and Bartlett, D. J., and others 'Chromosomes of Male Patients in a Security Prison', in *Nature* (1968), 219. For an account of research and findings see Escoffier-Lambiotte, 'Genétique et Criminologie', in *Le Monde* (16 October 1968). Jean Graven, *'Existe-t-il un* "Chromosome du Crime"?' in *Revue internationale de Criminologie et de Police Technique*, nos. 4 and 1, 1968 and 1969. The following may facilitate the understanding of the role of chromosomes: The human body cells contain 46 chromosomes of different shapes and sizes, constituting 23 pairs. Different chromosomes carry different genes; one pair of chromosomes called X and Y determine sex. The sex chromosomes in the human female are a matched pair, both X, while in the human male this pair consists of one X chromosome which is larger, and its partner, the Y chromosome. Two X chromosomes make a girl, one X and one Y a boy. A boy inherits his X chromosome from his mother, his Y from his father. Usually in bookplates the sex chromosome pair appears as the 23rd pair. Now, the normal combination XY male and XX female may be altered by the presence of an extra chromosome and become XYY

or XXY. Apparently the mosaic XYY/XYYY has been found in one case among 34 prisoners in Australia. It seems that the regulating function assigned to the sexual chromosomes X and Y which determine sex and to some extent growth and other somatic characteristics is disturbed by the presence of an extra one. However, it has been noted that this disequilibrium is not necessarily constant, that persons with an extra sex chromosome behave normally, and that this abnormal genetic condition is not hereditary. Dr Escoffier-Lambiotte mentions the case of the father with formula XYY who had six boys, all of them with the normal formula XY. As for detecting the formula of the karyotype, he adds that the procedure, which he describes, is relatively simple. Briefly, it consists in taking a small amount of blood and treating it through a series of manipulations in order to disperse, fix and colour the chromosomes so as to photograph and reconstitute them in 23 pairs; also *Proceedings of the Symposium on Chromosome Abnormality and Criminal Responsibility,* Institute of Criminology, Jerusalem, 1969, and Michele M. Carrera, *I fattori biologici della criminalita, La sindrome cromosomica,* 1970, with a clear exposé and well documented.

38 The teaching of Darwin's evolution theory was prohibited in some states. Only in October 1968, after having been held constitutional by the different state courts, was the Arkansas 'monkey law' declared unconstitutional by the Supreme Court of the United States at the request of a courageous woman teacher. The decision will no doubt affect similar laws still in force in Mississippi and Tennessee.

39 See Reckless, Walter C., *The Crime Problem* (4th Ed., 1967).

40 See Bauer, Raymond A., *The New Man in Soviet Psychology* (1959), and ch. 2 of Volman's *Contemporary Theories and Systems in Psychology* (1960), already cited. Like Section 1, this section should not be construed as a bibliographical exposé of socialist criminology. On USSR bibliography see, *Soviet Criminology,* 1969, by Peter H. Solomon, Jr, in Bibliographical Series No. 4, Institute of Criminology, Cambridge, which appeared too late to be considered in the text.

41 See 'Juvenile Delinquency' and 'Prevention of Juvenile Delinquency' in *The Annals of the American Academy of Political and Social Science,* (January 1948 and March 1959 respectively), with papers by Sol Rubin and Richard Perlman criticizing the 'extravagant expansion of the definition of juvenile delinquency' and its 'catch-all condition' respectively, while others support or accept it. Harry M. Shulman regards juvenile delinquency as indicative of an acute breakdown of normal family functions. Although attenuated, a broad concept of juvenile delinquency is also maintained by Sheldon and Eleanor Glueck in *Unravelling Juvenile Delinquency* (1950). Numerous reports of the U.S. Senate Subcommittees have dealt with juvenile delinquency, and in all the conclusions have maintained its wide concept. In the report of the 85th Congress Subcommittee dealing with juvenile delinquency in New York, a distinguished witness maintained that truancy was a general American delinquent pattern, due to the inability of the child 'to sublimate his instinctual drives through school study and activity'; another stressed the necessity of satisfying all emotional needs of minors; and another that understanding and permissiveness are

essential, as well as the abolition of legal responsibility. The Juvenile Delinquency Prevention and Control Act, 1968, is based on this philosophy. With respect to Britain, the *Report of the Committee on Maladjusted Children* (Ministry of Education, 1956) correctly states that maladjustment cannot be equated with delinquency; the *Report of the Committee on Children and Young Persons* (1960) makes recommendations, some of which show sensible approaches to the problem. However, its assertion that only a small proportion of children, less than 2 per cent, get into trouble is over-optimistic. See the Records of the Standing Committee E. Children and Young Persons Bill (1963) with interesting opinions about age limits; and López-Rey, Manuel, 'International Trends in the Prevention and Treatment of Juvenile Delinquency', in the *National Review of Criminal Science* (Cairo, 1968); 'Juvenile Delinquency, Maladjustment and Maturity', in the *Journal of Criminal Law, Criminology and Police Science* (May–June 1960; 'Present Approaches to the Problem of Juvenile Delinquency', in *Federal Probation* (1959); *Police and Juvenile Delinquency* (Lucknow, 1961); 'Considerations on the Formulation of Policies for the Prevention of Juvenile Delinquency in Developing Countries', XIIIth International Course on Criminology, Cairo, 1963, in *Bulletin de la Société internationale de Criminologie* (1964), and 'Youth and Crime in Developing Countries', XVIth International Training Course, Fuchu, 1967.

42 See Thomson, David, *England in the Nineteenth Century* (1950); Marx, Karl, *Capital* (1867), i, refers in some detail to the squalid conditions of children's work and quotes a country magistrate chairing a meeting in 1860 who stated 'children of nine or ten years old are dragged from their squalid beds at two, three or four o'clock in the morning and compelled to work for a bare subsistence until ten or twelve at night, their limbs wearing away, their frames dwindling, their faces whitening and their humanity absolutely sinking into a stone-like torpor, utterly horrible to contemplate . . .'; Teeters, Negley K., and Reinemann, John Otto, *The Challenge of Delinquency* (1950), with interesting data about delinquents and the child-rescue movement in England and the United States.

43 See *Jugend in der modernen Gesellschaft* (1965), edited by Ludwig von Friedeburg, with papers from different authors and countries of great interest for the criminologist. In particular, Karl Mannheim's 'Das Problem der Generationen' makes a series of distinctions of practical value for research; Tenbruck, Friedrich W., 'Moderne Jugend als soziale Gruppe', raises the question what is youth? Erikson, Erik H., 'Identifikation und Identität', makes a distinction between these conditions and opens the door to a series of criminological considerations which go beyond the generalities involving the thesis of maladjustment or deviation. The thesis of youth subculture evolved by Talcott Parsons is denied by F. Elkin and W. A. Westley as a myth of American sociology. With more political overtones, recent literature in France has stressed the growing role of youth in contemporary society: Fouchard, Georges, and Davrance, Maurice, *Enquête sur la Jeunesse* (1968), Gallo, Max, *Gauchisme, Réformisme et Révolution* (1968). For a good exposé of what is called *la révolte des jeunes*, see *France-Forum* (October–November 1968).

44 See Luther, Horst, 'Die Role des Jugendstrafverfahrens im complexen System zur Verhütung und Bekämpfung der Jugendkriminalität in der Deutschen Demokratischen Republik', in *Wissenschaftliche Zeitschrift der Humboldt-Universität zu Berlin* (1966), xv; *Jugendhilfe* (1968), No. 4, with informative short notes by several authors on different aspects of the functioning of juvenile courts; Alexejew, N. S., 'Die Besonderheiten des Jugendsstrafverfahrens in der UdSSR', in *Jugendkriminalität,* already cited; Y. P. Mironenko's 'New Legislation against Juvenile Delinquency', in *Bulletin of the Institute for the Study of U.S.S.R.* (1962), xi, No.6, who makes the important comment that since there are about 20,000 regular people's courts in the Soviet Union, which, besides dealing with adult offenders, also try juvenile offences, and about 6,000 juvenile commissions which are virtually juvenile courts, if each of these organs were to deal with only six juvenile cases each year the total number of cases would be greater than the hypothetical figures given by Soviet newspapers. According to Mironenko, juvenile delinquency in the Soviet Union is greater than in any Western country.

45 In the United States, although juvenile courts deal mostly with actual criminal cases, they are not regarded as criminal but as welfare courts. The fiction is based on the thesis that what matters is to save the 'child' from 'punishment and disgrace'. Accordingly, constitutional rights were ignored. Among many other cases typical in this respect was the decision of the Supreme Court of Pennsylvania *in re* Holmes (1955), according to which, 'since juvenile courts are not criminal courts, the constitutional rights granted to persons accused of crime are not applicable to the children brought before the court'. Holmes was sent to an industrial school for a long period for having been arrested in the company of another boy who had been operating a stolen car. On appeal, it was stated that the boy had not been represented by counsel, nor been informed of the charges against him, etc. All this was considered irrelevant by the Supreme Court of Pennsylvania. The case was brought to the U.S. Supreme Court, which refused to hear it. This welfare approach was maintained, with some exceptions, all over the United States. Only in 1967 did the U.S. Supreme Court change its views and agree to review *in re* Gault, the case which led to the decision.

46 See Bowlby, J., *Forty-four Juvenile Thieves, Their Characters and Home Life* (1946), *Psychiatric Aspects of Juvenile Delinquency* (W.H.O., 1951), where he makes the pertinent remark that not all delinquents are maladjusted, and the more debatable one that their common denominator is insecurity, and *Maternal Care and Mental Health* (W.H.O., 1951), where it is said that the lack of maternal care and love should be met with socio-economic aid, community programmes, etc. The need for love has also been stressed by Kharchev, A. G., 'The Nature of the Soviet Family', in the *Soviet Review* (May 1961), with the customary propaganda emphasis. Insecurity has been the substratum used by many authors to explain delinquency. This is the thesis of Fyvel, T. R., *The Insecure Offenders* (Revised Ed., 1963), where actually the thesis is overshadowed by remarks more apt to other aspects, such as a wanted sense of national purpose, the role of youth and educational

reform, the latter, however, still approached in rather traditional terms.

47 See Burgess, Ernest W., 'Mental Health in Modern Society', and Jahoda, Marie, 'Toward a Psychology of Mental Health', in *Mental Health and Mental Disorder* (1956), edited by Arnold M. Rose. The term is used in many studies, reports and papers as a catch-all concept which reflects a variety of causes or conditions leading to a lack of adjustment or adaptation to a particular environment.

48 Children and juveniles in need of care, assistance and control who have not committed a criminal offence should be dealt with by social and medical services. If their internment is required or parental rights should be suspended, the necessary procedure with adequate guarantees, including legal aid, may be devised. These proceedings are not criminal, but civil or administrative, and should be organized as such. The adjudication may be made on the information gathered by social and medico-psychological services and discussed in informal hearings. What is disadvantageous for everyone concerned, including society, is to transform juvenile courts into something which is neither one thing nor another, with all the inconveniences that this implies.

49 See *World Population Prospects* (United Nations Publication, Sales No.1966XIII.2); *The Population of South-East Asia, 1950-1980* (*idem*, 1959.XIII.2); *The Population of South America, 1950-1980* (*idem*, 1955.XIII.4); *The Determinants and Consequences of Population Trends* (*idem*, 1953.XIII.3); *The Ageing of Populations and Its Economic and Social Planning* (idem, 1956.XIII.6); *National Programmes of Analysis of Population Census Data as an Aid to Planning and Policy Making* (*idem*, 1964.XIII.4); *Statistical Yearbook* (*idem*, 1967.XVII.1); Demographic Yearbook (*idem*, 1965. XIII.1); López-Rey, Manuel, 'Guerra y Criminalidad', in *Revista de Criminología* (Montevideo, 1958).

50 See *International Action in the Field of Social Defence 1966-1970*, prepared by the Secretariat of the United Nations (Doc. E/CN. 5/C2/R2, 1966) and related documents, and *Progress Report on the Programmes in the Field of Social Development* (E/CN.5/409/ Add.4, 1967).

51 See *World Tension: the Psychopathology of International Relations* (1951), edited by G. W. Kisker; Wust, Peter, *Incertitude et Risque* (1957); Gellhorn, Walter, *Security, Loyalty and Science* (1950); Madge, Charles, *Society in the Mind* (1964); and López-Rey, Manuel, 'Características de Nuestro Tiempo', in *Sustancia* (Tucuman, 1942).

52 See *The Annals of the American Academy of Political and Social Science* (May 1926), devoted to 'Modern Crime; Its Prevention and Punishment', especially R. Moley's contribution; Wraith, Ronald, and Simpkins, Edgar, *Corruption in Developing Countries* (1963), most of which is devoted to Britain regarded as a developing country until the 1880s; *Report of the Committee of Corruption* (1964, Government of India, Ministry of Home Affairs), which in many respects reflects a condition existing in other developing countries.

53 See 'Women Around the World' and 'Sex and the Contemporary American Scene' in the January and March 1968 issues of *The Annals of the American Academy of Political and Social Science*. As on other occasions, these special issues make a valuable con-

tribution, and the Academy should be congratulated. As Lady Wootton has pointed out, the study of female crime has received scant attention. Probably the best exposés on current opinions are ch. 26 of Mannheim's *Comparative Criminology* and Section 6 of ch. iv of Mergen's *Die Kriminologie*. Clemens Amelunxen's essay, *Die Kriminalität der Frau* (1963), is interesting, but in the main follows the traditional approach. About the improvement of the status of women, see *The Annals* of January and March 1968, cited above, with valuable contributions by Jeanne C. Ridley, Julia J. Henderson, E. Sagarin, Erwin O. Snigel and Rita Seiden, Richard Udry and others. For the United Nations, see *Convention on the Political Rights of Women* of 1952 and the various reports and other publications on this and related matters. On North African countries, the series of surveys conducted by Nicole Bernheim in *Le Monde* (January 1969).

54 See López-Rey, Manuel, 'El Delito de Aborto en España y América Latina', in *Boletín del Instituto de Derecho Comparado de México* (Enero–Abril, No. 49, 1964), where, for comparative purposes, the situations in Sweden and Japan are studied. Family planning depends primarily upon the effectiveness of contraception methods. A survey conducted in Hungary in the years 1958–60 partly reproduced in *Semaine Médicale, Professionnelle et Médico-sociale* (No. 4, 1967) shows that *coitus interruptus* and Ogino-Knaus methods are still widely used in some socialist countries and the United Kingdom; the condom is widely used in the United States. Even assuming that the situation has been improved by the greater use of the 'pill', in these as well as other countries unwanted pregnancy is frequent. In the United States it has been said that about 5 million women were using the pill, a figure which, although impressive, is not very encouraging as far as the prevention of illegal abortion is concerned. The situation is worse among juveniles and young people, who as a rule are opposed to old methods or I.U.C.D. All this means that illegal abortion as a combined form of male and female crime is still widely practised.

55 See *The Determinants and Consequences of Population Trends* (United Nations Publication, Sales No. 1953.XIII.3); *The Population of Central America, including Mexico, 1950–1980* (*idem,* 1954.XII.3); *The Population of South America 1950–1980* (*idem,* 1955.XIII.4); *The Future of World Population* (*idem,* 1958.XIII.2); *The Population of South-East Asia, including Ceylon and China: Taiwan, 1950–1980* (*idem,* 1959.XIII.2); *Inquiry Among Governments on Problems Resulting from the Interaction of Economic Development and Population Changes* (E/3895/Rev.1.1944); *The Ageing of Populations and Its Economic and Social Implication* (United Nations Publication, Sales No. 1956.XIII.6); and *World Population Prospects* (*idem,* 1966.XIII.2). All these studies are of considerable value in criminological research. Also relevant are *National Programmes of Analysis of Population Census Data as an Aid to Planning and Policy-Making* (*idem* 1964.XIII.4); and *General Principles for National Programmes of Population Projections as Aids to Development Planning* (*idem,* 1965.XIII.2). See also Mannheim; *op. cit.* ch. 26.

56 See Hirsch, Charles A., 'La Criminalité des Nord-Africains en France est elle une Criminalité par Défaut d'Adaptation?', in *Revue internationale de Criminologie et de Police Technique* (No. 2, 1959);

Bottoms, A. E., 'Delinquency among Immigrants', in *Race* (1967), viii, 4; Ferracuti, Franco, 'European Migration and Crime', in *Collected Studies in Criminological Research* (1968), iii, Council of Europe; Bagley, Christopher, *A Comparative Study of Mental Illness among Immigrant Groups in Britain* (1968), and Hashmi, Farrukh, *Community Psychiatric Problems among Birmingham Immigrants* (1968), both in mimeograph and lent to the writer by courtesy of the authors before publication.

57 See 'Urbanization: Development Policies and Planning', in *International Social Development Review* (No. 1, United Nations Publication Sales No. E.68.IV.1), with excellent contributions by the Secretariat on urbanization and socio-economic problems of development in Asia, Africa, Latin America and Middle Eastern countries, as well as on policies and planning related to urban growth and problems of slums and shantytowns; *Social Change in Modern Africa* (1961), edited by Aiden Southall, with several contributions by different authors. Particularly interesting is the *Introductory Summary,* by Professor A. W. Southall, in which he refers to the many catchwords, such as 'detribalization', 'the breakdown of traditional authority', etc., frequently used in this kind of study. Important, but in some respects surpassed by recent events in the United States, is *The Moral Integration of American Cities* (1951), by Robert Cooley Angell; *The Annals of the American Academy of Political and Social Science,* March 1955, devoted to 'Contemporary African Trends and Issues', especially Daniel F. McCall's contribution on the 'Dynamics of Urbanization in Africa'; *Dynamic Urban Sociology* (1954), with such excellent contributions as 'Historical Perspectives in Urban Development', by W. E. Cole; 'Rural-urban Contrasts in Socialization', by E. L. Lively; 'Africa in Social Change, 1967', by P. C. Lloyd; and, with a more general character, *'L'Incertaine Bataille du Développement* (1967), by Jean Rigotard. 'Crime and Delinquency in Relation to Urban Growth' and 'Problems of Youth and Delinquency' were dealt with by the *Report on the World Social Situation* (United Nations Publication, Sales No. 1957.IV.3), but only a small part of the extensive material and comments prepared were included. The material gathered showed that, with some fluctuations and exceptions, urban crime was higher than rural crime, that collective attitudes play a definite role in the higher indexes, and that female and juvenile crime increased in urban areas. See also *International Review of Criminal Policy* (No. 25, 1967, United Nations), with contributions by the Secretariat, W. Clifford, Leslie T. Wilkins, David Carney and others on social defence and national development, crime and economic planning, crime and prevention costs, etc.

58 See José M. R. Delgado, M.D., *Physical Control of the Mind— Toward a Psychocivilized Society,* (1969) who, after years of work as Professor of Physiology at Yale, has developed techniques for electrical and chemical stimulation of the brain and has applied them to the study of primate and human behaviour. His remarkable book opens new avenues, particularly for criminology and penal systems. However, as he says, 'A host of medical, ethical, legal and political questions are involved in the possibility of intelligent choice among behavioral determinants and their control'. The main components of the psychocivilized society suggested are: social dependence, individual freedom, natural causality and intel-

ligent planning in the organization of human behaviour. Finally, he outlines in very general terms a tentative working plan. In my recent discussion with him of some of the problems involved, I learned that satisfactory results have already been obtained with some female offenders. The first question however, is what is the meaning of civilized society? Can the psychological approach evolve it and offer bases firm enough to plan it? The second question is, what kind of crime is being considered by those working on the control of mind? As far as I know from some of the existing literature on the matter only a minor part of 'crime in the street', but not crime committed under cover of official position, against international law and as sequel to patriotic, political, ideological or revolutionary action which far exceeds what may be called conventional crime. In this respect, the hypotheses and examples given by Albert Rosenfeld in his book *The Second Genesis. The Coming Control of Life* (1969), are attractive but misleading. This is the disadvantage of popularizing ideas and techniques which require serious revision. Although not the only aspects to be considered, scientific and technological progress are in many respects challenging criminology and the penal systems and criminal justice of our time. It would be advisable to start discussing the questions involved in the building of a new criminology, criminal law and criminal justice systems at national and international levels. I have in mind particularly the United Nations, UNESCO, the World Health Organization and leading foundations.

59 From the English translation *The Modern Theme,* 1961, by James Clough.

Index

compiled by Brian Hunter

Criminal Behaviour Systems, 32
Criminal constitution *see* latent
   criminality
'criminal exposure', 9
criminal justice, xiii, xv, 3, 16, 41,
   99, 100, 185, 238
  biased, 34
Criminal Justice Act, 1967, 75, 76,
   152
criminal law 3, 4–5, 16, 41, 62, 104,
   110, 111, 128, 205, 237
  inflation, 24, 63–4, 68
  reduction, 235
Criminal Law Act, 1967, 218
Criminal negligence, 9, 10
criminal policy, 2–3, 11, 14, 22,
   99, 100, 113, 121, 182, 187 188,
   207–8, 209, 212, 236–9
criminal procedure, 24, 53
criminal records, 7–8
criminal responsibility, 3, 9, 10,
   103, 140, 179, 185
  age of, 154, 169, 209, 211
criminal statistics, 1, 6, 13–14, 16,
   21, 52, 54–8, 99, 120, 181, 183,
   208, 230
criminal typology, 131
Criminalité à Paris, 229
Criminality of Women 199
criminogenesis, 116–7, 133
*Criminologie et Science Pénitenti-
  aire*, 216
criminology, xiii–xv, 3, 8, 9, 14, 20,
   100–2, 115, 137, 146, 186, 187,
   234, 235, 236–9
  in developing countries, 21–2,
  in East Germany, 142–3, 145
  in France, 146
  in Germany, 10–12
  in Hungary, 144
  in Japan, 146,
  in Poland, 143–4
  in UK, 146
  in US, 15, 17–18, 139
  in USSSR, 141–2
  in Scandinavia, 12, 146
  in Yugoslavia, 143, 144–5
  see also Institutes of Criminology

culture, 124–5
  conflict, 102, 104–11, 139
  feminization, 149
  immigrants, 222
Culture of Youth, 149
Cuzco prison, 94
Czechoslovakia, 48, 142, 184

Dahomey, 95
Daily Life in Ancient Rome, 226
Dallemagne, J., 130
damage, 30, 32
Damascus
  juvenile court, 176
  prison, 68, 91
Dar-es-Salaam, 95
'dark figures', 7, 8, 22, 61, 205
Dartmoor prison, 74
debt collection, 27
Declaration of Human Rights, 29
defamation, 203
'De Fleddervoort', 86
Deir-ez-Zor prison, 68, 91
Delgado, José M. R., 237
Delinquency and Drift, 139
Delinquency and Human Nature,
   173
'delinquent areas', 231
'delinquent generations', 220–1
Denmark, 178, 227
  see also Scandinavia
Deprivation of Maternal Care, 168
Detection of Secret Homicide, 25
Detroit House of Correction, 81
Deuel Vocational Institution, 80
developing countries, 1–2, 13, 14,
   21–2, 25, 44, 167, 181, 185,
   187, 188, 189, 191, 194, 203,
   208, 218, 219, 238–9
deviance, 171, 180, 237
differential association, 102, 136–7
diplomats, 39, 40
  expulsion, 42
discrimination, 24, 39–40, 43, 46,
   100, 108, 172, 223, 224, 233
divorce, 9, 103, 167, 200
documentary system, 15
Dominican Republic, 43
drift thesis, 139

INDEX

public order, 32–4, 45, 63, 129, 230
  see also legitimate order
Puerto Rico, 173, 187, 227
Pujasol, Esteban, 130
Pulan Senang settlement, 89
punishment, 235–6
Punjab Children's Act, 175
Put Away, 236

40,000 Heures, 206

questionnaire, 12, 15, 18, 22
Quinney, Richard, 32
Quirós, Bernaldo de, 130
Quito prison, 94

racialism, 34, 223–4
Radbruck, Gustav, 130
Radzinowicz, Leon, 237
raison d'état, 40–1
Rank, O., 128
Rao, S. Venngopal, 207
rape, 9, 15, 17, 58, 59–60, 154, 174
rebellion, 39
receiving, 9, 60, 63, 210
recidivism, 8, 11, 31, 72, 120, 121
Reckless, W. C., 105, 136, 137–9
reductivism, 235
Reformatory Schools Act, 1893, 148
rehabilitation, 3, 8, 72, 81, 125
  political, 41, 51
Reik, T., 128
Reinemann, J. O., 148
Reiss, R. A., 17
Reiwald, P., 128
religion, 51, 114, 191, 204
remand, 71
  centres, 75
research *see* criminology
resistance organizations, 50–1
Revija za Kriminalistiko in Kriminologijo, 145
Rezaieh prison, 68
Rhode Island prison, 82
Rhodesia, 96, 224
Richmond Criminal Court, 65
Rio Grande do Sul, 92
riot police, 44

riots, 32, 33, 39, 40
robbery, 17, 63, 198, 227, 230
Robbery in London, 39
Roheim, G., 124
'romantic sociology', 112
Rome, Ancient, 110, 112, 226
Royal Commission on Assizes and Quarter Sessions, 235
Rumania, 184
Ruth, Henry S., jr., 37, 38, 39, 195

sabotage, 39, 40
Saginalcilar prison, 89
Saharov, A. B., 142
Saigon, 52
St. Gilles prison, 84
Sampurnanand Camps, 89
San Juan de los Morros Penitentiary, 93
San Quentin prison, 80, 82
Santa Cruz de la Sierra prison, 94
Santiago Penitentiary, 93
Sao Paulo, 92
Sardinian penal code, 1859, 22
Saudi Arabia, 29
Sauer, W., 8, 104
Scandinavia
  Criminal statistics, 19
  homicide, 109
  increase in crime, 184
  Juvenile crime, 190
  unknown crime, 12, 13
  Welfare Boards, 175, 177
Scandinavian Research Council for Criminology, 12
Schlapp, Max G., 130
Schmideberg, Melitta, 129
school-leaving age, 215
science and technology, 109, 113, 114, 192, 193, 215, 237, 238
  see also improvement of material conditions
Scotland, crimes v. offences in, 61, 64
Secret Army Organization, 50
secret organizations, 34
security, political *see* State security
security, psychological, 112, 124, 191–3